Basking with Humpbacks

GIFT OF

The Earle F. Jenkins
Memorial Book Fund

In Memory of
Earle F. Jenkins
Class of 1927

Basking *with* Humpbacks

Tracking Threatened Marine Life in New England Waters

Todd McLeish

UNIVERSITY PRESS OF NEW ENGLAND

HANOVER AND LONDON

University Press of New England,
One Court Street, Lebanon, NH 03766
www.upne.com
© 2009 by University Press of New England
Printed in U.S.A.

5 4 3 2 1

Library of Congress Cataloging-in-Publication Data
McLeish, Todd.
Basking with humpbacks : tracking threatened marine life in New England waters
/ Todd McLeish.
    p. cm.
Includes bibliographical references.
ISBN 978-1-58465-676-0 (cloth : alk. paper)
1. Marine organisms—New England.   2. Endangered species—New England.
I. Title.
QH104.5.N4M35 2009
578.680974—dc22   2009015170

University Press of New England is a member of the Green Press
Initiative. The paper used in this book meets their minimum
requirement for recycled paper.

For Renay, again

Contents

Introduction

The world beneath the surface of the ocean is a realm like none other, and a lifetime of nature documentaries and Discovery Channel programming could never provide a true sense of its beauty, complexity, and immensity. Not only is it home to a remarkable array of bizarre plants and animals, from microscopic creatures at the base of the food chain to ferocious predators more dangerous than almost any on land, but its physical structure includes spectacular geologic formations, like active volcanoes and hydrothermal vents spewing boiling hot water from the earth's core. And its unique chemical and physical properties create a challenging environment that forced inhabitants to develop a myriad of astonishing and unexpected evolutionary adaptations to survive.

Yet, while the oceans make up about 70 percent of the planet's surface, the undersea world has been only minimally explored, especially the deep seas far off the continental shelf. There is even much that is still unknown about the creatures that live in our coastal waters, where they go when they leave, and how abundant they are. Because of the inherent challenges and expense of spending time beneath the surface, the ocean's life forms cannot be studied as readily as those found on land. Marine biologists cannot just walk into the appropriate habitat and observe their target species at length like those studying trees or birds or reptiles. Most of the historic data that scientists have about fish populations, for example, comes from the records of the fishing industry. And while methods for surveying marine life have improved dramatically in recent decades, it is still nearly impossible to derive an accurate population assessment for most marine species because they are so difficult to find and count. That's why, with the exception of the air-breathing marine mammals and sea turtles, so very few marine creatures are included on the U.S. endangered species list (and why we don't know for certain whether any have become extinct). A species cannot usually be declared endangered if scientists cannot say with confidence how many there once were and how many there are now, but there is no way to determine those figures in most cases. So those trying to protect and manage populations of marine life are doing so with very little hard data to work with. It's a challenge that is not likely to be overcome anytime soon.

Nonetheless, scientists are learning more and more about the marine environment every day. While it would be easy to assume that the oceans are all quite similar in their geology and wildlife and other characteristics, this just isn't true. The waters around New England are a perfect example of the differences among marine environments from place to place. Perhaps the most common complaint about the region's salt water—besides how cold it usually remains, even in the summer—is how cloudy it is. We visit Florida or the Caribbean and envy the clear tropical waters where visibility is 100 feet or more, and then we return home to 10-foot visibility on a good day. But we should celebrate our murky water, because that's why we have so much more marine life than elsewhere. It's why so many whales and other species visit coastal New England in the summer. That murky stuff in the water isn't dust or dirt or pollution but life—tiny plants and animals collectively called plankton—that drives the marine food chain and explains why the fishing industry in New England is so much more successful than most other places in the country.

"The clear waters in the Tropics are clear and beautiful because there's not a lot swimming in them," explained marine biologist Greg Skomal, who has studied sharks in a wide range of marine conditions around the world. "There are limited resources in clear tropical waters. The elevated water temperatures there make it incompatible to a lot of phytoplankton and zooplankton. Up here in New England, it's the dense concentrations of plankton that give us the green coffee water we have."

But that's not all that differentiates New England's marine environment from the Tropics and elsewhere. Fish that spend most of their lives in New England waters are larger, on average, than those found further south, because most large fish have difficulty surviving in warm temperatures. The region also has a broad and shallow continental shelf with more species that live or feed on the bottom than higher in the water column. And offshore of New England is a thermal transition zone, where the warm waters of the Gulf Stream from the south converge with the cold northern waters arriving on the Labrador Current, resulting in an unusual commingling of warm-water-adapted species with cold-water-adapted species.

One thing that is not unique to New England waters, but that is instead a common feature of almost all of the oceans and bays of the world, is the wide range of human-caused problems they face. The Pew Oceans Commission report of 2003, the first thorough review of ocean policy in more than three decades, highlighted many of these issues, as did a report a year later by the U.S. Commission on Ocean Policy. The latter report noted that "human ingenuity and ever-improving technologies have enabled us to exploit—and significantly alter—the ocean's bounty to meet society's escalating needs. Pollution runs off the land, degrading coastal waters and harming marine life. Many fish populations are declining and some of our ocean's most majestic creatures have nearly disappeared. Along our coasts, habitats that are essential to fish and wildlife and provide valuable services to humanity continue to suffer significant losses. Non-native species are being introduced, both intentionally and accidentally, into distant areas, often resulting in significant economic costs, risks to human health, and ecological consequences that we are only beginning to comprehend."

The Pew report adds that "climate change over the next century is projected to profoundly impact coastal and marine ecosystems. Sea-level rise will gradually inundate highly productive coastal wetlands, estuaries, and mangrove forests. Coral reefs that harbor exceptional biodiversity will likely experience increased bleaching due to higher water temperatures. Changes in ocean and atmospheric circulation attributable to climate change could adversely affect coastal upwelling and productivity and have significant local, regional, and global implications on the distribution and abundance of living marine resources."

Yet there remains a great deal of optimism among the scientific community and public policymakers about the ability of the ocean to withstand this onslaught and bounce back. Again, the waters around New England are a good example. Despite the huge number of people living along the region's coastline and the harm that the population causes the marine environment, there is still an abundance of marine life here. As the following eleven chapters will attest, even species that are considered rare or threatened or of special concern may also be thriving in our waters. The stories told in these pages give a face to some of these lesser known species that have endured significant declines in abundance and overcome obstacles to rebuilding sustainable populations. They include stories of creatures we have all seen on our dinner plates or on beaches, species we would never have imagined were rare in the wild or threatened in any way. And they illuminate the lives of a suite of species that have unique life cycles, unusual appearances, and interesting behaviors, all of which call New England home for a good portion of their lives. Each chapter also tells the stories of the admirable men and women who spend their days trying to learn more about these marine organisms so they can protect wildlife populations from depletion and gain insight into their lives.

For me, the experience of researching and writing this book was an extraordinary and somewhat worrisome undertaking. Having spent more than 20 years joining biologists in the field as they study rare species on land, I was unprepared for the range of very different issues involved in studying marine species. Not only did I have to overcome my lifelong concern about the seaworthiness of any boat I was about to climb aboard, I also had to confront the discomfort I felt ordering from a restaurant menu that listed two species about which I was writing. Nonetheless, I had some wonderful times talking with fishermen, riding on boats of all sizes, learning scuba diving, and seeing my first shark. Along the way, a turtle kicked sand in my face, a whale appeared to spit at me, a scallop clamped its shell down on my finger, and I stuck my arm deep into a hole in the ground and waited for a seabird to bite my hand. Which it eventually did. In examining the natural history of these creatures and the role they play in their ecosystem, I also gained a better understanding of the physics of waves and currents, the geology of the seabed, the chemistry of sea water, and other natural factors influencing the lives of New England marine life.

Despite having lived almost my entire life within a few miles of the coast, with this project I finally developed a kinship with the sea and its creatures, an emotional connection that I vow to hold on to for the rest of my days. It's a connection and appreciation that I hope readers will share as they flip through these pages and learn about a remarkable group of marine plants and animals that just may need a few concessions from the human inhabitants of Earth to prosper.

I

Humpback Whale

We were less than a third of the way through our day-long whale-watching expedition when the naturalist on board the *Captain John II*, Krill Carson, made an unexpected announcement. We were approaching a humpback whale that was entangled in fishing gear, and, as regulations dictate, we were going to stand guard over the whale while a disentanglement team was dispatched from Provincetown to try to remove the gear from the animal. It was September 2005, and my wife Renay and I had been enjoying what had become an annual activity for us. Having departed from Plymouth, Massachusetts, we had already seen a couple of humpback whales and were destined to see many more on the trip, but when we finally got a clear look at the entangled whale, it was quite disturbing. Her dorsal fin had been shredded by a boat propeller and looked more like a hand with pudgy fingers than a sleek fin, and a rope and monofilament netting was stuck between the "fingers" and extended around her belly. In addition, more rope was wrapped around a flipper and in her mouth like a gag, making it impossible for her to close her mouth entirely.

Carson told those of us on board that the whale was named Fulcrum, and she was a regular visitor to the waters of Stellwagen Bank, north of Provincetown. She was born in 1997 and is one of the few whales in the region whose lineage can be traced back two generations—her mother, Chimney, has borne three other calves, and Chimney is the daughter of a whale named Ebony. The vessel strike that caused the damage to Fulcrum's dorsal fin occurred sometime between October 2002 and March 2003 and made her perhaps the most easily identifiable whale in the Gulf of Maine. But the entangled fishing gear appeared to be jeopardizing her life.

"That was the summer of Fulcrum and a right whale called Regulus," said Scott Landry, a member of the disentanglement team from the Provincetown Center for Coastal Studies. "Both had very difficult-to-deal-with entanglements. They also spent a lot of time on Stellwagen Bank, so we received a lot of reports from people who had sighted them. That meant we had to keep responding over and over again, and we were unsuccessful at disentangling either of them."

Part of the challenge of disentangling Fulcrum was that there wasn't a length of rope trailing behind the whale that the team could get hold of, and given her earlier run-in with a boat, it was likely that she was more sensitive to approaching vessels than are many other humpback whales.

"It added up to a lot of frustrating days at sea. We tried to get as close as we could, but then she would take a dive, hold her breath for fifteen minutes, and come up half a mile away," said Landry. "With humpbacks we have a ninety percent disentanglement success rate if we find the whale. Usually we can disentangle them on the first try. But we went out for Fulcrum six times, we tried really hard, but despite our best efforts, she got away from us."

By the end of the summer, however, the disentanglement team had been close enough to Fulcrum often enough to determine that the gear was likely to fall off on its own eventually, and according to Landry, the rule of thumb is not to continue to pursue whales that do not have what are considered lethal entanglements. It was a good call. By the following summer, Fulcrum was sighted again in the same general area, but this time she was completely free of any ropes or fishing gear.

Ship strikes and fishing gear entanglements are believed to be the primary source of human-caused mortality for humpback whales and North Atlantic right whales, and while Fulcrum survived both events, many whales aren't so lucky. Yet it is difficult to calculate how many whales are killed by these means each year. Whales struck by ships often die out at sea without anyone ever knowing about them. The probability of seeing an entangled whale is much higher, partly because more than 50 percent of humpbacks and 70 percent of right whales become entangled at some point in their lives, and many live for years with ropes around them before eventually shedding the gear or succumbing to infection or exhaustion. The popularity of whale watching around the world also ensures that many entangled whales will be observed and reported. Efforts to resolve these issues and reduce the threats to the whales are being driven by concern for right whales, which are critically endangered, with only about 350 animals in the entire population. Reducing the speed of ships traveling through known whale feeding grounds, relocation of shipping lanes, reconfiguring fishing gear, and requiring the fishing industry to use breakaway ropes are all strategies being used in various places to protect right whales, and humpbacks are benefiting as well. Yet the threat remains high.

Humpback whales are among the best known whales on the planet. They are found in all the world's oceans, they travel thousands of miles annually from their tropical breeding grounds to their summer feeding areas—the longest mammalian migration on Earth—and their unique songs and acrobatic behaviors make them popular among scientists and the general public alike.

Jooke Robbins is one of their biggest fans in New England. She is director of humpback research for the Center for Coastal Studies and a member of the U.S. delegation to the scientific committee of the International Whaling Commission who studies humpbacks throughout the Atlantic and Pacific Oceans. "From a personal perspective, when you compare humpbacks to other whale species, they're definitely more expressive in a sense," she said. "In the Gulf of Maine, individual whales make a lot of noise, which is very different from fin whales that are more businesslike. They're playful, they're curious, and these are things we can identify with. We once saw a young female playing with a full oil bucket, trying to balance it on her flipper, trying to put it on her head. After we took the bucket away, she followed us and trumpeted at us. You don't get that from other species."

Looking at the illustrations in any field guide to the whales of the world, two things are quite unmistakable about humpbacks. First, they have tremendously long, mostly white flippers—one-third the length of their body, the longest by far of any whale—which are easy to see from a boat even when the whale is more than 20 feet below the surface of the water. It is these distinctive appendages that provide humpbacks with their scientific name, *Megaptera novaeangliae*, which Robbins said translates to "big-winged New Englander." The other physical characteristic that makes humpbacks unique on first glance is their overall shape. They aren't nearly as sleek and streamlined as almost every other whale, most of which are shaped like torpedoes. Instead, humpbacks are all angled and bumpy. Their dorsal fin is located on a hump on their back, which gives them their common name; the edges of their flippers and the trailing edges of their tail or flukes are somewhat irregular or serrated; and their head and lower jaw are covered in lumps called tubercles—somewhat like a giant dill pickle—from each of which grows a small hair follicle called a vibrissa that may have a sensory function. Coupled with their gangling flippers, these bumps and lumps make humpback whales one of the more slowly moving whales.

Mostly black above and white below, they grow to about 55 feet long and can weigh up to 45 tons, and they feed on small schooling fish like herring, sand lance, and mackerel that they find in the relatively shallow waters of the continental shelf. After putting on a thick layer of blubber during the summer, they only feed opportunistically on their breeding grounds, where they live mostly off their fat reserves. According to Robbins, the Gulf of Maine population of humpback whales is one of six distinct populations that feed in the North Atlantic between April and December, with others located off Norway, western Greenland, Iceland, Newfoundland, and the Gulf of St. Lawrence. However, all six populations share a breeding range in the Caribbean between Cuba and Venezuela, with the biggest concentration being just north of the Dominican Republic. This shared breeding site "makes sense to reduce the chance of inbreeding," Robbins said. "In February when all the populations are together, a whale from the Gulf of Maine can mate with a male from Norway." Calves 14 feet long and weighing 1,500 pounds are born a year later and then follow their mothers along unknown migratory routes to the northern feeding grounds they will return to year after year for the rest of their lives.

In New England waters, one of the most preferred humpback whale feeding sites is Stellwagen Bank, part of a national marine sanctuary of the same name that stretches between Cape Ann and the mouth of Massachusetts Bay. Nearly the size of Rhode Island, the sanctuary protects 842 square miles of open ocean and varied seafloor topography that supports a diverse array of species. The bank itself is an underwater plateau that was formed by the retreat of the glaciers at the end of the last Ice Age and that was above sea level as recently as 12,000 years ago. Named for a former U.S. Navy lieutenant, Henry Stellwagen, who discovered the bank during an 1854 survey to find potential sites for constructing lighthouses, it is a rich and productive fishing ground for species of commercial interest, and it has an abundance of sand lance—small eel-like fish—that burrow into the seafloor and provide a nutritious diet for whales every summer.

According to a 2008 draft management plan for the sanctuary, "sand lance numbers in the sanctuary are the highest and most concentrated anywhere in the southern Gulf of Maine and the sanctuary is in an area of high relative abundance of herring. Accordingly, the sanctuary is one of the most intensively used whale habitats in the northeast continental region of the U.S." It has been named one of the top ten premiere places in the world to watch whales.

Unfortunately, nearly every square kilometer of the sanctuary is physically disturbed by fishing gear every year. "Fishing has removed almost all of the big old-growth individuals among biologically important fish populations and reshaped biological communities and habitats in the process," the management plan states. "Commercial fishing lands 17.0 million pounds to 18.4 million pounds of fish and crustaceans from the sanctuary each year on average (1996–2005), yet discards approximately 23% of the total catch as by-catch . . . . Fishing removes 3,200 metric tons of herring from the sanctuary each year on average, an amount sufficient to potentially deplete the forage base for whales and other sanctuary wildlife. The area in and around the sanctuary has the highest use of fixed-gear vessels anywhere along the eastern seaboard of the U.S., and the sanctuary area has the highest number (41%) of reported whale entanglements in the Gulf of Maine."

If that's not enough to worry whale biologists, the shipping traffic through the sanctuary causes about 10 percent of the whale/ship collisions in the entire world. Worse yet, the whale-watching industry in the region is among the biggest offenders. Its boat speeds have doubled in the last 20 years, as has their rate of whale strikes. And 78 percent of whale-watching companies are out of compliance with whale-watch guidelines established by the National Oceanic and Atmospheric Administration. As a result of these concerns, the sanctuary managers are calling for a host of regulatory initiatives designed to better protect the site and the species that live there. These include tighter management regulations for the whale-watching industry, steps to prevent depletion of key forage species, and instituting habitat zoning and compatibility analyses.

To get a close look at some of the humpback whales that enjoy the cornucopia in New England waters, I joined Jooke Robbins in August 2007 for a long day of seeking humpback whales as part of her research to better understand the population dynamics of humpbacks in the North Atlantic. We left Provincetown harbor aboard the *R/V Shearwater* at 8 A.M. with Scott Landry and three interns. The plan was to travel around the tip of Cape Cod and head straight south, paralleling the Cape shoreline, then veer eastward toward the Great South Channel to a point 10 miles east of Chatham, a total distance of about 50 miles. Along the way, Robbins had the interns practice judging distances from the boat to other objects to get them to gain skill in determining how far away a whale is located. I was amazed at how remarkably well they did and at how poorly I did, always underestimating the distance by a large margin, which is apparently typical of beginners.

An hour into the trip, long before we reached our destination, the interns announced that they saw a whale breach in the distance, so we headed after it, even though Robbins worried that we would waste too much time chasing individual whales rather than going to where she believed we would find large congregations of them. Approaching the area where the whale had been seen, dozens of sooty shearwaters and a few greater shearwaters began to appear, suggesting that the area had a wealth of food near the surface. As the boat slowed to a crawl, the whale surfaced nearby and Robbins quickly identified it as a humpback named Freckle traveling with her new calf. It was the first sighting of Freckle in 2007, and Robbins noted some scarring on her tail stock that suggested that she had previously been entangled in fishing gear. While still at the surface, Freckle lifted her flukes and flapped them down on the water in a behavior called lob-tailing; then she raised one long white flipper in the air as if to wave to us. These are two of the behaviors that few other whale species engage in and are among the reasons the whale-watching public is so enamored of humpbacks. As we waited for Freckle to surface once more, her calf breached just 20 yards off the starboard side of the boat, then resurfaced on the port side. The crew let out a collective groan, worried that the calf was unaware of how dangerously close it had come to hitting the boat, but to me it looked like it was playfully trying to splash us.

As Freckle raised her tail to go for a deep dive, most of the seabirds seemed to suddenly disappear, and when the whales resurfaced, the birds appeared again out of nowhere. With her calf at the surface, Freckle created a circle of bubbles from below called a bubble net, which, when the bubbles rise to the surface, traps potential prey within the circle. As I watched the bubbles reach the surface of the water, Freckle swam straight up through the middle of the circle, emerging above the water line with a big splash, her mouth wide open and her throat pleats extended as if she had a huge mouthful of something good. It was the first time in more than twenty whale-watching expeditions that I had seen the bubble-netting behavior, and I was amazed by it. It's hard to imagine how a whale could create what appears to be a constant stream of bubbles rising in a perfect circle, and then know to swim upward through the circle. How much experimentation was required for the first whale to successfully accomplish the feat, and how is that feeding strategy passed on from generation to generation? The second question was answered even before I could think to ask it, as I saw another bubble net rise to the surface and then both Freckle and her calf emerged at the surface within the circle of bubbles. As they did, a mad dash of seabirds flew in to try to capture any tiny morsels of food the whales left behind.

While I was enjoying the bubble net show and noting that sometimes the bubbles are still reaching the surface long after a whale has left the immediate area, Landry had been preparing a low-power crossbow and a custom-made arrow with a tubular tip. When the arrow strikes a whale, it collects a one-inch sample of skin and blubber before a rubber bulb an inch from the tip makes the arrow bounce off the animal and float on the water's surface, where it is easily retrieved with a long-handled fishing net. It's the way that whale biologists collect biopsy samples for DNA analysis and other health assessments, and it was the primary purpose of the research expedition that day.

As Freckle and her calf surfaced once again and went for a deep dive, Landry shot the arrow at the calf from just 20 yards away. It bounced right off, as if it were a child's toy arrow, and the boat's captain called out "Nothing but net!" It was a perfect shot, and within minutes we had retrieved the arrow and unscrewed the tip, containing a blubber sample the color and consistency of a soft-boiled egg. After storing the sample in a cooler for later analysis, we returned on deck just in time to see Freckle and her calf break the surface in the middle of another bubble net, providing one last opportunity for a photograph before we turned to leave.

According to Robbins, bubble netting is usually a group feeding strategy among humpback whales in the Pacific Ocean, but more often than not it is used by individual whales in the Atlantic. "Every whale seems to have its own preferred feeding method," she added, "and Freckle apparently really likes to bubble net."

As we continued on a southeasterly heading, we passed by our only sei whale of the day, then stopped for what we thought were two humpbacks surrounded by hundreds of seabirds—mostly shearwaters, but several gannets and storm petrels as well—but they turned out to be fin whales instead. Further on, a minke whale surfaced 50 feet off the port side of the boat. Then the wind died down, the sun came out, and the research team and I spent the next hour on the upper deck watching birds while searching in vain for whales.

. . .

The biopsy samples that Robbins collects with her crossbow are used for a wide variety of research purposes. Originally it was for genetic analysis simply to determine the gender of each whale. "Unless it rolls over for you, you don't know their sex, which is pretty limiting when you're trying to do population monitoring and you don't have that basic information," explained Robbins, a native of Pennsylvania who started her career as a geologist. Over time, other applications for genetic analysis have been developed, including determination of age, parentage and other relationships, toxicology, and foraging ecology. "Techniques are now being developed to look at various aspects of their health to help us piece together the status of the population," she added.

Determining how many humpback whales are in the population is one question that Robbins hesitates to try to answer. "I can tell you, there are very few good estimates of populations. Rates of survival are easier to study than total number of whales. We don't even have a reliable estimate of the number of humpbacks in the Gulf of Maine, and this is the best studied population there is. The best estimate we have for the North Atlantic is from a study from 1992–93, and that was about twelve thousand animals. We've looked at population growth rate, which is about 3 percent, so the trend is upward. But in every ocean, the dynamics are different, so there isn't good data, even about growth rates. The only other growth rate we know is for the population along the coast of Australia, which is growing at about twelve percent per year, but it can be quite variable. For most areas, we don't have good growth-rate data. Often that's because they are in places where there aren't very many animals to study. In Oceania, the population sizes are not thought to be increasing, though they may be stable, but they are at a very low density. It takes a long time to get at a population number, and by the time you do, it has probably changed."

Despite her hesitancy, Robbins guessed that the North Atlantic humpback whale population probably numbers somewhere around 12,000. Other sources place the North Pacific population at between 18,000 and 20,000 and growing, while those in the Southern Hemisphere may total about 17,000. Some estimates suggest that these numbers are only 10 percent of the number of humpbacks plying the world's oceans before the onset of whaling.

Besides biopsies and genetic analysis, the other primary research strategy being used by marine mammalogists around the world to study whales is a photographic database of individual whales. Since every humpback whale has unique markings on its tail and many dorsal fins are quite distinct, individual whales can be identified in the field.

"It's mainly used to keep track of the population, to determine who's alive, who's entering the population, who's leaving the population," Robbins said. "It's used in studies of survival and other population dynamics. And it's important that it is done every year so we can identify calves being born each year and so we can know which mother they are related to. It also gets at reproductive rates of mothers, tells us the age when they first give birth, and that tells us about the health of their environment. How quickly in life you acquire enough resources to have a calf, provide for it and stay alive yourself depends in large part on the availability of resources in the environment. As the environment changes, population abundance changes. The photo database helps us get at all these questions."

The database also contributes to an understanding of the frequency of entanglements. While many entangled whales shed the gear themselves, the ropes leave scars that can be identified in photographs. By studying which whales have entanglement scars and which do not, biologists can determine the rate of entanglement. "It tells us about the survivors," Robbins said, "but what we really want to know is who didn't survive."

Every humpback whale in the photo database is given a name based on the distinctive pattern of markings on its fluke. But getting all of the biologists and whale-watching boat naturalists to agree on a name has become quite a challenge. The first person to name a whale in New England waters was Aaron Avellar, former owner of the Dolphin Fleet whale-watching company, who thought the white scarring on the dorsal fin of one whale looked like a coating of salt, so he called her Salt. That started the trend of assigning names to every humpback in the region, which has continued for more than 30 years. Before his death, Avellar named all of Salt's subsequent calves and their offspring, and now Avellar's son carries on the tradition. But names for the rest of the whales in the region are decided through a democratic process whereby all participating biologists and naturalists can submit suggested names. Robbins moderates the process, which she said started out as a small gathering during which names were debated over notable quantities of alcohol, but as the scientific community increased, the process became somewhat formalized. In 2008, names were decided through an electronic vote.

"Everyone who participates comes up with suggestions based on a mark on the whale's flukes that, when you see it in the field, is obvious," Robbins said. "It can't be a person's name; it can't be a name that indicates gender; and it can't be a name that's been used before. And you don't want it to be a bad name. We did name one Roadkill, but we regretted it due to the educational component that all these whales play. And then we vote on them . . . People sometimes disagree, or they strongly want the name they suggested, and sometimes nobody likes any of the suggested names. Then we try to come up with an alternate. There are some years when we have to name seventy whales at a sitting, so it can be a long process. But the important thing is that it's a community process because names are a shared system of communication that is used by every naturalist from here to Maine."

Much of the other research on humpback whales in New England is focused on trying to come up with answers to the two most pressing threats the animals face—ship strikes and fishing gear entanglement. According to Dave Wiley, research coordinator at the Stellwagen Bank National Marine Sanctuary, in order to understand these threats, it's important to understand how the whales forage. That's because when the animals feed at the bottom they are at risk of becoming entangled in fishing gear, and when they feed at the surface they are at risk of being struck by passing ships.

"The whales come to our waters exclusively to eat," he said. "To understand the water column and what puts them in jeopardy, we have to have a really good idea of how they forage."

So Wiley tags humpbacks in the sanctuary with a revolutionary tool called a D-tag that attaches to the animal's back with a suction cup and has provided the first clear understanding of the subsurface behavior of these large whales. By measuring the whale's pitch, roll, heading, and depth multiple times every second, researchers can process that data into a three-dimensional visualization and create a virtual whale on their computers. The 300 hours of data Wiley and his

team collected between 2004 and 2007 finally confirmed the speculation that humpbacks often dive straight to the bottom to scoop up
sand lance buried in the substrate.

"From the abrasions we've seen on their lower jaw, we figured that
they sometimes went down to the bottom, but the fact they did it for
hours and hours on end was unknown," Wiley said. In 2006, the
whales he tagged fed high in the water column by day when sand
lance were swimming there, but the humpbacks fed at the bottom all
night long because that's when the sand lance bury themselves in the
sediment. But not all the whales he tagged did that.

"The data showed us that they do a lot of different things based on
local conditions," Wiley said. "These are long-lived predators covering
a lot of area, so to be successful they need to employ different strategies depending on local conditions. Some whales we tagged in the
Great South Channel fed on the bottom twenty-four hours a day,
while others were at the surface all the time. Humpback whales are extremely plastic in their foraging behavior, so they will adapt their foraging behavior to whatever strategy will be successful at that moment."

Because the D-tags are also equipped with hydrophones to record
sound, the researchers can, for the first time, match the sounds the
whales make to the behaviors they exhibit. The tags can also detect
other sounds in the marine environment, which may help determine
whether the whales change their behaviors in response to the sounds of
ships. One thing the researchers have already learned is that humpback
whales sing a great deal more in New England waters than anyone expected. They also detected a previously unknown clicking and buzzing
sound used only at night that appeared somewhat like a bat's echoloca-
tion and that may be used to help them find food, though it may also
be simply a method of finding the seafloor in extreme darkness.

One outcome of this research has been a successful shifting of the
shipping lanes that cut through Stellwagen Bank National Marine
Sanctuary for ships on their way to Boston Harbor. Wiley said that in
their previous location, the shipping lanes cut across habitat that was
48 percent sandy bottom, the preferred foraging habitat for humpbacks because that's where the sand lance are found. After the shift,
only 18 percent of the shipping lanes cross sandy bottom habitat, considerably reducing the risk that humpbacks will be struck by ships.

Wiley has also worked in collaboration with Chris Clark, director of Cornell University's bioacoustics laboratory, to deploy a system of ten acoustic recording units on the seafloor to collect whale sounds. Their aim is to examine the distribution of whales based on acoustic data by studying the different calls they make and determining whether those calls are impacted by shipping noises. These submerged listening posts can also relay information to shore via satellite to warn ships' captains when whales are in the shipping lanes. Currently, the system only issues warnings when North Atlantic right whales are present, but it may soon be programmed to warn of humpbacks in the vicinity as well.

Back aboard the *R/V Shearwater*, we approached a juvenile humpback feeding continuously at the surface, but it was zigzagging so much that it was difficult to determine where it was going to turn up next. Every time it took a breath, we could see that its throat pleats were distended, which the biologists thought suggested it was taking in large mouthfuls of water and plankton, an unusual feeding strategy since most adults prey on small fish. And each time it dove beneath the rolling waves, it left a large footprint—a slick spot on the water produced from the energy of its tail movement—then changed direction again and reappeared in an unexpected location. The biologists quickly tired of trying to track this unidentified whale to get close enough to shoot for a biopsy. As the captain continued to maneuver the boat into position, we saw the blows of two fin whales in the distance, but we paid little attention to them. After 20 minutes and one missed shot with the crossbow, Landry finally got a good angle (though it was longer than he would have preferred), pulled the trigger, and the arrow struck the whale just below the dorsal fin as the animal sunk beneath the surface.

Just after noon, another pair of humpbacks was spotted and identified as Scratch and her calf, and since the biologists already had a biopsy from her, they just took a quick photograph and continued on. Soon after we found another pair, but Robbins looked confused as she tried to process who they were. She was certain by its fluke markings that the mother was Tilt, but she was traveling with a small juvenile that Robbins couldn't identify. Robbins thought it might be Tapioca, but the young whale never showed its flukes well enough to identify it confidently despite more than 30 minutes of watching the whales and cross-referencing the juvenile's features in the photo database in an on-board laptop computer. While Robbins tried to make the identification, Landry repeatedly attempted to get a biopsy, but the rocking of the boat in the deep swells and the distance the whales remained from the boat made it challenging. Twice the arrow hit the water just inches from the whale but didn't penetrate enough to collect a sample. Clearly frustrated at his lack of success, Landry turned the crossbow over to Robbins as the boat continued on its way.

An hour later, we finally found what Robbins was looking for—a large concentration of humpbacks. Located about 10 miles east of Chatham in waters about 180 feet deep, we stumbled across more than a dozen humpbacks in relatively close association, and all hands were called on deck to try to keep track of them. A quick 360-degree scan around the boat found five whales blowing at once in one direction and four more blowing simultaneously perhaps a mile away in the opposite direction, causing Robbins to excitedly shout out, "We're surrounded!" She repeatedly called out whale names and certain behaviors, while the interns jotted down notes on a spreadsheet in complex shorthand. I was amazed at how quickly Robbins could identify each whale based on very brief glimpses of mostly submerged body parts far in the distance. As she did so, the students also shot hundreds of photographs, noting the identity and position of each whale and whatever else they thought might be useful. It was an exhilarating and somewhat stressful time.

Among the whales in the group were Seal, Canopy, Circuit, and Snowplow; mothers Fern, Ursa, and Pogo, each with a calf; and Dyad with a yearling, which was quite unexpected. Most whale calves separate from their mothers before they are a year old, and Robbins said that she knows of fewer than ten humpbacks since the 1970s that were seen associating with their mothers in their second year. As unusual as that is, Robbins was somewhat disappointed that the whales seemed to be feeding as mother/calf pairs and not interacting as a large group, which usually leads to interesting group behaviors. Nonetheless, to be so close to so many whales at once was quite spectacular. As I turned to scan the horizon, one of the mothers surfaced right next to the stern of the boat. A second too late, I heard the captain call out "watch out for your glasses," a reference to the mucus that sprays from a whale's blowhole and that, when it lands on your sunglasses, becomes smeared and is difficult to remove without soap and water. A close encounter with a whale blow is also a disturbing assault on one's olfactory system. But I was too focused on the sound of the blow to worry about my glasses or the smell. At a distance, a whale blow sounds like exactly what it is—a forceful exhale of air from a massive creature—but up close I could hear a bit of a squeak or whinny sound as well, as if the crush of air swirled through its blowhole like the release of the air brakes on a tractor trailer.

Unfortunately, the wind had picked up as we continued watching the whales, making the conditions difficult to take pictures and even more difficult to shoot for biopsies. And as we moved around looking for more, we just kept re-sighting the same individuals. So Robbins decided it was time to head off to another target area, and I decided it was time to take a nap.

On a recent visit to the New Bedford Whaling Museum, I was surprised to learn that while humpback whales were hunted extensively in the late eighteenth and early nineteenth centuries, they were never the preferred target of whalers because they produced inferior-quality oil and baleen. Nonetheless, because the whaling industry was centered in New Bedford, Massachusetts, and because so many whaling ships plied the North Atlantic where humpbacks were once abundant, tens of thousands of humpback whales met their deaths at the point of a harpoon. In the Southern Hemisphere, where the hunt continued until 1983, much of it illegal, more than 200,000 humpbacks were killed in the twentieth century alone.

The whaling industry reached its peak in the 1840s when 739 whale ships were registered around the country, 400 of which were based in New Bedford. As the population of the preferred whales—North Atlantic right whales—bottomed out and ships had to travel farther and farther away to find other species of whales, the industry declined and sailors switched careers and went to work in the textile mills that had sprung up around the region. When thirty New Bedford-based whaling ships were crushed by Arctic ice in 1871 and twelve more met the same fate the following year, it was clear that the whaling industry was on its way out. The last American whaling ship sailed from New Bedford in 1924, only to run aground and sink off Cuttyhunk Island at the entrance to Buzzard's Bay.

Seventeen years previously, the New Bedford Whaling Museum opened its doors, and since 1935 it has exhibited the skeleton of a 35-foot-long male humpback whale that had been found dead off Martha's Vineyard. Its skeletal flippers look like four-fingered hands, with the middle two fingers considerably longer than the others, and its upper jaw looks somewhat like the massive beak on the world's largest bird. The gray and dried humpback skeleton is dwarfed, however, by the skeleton of an adolescent blue whale that hangs beside it in the museum's main entryway. Measuring 66 feet long and weighing 4 tons—more than ten times lighter than the living whale was when it was struck by a ship in 1998—the blue whale skeleton is only two-thirds the size of that of an adult. The rest of the museum is equally impressive, including figureheads from whaling ships, tools and equipment for processing whales, paintings and etchings of whaling scenes from the 1500s to the 1900s, and beautifully crafted log books. For me, what was nearly as impressive as the blue whale skeleton was the skeleton of a sperm whale, whose head looked like that of my childhood-favorite dinosaur, a triceratops, complete with a shield-like protuberance rising up from the back of its skull and a massive line of teeth in its jaw.

Walking away from the museum, I thought to myself how glad I was that the era of whaling had ended long ago. But it really hasn't. In fact, some countries—led by Japan—are trying to make it respectable again. Despite an international moratorium on commercial whaling enacted in 1982, Japan has exploited a loophole in the agreement and continued to harpoon whales, contending that the hunt is entirely for scientific purposes, even though all of the whale meat ends up on the dinner plates of Japanese consumers. There is little evidence that their science holds up to review by the international scientific community, yet their hunts continue. The Japanese have killed more than 25,000 minke, sei, Bryde's, and sperm whales in the Southern Ocean and the North Pacific since 1987. In the 2007–2008 season, Japanese whalers planned to kill 935 minke whales, 50 fin whales, and—for the first time since the moratorium went into effect—50 humpback whales. Public outcry, international condemnation, and formal diplomatic objections didn't stop the hunt, though interference by activists from Greenpeace and the Sea Shepherd Conservation Society delayed it long enough that the whalers were unable to kill as many animals as they had hoped. Yet the Japanese intend to continue hunting whales every year, even though just 1 percent of Japanese consumers choose to eat whale meat and 4,800 tons of surplus whale meat sits stockpiled in freezers. Even the five seafood companies that owned the whaling fleet got out of the business, citing poor consumer demand.

Thankfully, targeted hunting of humpback whales is not a concern in the North Atlantic. What is a growing concern, however, is the increasing amount of human-caused noise in the ocean, which may be affecting humpback whales, other marine mammals, and perhaps even fish. Humpbacks have become known as the "songsters of the sea" for the wonderful variety of creaks, moans, squeaks, and groans they make to communicate with one another. Produced primarily on the breeding grounds, their songs can last for as long as 20 minutes, and they may repeat them over and over again for hours. Humpback whales in different geographic regions have even developed unique dialects that gradually change over a period of years. Yet no one seems to know how they produce the sounds or what they mean. Some scientists suggest that the song is designed to attract a mate, while others say it may be their way of issuing a threat. It may even simply be an inquiry to find out who else is in the neighborhood.

Regardless of its purpose, the sounds made by humpbacks apparently play an important role in their lives. Sadly, military sonar, seismic air guns used in oil and gas exploration, pile driving to build bridges and offshore energy facilities, and ship engines are flooding the marine environment with a constant racket that is likely interfering with whale communication, affecting their behavior, and in some cases causing physical injury and even death.

Brandon Southall, director of the Ocean Acoustics Program for the National Oceanic and Atmospheric Administration, divides these sources of noise into what he calls acute noises and chronic noises. Acute noises like sonar and seismic air guns are typically rare events but are especially loud—military tactical sonar systems can generate sounds as high as 235 decibels—and have been documented to cause a wide variety of severe impacts, primarily on small beaked whales, which are more closely related to dolphins than to humpbacks.

"Beaked whales are deep divers that spend a lot of time under the surface approaching a mile deep," Southall said. "It's possible that their diving characteristics make them especially sensitive to these acute sounds. The general hypothesis is that the sounds don't harm them directly, but that it probably causes some behavioral response that may disorient them into stranding or result in the formation of the bends or other physical injuries. No one will deny the fact that there have been a number of stranding events of beaked whales [caused by military sonar] . . . The dispute is over how common it is, whether that effect is isolated to a subset of marine animals or whether all marine animals are affected, and what to do about it."

Mid-frequency military sonar systems are primarily used in training exercises in areas of the ocean near U.S. Navy shipyards, like Hawaii, Southern California, the Bahamas, and Virginia. The crews on Navy ships must be certified to operate sonar systems, so they conduct war games to learn to use sonar to detect submarines. Over the years, submarines have gotten progressively quieter, making it more and more difficult for Navy personnel to detect the vessels simply by listening, and as the background noise of cargo ships in the ocean has increased, the Navy has placed more emphasis on the use of active sonar.

According to Southall, there is no evidence of humpbacks having been negatively affected by sonar or other acute noises, but that doesn't mean that it isn't an issue for them. "We have no direct evidence of large whales reacting to sonar the way the beaked whales do, but it also hasn't been looked at all that closely. Of the large whales, humpbacks would presumably be the most likely ones to be impacted because they make sounds that cross over into the same frequency range as the sonar. They have the broadest range and highest frequency of any of the large baleen whales."

While concerns over the acute noises get most of the attention from environmental groups and the news media, Southall thinks that the chronic noises—primarily from the engines of cargo and tanker ships—could be more significant because of the wide range over which the noise occurs and the continuous nature of the sounds. More than 90 percent of world trade is transported by ship, and according to the Roundtable of International Shipping Associations, in 2004 alone more than 6.7 billion metric tons of cargo were hauled a total of four million ocean miles. And the continuing boom in international trade is likely to drive demand for more and bigger ships going to more and more ports.

"Big ships driving around the oceans delivering things are unintentionally making sounds, and it's like living near a highway—it's just constantly noisy," Southall said. "The effects from these chronic noises are more difficult to identify and to differentiate from other stressors. We have better information on the acute effects than the chronic effects . . . The sound of ship engines can travel hundreds of miles, and with so many ships traversing the world's oceans, the conglomeration of the noises from these ships make up a background noise like an acoustic fog. Whales are used to operating in a world with a certain background clarity that is being clouded by this din."

Most ship noises occur in the same low frequency range that most whales use to communicate—what Southall calls their "bread and butter range"—so it is quite likely that these chronic noises may affect the whales' ability to communicate. Due to the increased background noises in the ocean, whales that could detect each other from 1,000 kilometers away 100 years ago can now only detect each other from 10 kilometers.

"What that background interference means remains somewhat uncertain," said Southall. "We know these are acoustic animals that use sound for crucial life functions like breeding and avoiding predators. So at some point you get to where you really are changing the way they live and survive."

Southall is optimistic, however, that the background noise created by ships is a problem that can be addressed with new engine technologies. "All the shipping companies care about is getting a box from point A to point B, so I think the best chance for making progress on this issue is with those sources where the introduction of sound is unintentional. But the military sonar and the seismic air guns are going to continue to be difficult to manage, controversial, political, and contentious for the foreseeable future."

I awoke from my nap to what sounded like celebratory shouts from Robbins and Landry, and when I emerged from below deck, the biologists reported that Fulcrum was up ahead. It was the first time the formerly entangled whale had been seen in 2007, so her propeller-damaged dorsal fin was a pleasure to see. And even better, she was traveling with her first calf. Given the stresses she underwent during her long entanglement, no one expected that she would give birth for at least another year or two, so Robbins speculated that she must be a strong and healthy animal.

As we happily watched Fulcrum cavort with her calf, we noticed a massive cargo ship—undoubtedly the largest ship I had ever seen—as it appeared on the horizon from the south and slowly powered north toward Boston Harbor. Labeled NYK in large red letters for Nippon Yushen Kaisha, a global shipping company based in Japan, it was probably transporting automobiles for the U.S. market. It took the ship nearly an hour to disappear from view, and when it was nearly gone, Landry wondered aloud how many whales it had unknowingly struck along the way.

At 6 P.M., while I was taking yet another nap, Robbins decided to call it a day and the boat turned northwest toward Provincetown. Along the way on the three-hour return trip, we slowed occasionally to view other humpbacks, including a solitary mature male named Thread and a young male called Summit, whose dorsal fin had been partially broken or sliced off. We stopped to get a photograph of the new shape of his fin so it could be included in the photo identification catalog. Summit had last been seen 3 years previously, so it was impossible to know when the damage was done, but Robbins speculated that it may have been a blunt-force injury caused by the tail of another whale during periods of aggression. "It's not unusual to see dorsal fins that are a little droopy because of that kind of behavior," she said.

Halfway home, we stopped again for two very active humpbacks, which turned out to be Tulip and her calf. Tulip appeared to be calmly feeding while the calf exhibited almost all of the most entertaining behaviors humpbacks are known for—flipper waving, lob-tailing, and repeatedly breaching and flopping back into the water with a loud splash. It was clearly having a ball. Landry took the opportunity to get a biopsy of the calf with an easy close-up shot, to which the whale seemed to object. It immediately raised its tail straight upward and aggressively slapped it down hard and loudly. "That's the biggest reaction I've ever seen to a biopsy," Robbins said, "though it's not totally unexpected from a young one. Most adults are used to being nudged by their calves or by other adults, so they don't even notice the arrow hitting them. But calves more often do, just as young children sometimes overreact from something that is unexpected."

As if to defend her calf, Tulip surfaced near the boat with her mouth wide open and full of seawater, her frayed baleen clearly visible. She then quickly closed her jaws, and like a mischievous child poking its engorged cheeks to spray those nearby, the massive whale nearly doused us with water. We clearly deserved it.

© Pat Morris / ardea.com

2

Atlantic Halibut

Nearly every one of the thirty-plus boats in the Jonesport, Maine, harbor in July is a workboat, mostly those of lobstermen, but also scallop draggers, otter trawlers, and a few others I couldn't identify. But on a Sunday night at eight o'clock, with the sun sinking low in the pastel sky, just one boat—the *Aspiration*—had any activity onboard.

I had just arrived in town after a six-hour drive from my home in Rhode Island, and my lodging for the night overlooked the harbor. Gazing out my window I watched as Jason Alley pulled his pickup into the harbor parking lot, tossed a few buckets of gear into a rickety rowboat, and silently glided among the moored vessels until he reached his 33-foot lobster boat. Alley described the boat as "nothing special," just a middle-of-the-road workboat he acquired 10 years previously. That Sunday night, he spent 90 minutes baiting hooks to be used the following day in hopes of catching Atlantic halibut (*Hippoglossus hippoglossus*), the largest flatfish found in the North Atlantic. Wearing bright orange oilskins that contrasted sharply with the white and mint-green boat, the 31-year-old fisherman looked somewhat lonely as he went about his solitary job, but Alley certainly wouldn't describe it that way. He has an incredible passion for halibut fishing (though he seldom eats what he catches), which he struggles to explain and which those like me who don't fish for halibut have difficulty comprehending.

"Some people want to hunt an elephant, some want to hunt a big moose, I want to hunt a halibut. It's kind of indescribable the drive to just see one," he said, struggling to find the right words. "I'm a local history buff, and I love seeing the pictures of the old guys with the big fish, and that's what I want to see."

He paused for a few moments, then a genuine smile came to his boyish face and he tried again to describe the feeling. "When I set my trawls on May first when the season opens, I don't sleep that night. I don't sleep at all, and I don't really settle in to start to sleep until a couple weeks later. It's a thrill to get a small one, but it's awesome to get a nice one." Later, after admitting he hardly makes any money fishing for them, he noted with embarrassment that he dreams about halibut, even imagining a system where a buzzer goes off in his bedroom the moment he has hooked a fish so he can immediately race out to retrieve it.

Alley is not the only halibut fisherman to get tongue-tied and feel sheepish while trying to describe the overwhelming anticipation, uncommon exhilaration, and immense pleasure of fishing for and catching halibut. But he was the only one out there in the Jonesport harbor baiting hooks until after nine o'clock that Sunday night before a very early morning of fishing.

I met him for the first time the next morning at four o'clock in the harbor parking lot, along with Kohl Kanwit, a fisheries biologist with the Maine Department of Marine Resources. The two looked and acted like brother and sister, dressed as they were in identical faded blue sweatshirts, brown knee-high boots, and orange oilskins, their good-natured ribbing and engaging banter filling any voids in the conversation. Five minutes later we were on the *Aspiration*, and five minutes after that we had left the harbor.

It gets bright quite early in Downeast Maine. Sunrise didn't officially come until 4:45, but it was bright enough to read by well before that, particularly since my visit coincided with a full moon. The weather conditions were perfect for a day on the water—calm winds, no swells, bright sunshine, and temperatures topping out at 65 degrees. As we steamed east toward Machias Seal Island, the sun rose directly ahead of us, forcing us to stare everywhere but in the direction we were traveling. The noise of the engine made it challenging to hear the conversation between Alley and Kanwit—I think it was mostly gossip about fishing regulations, other fishermen, and the fishing industry—so I scanned the water for seabirds and enjoyed the scenery. Approaching the town of Cutler, one of the easternmost communities in the United States, Alley pointed out the twenty-five Cold War-era radio antennas standing side-by-side on the horizon, each reaching between 800 and 1,000 feet high, remnants of the town's history as one of the most important military facilities for communicating with submarines in the North Atlantic, Arctic, and Mediterranean.

At 6:10, I saw the first Atlantic puffin of the trip, and regularly thereafter more of the clown-like birds flew by in groups of three or four, but not close enough to get a good look. Occasionally a lone razorbill fluttered by as well—looking somewhat like a fat black-and-white torpedo skimming inches above the waves—but no ducks or loons were about and very few gulls made an appearance. A mile or two west of Machias Seal Island, Alley slowed the boat and began to scan the water more intently while repeatedly glancing at his electronic equipment. And then he went to work.

First he tied three colorful 100-foot coils of rope together with two buoys at one end and an anchor at the other. He then connected another line, which had been carefully coiled in a bucket, to the anchor and tossed the anchor overboard. The latter line was 2,000 feet long, with a hundred 16/0 circle hooks connected to the ground line with 2 feet of heavy monofilament at 18-foot intervals. Each hook was baited with half a mackerel, thanks to the time Alley had spent in the Jonesport harbor the night before. The weight of the anchor, along with the slow forward speed of the boat, pulled the full length of the line into the water in a well-coordinated manner, each baited hook leaping over the stern like choreographed performing dolphins. The end of the line of hooks was connected to another anchor and another 300 feet of rope and two more buoys, all of which were also tossed into the water.

It was an impressive operation, particularly since Alley did it all by himself. Most halibut fishermen have a "sternman" to help coordinate the job from the back of the boat while the captain remains at the controls, but Alley prefers to do it himself, partly because he doesn't trust anyone else to do it right, and partly because he doesn't want to pay someone to do what he can do just as well without assistance. "It's not particularly safe to be out here by yourself," he said, "and I wouldn't let my kid do it, but I choose to fish alone anyway. Nobody else I know goes halibut fishing alone but me." Kanwit and I had offered our assistance, but we knew we would just be in the way, so we were pleased when he waved us off.

After the first 100 hooks were in the water, Alley raced off to find another site to set two more lines. The research project I had come to observe called for him to set one line of hooks at precise coordinates, but the other two lines could be placed anywhere within 2 miles of the coordinates, at the fisherman's discretion. So Alley repeatedly glanced at his electronics to give him an idea of the terrain of the seafloor while studying the water surface. Choosing the right location for setting the line may be the biggest challenge to fishing for halibut. It's important to avoid dropping the line too close to the abundant lobster traps and other fishing gear, and ideally Alley sought to set it on a slope or hole about 200 feet deep. Kanwit said that halibut prefer an edge habitat, like the dividing line between a rocky bottom and a sandy bottom. Later, though, they both admitted that they really weren't exactly sure what kind of habitat attracts the most halibut.

"I've found them on almost every kind of bottom," said Alley. He noted that on one trip with Chris Bartlett, Kanwit's partner in the research project and the man Alley jokingly refers to as "the good observer" of the two, "we set a grid in three hundred feet of flat soupy mud, and that's the kind of place I would have avoided like the plague if I was fishing commercially. But we did it because that was our coordinates and it was lightning and thundering like Gilligan's Island. And we were surprised that there were four fish on it—four decent keepers, the largest one was forty-five inches and the smallest one was thirty-eight. We were both stunned. The mud was soup. So I found them on that, I found them on old shell bottoms, I find them everywhere."

Yet it still took Alley 20 minutes to make up his mind about where to lay the second set of hooks, but when he did, it went out just as easily as the first. As the hooks jumped into the water, a northern fulmar glided in to try to grab an easy meal. The rugged seabird with the gull-like plumage appeared to beg for a bite, but when Alley obliged, the bird hesitated too long before reaching for it and the bait sank below the surface.

After steaming south for five minutes, Alley quickly decided on the site to set the final line of hooks, and just as the last anchor hit the water, Kanwit said it was time to break for lunch. It was just seven o'clock in the morning, and we had five hours to kill before we could haul in the lines.

Next to swordfish, bluefin tuna, and some of the larger sharks, Atlantic halibut are the largest fish in the northwest Atlantic Ocean. Growing up to 7 feet in length and weighing 600 pounds, they range from Greenland to Virginia, but they are seldom found south of Cape Cod any longer, and the bulk of their population appears to be in the northern Gulf of Maine and the waters off the Canadian Maritimes. To a biologist, it's an unusual looking fish, with both eyes located on the right side of its body instead of its left, an arched lateral line, a large mouth full of sharp, curved teeth, and a concave tail. But to a fisherman like Jason Alley, it's a muscular and elegant animal.

"Most people can picture a flounder," Alley said, "so a small halibut is a flounder times a hundred. It's kind of awkward to see something so large when you might be used to seeing something smaller. They're more unique than cod and haddock because their color changes a little bit on the different types of bottom. Sometimes you get some that are a pretty ocean green, or sometimes one with a calico gray, or a green and black. They have really unique colorings on the top. The bottom on a pretty specimen is ultra pure white, and it's really quite interesting to see. You can really see the muscle definition on a halibut on the white side, whereas on most fish you can't. A big halibut you can see the muscle ripples, sometimes even on the dark side. So it gives you a little respect for the fish."

Unfortunately, Atlantic halibut are among the rarest fish in the Atlantic. The National Marine Fisheries Service listed it as a species of concern in 2004, while the American Fisheries Society has designated it as threatened and the International Union for the Conservation of Nature calls it endangered. Regardless of how it is labeled, it's a hard fish to find today, and it's been that way for more than 100 years. Prior to the 1820s, it was, as Kohl Kanwit called it, a "trash fish." But when a market for halibut developed in Boston, a commercial fishery soon followed suit. Halibut were apparently abundant in the inshore waters of Barnstable Bay, Nantucket Shoals, the coast of Cape Cod, and Massachusetts Bay, where one vessel reported catching 15,000 pounds of halibut on a 2-day trip in 1837. As halibut abundance declined inshore, the commercial fishing fleet moved offshore to Georges Bank, where Captain Epes Merchant claimed in 1884 that 50,000 pounds could "easily" be captured in 2 days. Twenty years later, the fishery collapsed and halibut became one of the first fish to be considered depleted or overfished. It has yet to recover. In fact, it continues to decline, if you believe the data. Annual landings of halibut in the Gulf of Maine/Georges Bank area from 2000 to 2005 were just one-third of those caught from 1977 to 2000. As a result, federal regulations prohibit targeting halibut for capture in federal waters (from 3 to 200 miles off shore), and just one fish of at least 36 inches can be caught as by-catch per trip, even if the trip lasts 10 days or more. The state of Maine has a 3-month halibut fishing season in state waters (up to 3 miles from shore), where fishermen can catch up to four fish per day and fifty fish per season.

"One reason why the fish have never recovered," explained Alley, "is that the fish draggers from the nineteen-thirties to the nineteen-seventies would just take everything at the bottom, and they took a lot of small fish of every species, but especially halibut. Trawling irresponsibly wiped out many, many future generations [of halibut]. They're just not reproducing any more."

They're not reproducing in part because halibut are very slow to mature. Female halibut spawn for the first time at age 10 to 12 years, with males maturing a couple years earlier. Spawning occurs in late winter and spring on the soft, muddy bottom off the edge of the continental shelf in water 2,000 to 3,000 feet deep. Females produce several batches of eggs each season and can produce up to 7 million eggs in a single year, each about 3 to 4 millimeters in diameter and appearing pinkish in color. The eggs are buoyant, so they float freely in the water column. In about 16 days, they hatch, and the 6-millimeter-long larvae slowly begin moving into shallower water, obtaining nourishment from an attached yolk sac for their first 4 or 5 weeks until their mouths become fully functional and they begin feeding on tiny planktonic organisms. The larvae look much like the larvae of other fish, swimming vertically in the water with one eye on each side of their head. But when they approach 20 millimeters in length, the left eye begins to migrate over the top of its head toward the right side, completing its unusual journey by the time the fish is about 44 millimeters long. During this eye relocation process, pigment begins to appear on the right side of the body, and when the juvenile fish achieve a length of about 50 millimeters, they flop over with the white side down and live the rest of their lives as bottom-dwelling creatures. They then grow quite rapidly while feeding on progressively larger organisms, beginning with worms and small crustaceans, and eventually graduating to a diet consisting exclusively of other fish, including redfish, haddock, cod, and lumpfish, depending on seasonal availability.

Anecdotal evidence from fishermen suggests that the diet of adult halibut isn't as narrow as that, however. Alley said that one of the halibut he caught earlier in the season had not only his mackerel bait in its stomach, but also a small halibut and a spawning green sandworm, while another had a tiny halibut and a sand lance. He said that most of the large halibut—those over 50 pounds—appear to feed predominantly on what he calls bunny crabs.

Despite all of these details about the life history of halibut, very little is known about their biology and ecology, particularly about spawning locations, movement patterns, and preferred habitat types. That's the main reason why the Maine Department of Marine Resources conducted an experimental fishery in federal waters from 2000 to 2004. A wide range of biological data was collected from the 900 mature halibut that were captured and tagged during the project, and nearly 100 of the fish were later recaptured by fishermen, enabling the biologists to assess their movement patterns. One unexpected outcome was a realization that there are two female halibut to every one male halibut in the Gulf of Maine, yet the ratio is the reverse in Canadian waters. The big finding of the research, however, contradicted the previously held belief that fish stocks from Maine and Canada were not mixing. In fact, 30 percent of the fish originally tagged in Maine waters were later recaptured in waters off the Maritimes, especially off Nova Scotia.

"The bizarre thing about the tag returns is that either all the fish are coming back to the location where they were originally tagged—almost dead on to the spot that they were caught the first time—or they are going to the East," noted Kanwit, who earned a college degree in ancient Greek history before volunteering on a lobster research project and starting a career in fisheries research. "There's no westward movement at all. Out of the ninety or a hundred fish that we've had back, only two of them moved west, and only by five or ten miles. That's it. The rest of the fish have all moved east. There's a theory on the West Coast that there's a compensatory migration, that because they are buoyant eggs and buoyant larvae, the fish spawn out and the current carries the eggs and larvae to wherever the current is flowing, and then once the juveniles settle [to the bottom] and grow a little bit, they have to swim back to maintain the population where they came from. If that's true, maybe that's happening here and there's actually a spawning body off Nova Scotia, the current brings them this way and dumps eggs and larvae on the coast of Maine, and then some of the fish have to move back to the East to keep that population viable. That's a theory we've proposed."

My visit with Kanwit and Alley aboard the *Aspiration* was part of a follow-up research project designed to determine the abundance and distribution of halibut in the Gulf of Maine. The state's coastline was divided into five sectors, and a fisherman from each sector was contracted to fish for halibut for 1 day at each of thirteen sites. Alley's sector encompassed the easternmost part of the state, where halibut are believed to be most abundant. Every fish caught was tagged, weighed, and measured, and a DNA sample was collected to determine gender. One of the tags collected data on the temperature and depth of the water where the fish traveled, which will help determine how far offshore they wander. Each of the participating fishermen was paid $1,000 for each of the thirteen sites they visited, plus the cost of bait, but they paid for fuel themselves, as well as for other expenses like hooks, ropes, and buoys. The money isn't why Alley signed on, though.

"Fishing in state waters is exciting," he said, "but most people believe that the best fishing is offshore, maybe three miles to ten miles off. Traditionally that's where my family has caught the fish. There's a better type of bottom there, and maybe a little less pressure [on the fish]. This project is kind of like a ticket to do something no one else can. Kohl doesn't know this, but I would have done it for free anyway."

Before he could continue, Kanwit interjected, "I would have bet on that, Jason."

"It's a chance to go somewhere and fish in a closed area," the fisherman added. "It's not as easy as shooting fish in a barrel, but I don't have any competition out here."

The research project requires that the lines of baited hooks remain on the seafloor for a minimum of 5 hours and a maximum of 24 hours before they are retrieved. According to Kanwit, evidence from the halibut fishery in the Pacific Ocean suggests that additional fish are not captured after the bait has been in the water for more than 5 hours, and hooked fish either die or figure out how to escape after 24 hours. So to kill time while we waited for halibut to take the bait, we shared stories, took a nap, cut bait, and watched as Alley pulled out a hand line, baited the hook, and dropped it to the bottom in another effort to catch a fish. He said he often tries using a hand line to catch halibut, and while he has never caught one that way, it's worth the effort just to pass the time.

But this time, he wished he hadn't bothered. While straddling the side of the boat, Alley kicked the line repeatedly to make the bait dance at the bottom, but less than a minute after he started, his line broke and his heavy lead weight and baited hook were lost. The frustration on his face was clear, but a bit of sisterly encouragement from Kanwit convinced him to try again. Using an old, rusty monkey wrench as a weight, he tried in vain for 30 minutes before giving up and reaching for a snack instead.

With 2 hours still left to kill, Alley began a long slow ride around

Machias Seal Island, a somewhat famous seabird nesting site that is also the center of a somewhat less famous boundary dispute between the United States and Canada. The treeless, teardrop-shaped island—essentially a 10-acre pile of rocks—appears to have little value economically or politically, so one wouldn't suppose it would be the source of an international argument for more than two centuries. But its location at the boundary between the Gulf of Maine and the Bay of Fundy has led to numerous legal claims from both countries. The dispute is clearly visible simply by looking at a map—the boundary lines on American maps angle eastward around the island to make it part of Maine, while Canadian maps have a similarly angled boundary line that includes it as part of Nova Scotia.

The dispute apparently arose as a result of vague language in the 1782 Treaty of Peace that ended the conflict between the newly formed United States and Great Britain following the Revolutionary War. Article Two of the agreement establishes boundaries, but the language can be interpreted several ways, and of course each country interprets it to its own advantage. Efforts to resolve the dispute in international courts have been fruitless. Since neither country intends to alter its interpretation of the treaty, they both have made additional claims based on policies and actions they have taken that meet legal precedents from other international boundary disputes. Canada, for instance, claims that the lighthouse it constructed on the island in 1832 and has manned continuously since then—the only Canadian lighthouse still staffed—is proof of its ownership, especially since the United States has not contested occupation of the lighthouse. Both countries claim that their actions to police the waters around the island strengthen their claims. Neither country seems willing to or interested in compromise. In fact, Machias Seal Island was intentionally left out of the 1984 World Court agreement that divided up the fishing grounds on George's Bank between the two nations. That would have been an appropriate time and venue to settle the dispute, but neither country chose to press its luck and potentially have its interests invalidated. So the controversy remains. And fishermen laugh every time they see a U.S. or Canadian Coast Guard vessel parading around the island in a farcical show of force.

The real war games that take place over ownership of real estate on the island involve seabirds. Machias Seal Island is home to the largest breeding population of Atlantic puffins in the United States, while also serving as a nesting colony for razorbills and common murres—both close cousins of puffins—as well as common eiders, laughing gulls, Leach's storm petrels, and common, Arctic, roseate, and black terns.

As we approached the island, hundreds of the colorful puffins floated on the water's surface and repeatedly dove in search of sand lance and other tiny fish to feed to their nestlings hiding in burrows back on the island. Their oversized red, orange, and blue beaks appear Jimmy Durante-esque and make me wonder if the weight of their beak is the reason for their unstable gait on land. Mixed in among the puffins were small numbers of razorbills and murres, both similarly attired in black and white plumage but with distinct differences in size and shape. Razorbills have a stocky build and a weight-lifter's "neck-less" appearance, and they always seem to point their heavy, rounded black beak at an upward angle. Common murres have a much slimmer appearance and a narrow, pointy beak, and most of the ones I saw were of the uncommon "bridled" form, which have white eye-rings and a thin white line extending backward from the eye like elegant eyeliner. All three species are alcids, the Northern Hemisphere's version of penguins, with legs set well back on their body so they stand in an upright position. Predominantly found in the far north, there are few locations south of Machias Seal Island—all uninhabited islands off the coast of Maine—where these birds nest.

I was thrilled as we continued our tour around the perimeter of the island. My first vacation as an adult was to see puffins in Nova Scotia in 1985, and despite becoming somewhat obsessed with birding soon afterward, I had never seen an Atlantic puffin again until that day. To see 6,000 to 7,000 of them swimming nearby, diving beneath the boat, flying nearly within arm's reach, and standing guard on adjacent rocks was a tremendous feeling. And while razorbills are regular winter visitors to my usual birding haunts along coastal Rhode Island, those sparse sightings couldn't compare to seeing so many of them dressed in their elegant breeding plumage.

A glance at his watch and Alley knew it was time to get back to work. But as we approached the buoy marking the end of our first set of hooks, he looked worried. Based on the location of the buoy at the opposite end and a nearby buoy marking another fisherman's lobster traps, Alley was concerned that his hooks might have snagged a trap. So he decided to retrieve his line in reverse, hoping to avoid an entanglement. Using a long-handled gaff, he grabbed his buoy and used the boat's mechanized pothauler to slowly pull up the anchor, the rope automatically coiling into a plastic bucket at his feet, followed by his line of hooks. The water was calm and clear, so Kanwit and I leaned over the edge of the boat with great anticipation and stared into the water to see if a fish was hooked. Although the hooks are 18 feet apart, we could see three hooks deep, and almost every one came up with nothing but a mass of seaweed. Most of it was what Alley calls maidenhair and which Kanwit knows as gorilla hair. At one point, Kanwit called out, "You caught a kelp forest," as several hooks in a row came up with a particularly long and heavy species of kelp called sea colander, which is dotted with holes to give it its common name. As some of the seaweed reached the surface, it still had tiny crabs and other marine life crawling on it, none larger than a fingernail. We got excited for a moment when an unusual shape arose from the depths, but it turned out to be a "ghost trap"—the lid to an old, barnacle-encrusted lobster trap that appeared to have been lost on the bottom for years.

Not one fish was found on our first 100 hooks, but Alley didn't seem particularly surprised. A glance at his daily log in which he records where he has gone fishing and how many fish he caught shows that many dates have a big X over them, indicating that nothing at all was caught. On particularly frustrating days, he sometimes wrote "skunked" in large letters across the page. Alley protects his log from the eyes of other fishermen so they don't discover his favorite fishing spots, and perhaps also so they don't know how many unsuccessful days he has. Nonetheless, he still had an optimistic smile on his face as we arrived at the second set of hooks.

Alley retrieved this line in a more typical manner—by hand—though it's not the typical process for most other fishermen. He used his pothauler to pull up the anchor at one end, then released the line back into the water and retrieved the anchor from the other end, allowing him to more easily pull in the line by hand. He said this method allows him to feel the weight of any fish that might be caught, and it's easier to coil the ropes and re-bait the hooks as they come aboard so they are ready to be dropped back into the water again. Kanwit asked if he felt a fish on the line, and Alley just shook his head and continued pulling. Some of the hooks still had part of the bait on them, but he put a new piece of mackerel on all of them anyway, tossing the remaining bits to the shearwaters floating nearby.

Jason Alley grew up in a fishing family in Jonesport, where, according to Kanwit, just about every other person in town is named Alley. He said the town was "a fishing place before it became a lobstering place. So my great-grandfather and his father were real fishermen—they actually caught fish, not lobsters. And they passed it down to my dad, who halibut fished. When I got out of high school and went to college, all the time I had lobster traps. I got out of college and was working on my own boat and on my dad's boat. I'd watch my home movies every once in a while and look through dad's pictures where he had halibut in the back of the truck. There's one where I'm on the tailgate and my little brother's on the tailgate and we're just looking at [the fish]. I find that the coolest thing . . . I've got a little boy now, and I want to catch a big fish and take a picture of it with him on the tailgate."

Alley hasn't yet caught a really big fish. Not like the guy 2 weeks before my visit who caught a 245-pounder and became a local hero. His photo appeared in all the local newspapers and in the fishing trade publications. A fish that big is quite rare. Kanwit said only one halibut a year tops the scales at more than 200 pounds. But that's Alley's goal, and based on his optimism and his determination, I'm confident he'll get that big fish. Unfortunately, to pay his bills he can't spend all his time fishing for halibut, so, like most of the rest of the fishermen in Jonesport, he sets lobster traps.

"Lobstering is fun, but it's not a good second choice to halibut," he said. "It's exciting, it keeps you busy, you make pretty decent money, but it's a dull, boring routine. There's no suspense. If I haul up a trap, I don't get too excited if there are three or four lobsters in there. But if I can have some hooks on the bottom and I never know what I'm going to get and I'm dreaming of the three-hundred-pounder . . ." His voice tailed off and he paused before continuing, clearly dreaming of that big fish. "Kohl asked me the other day when we were out if I wanted a minimum size restriction on halibut or a maximum restriction." He paused again his voice became soft. "If you have a maximum restriction, you kill my dreams."

Soon after my visit, the Department of Marine Resources proposed changing the regulations for halibut fishing in state waters, and while the changes probably won't make Alley happy, at least they won't kill his dreams. The primary changes would be an increase in the minimum size from 36 to 38 inches and an elimination of the four fish daily catch limit. Kanwit's research partner Chris Bartlett, a fisheries biologist with Maine Sea Grant and the University of Maine Cooperative Extension, said the increased minimum size was designed to ensure that more fish reached maturity and reproduced before being captured. Based on research from the experimental fishery, half of the female halibut didn't reach full maturity until they were 40 inches in length, and half of the males achieved maturity at 36 inches. "I've heard a lot less grumbling from the fishermen than I expected," Bartlett said of the reaction to the proposed changes. "Many of them think it's a good idea. They know that when they clean a thirty-six-inch fish, most of them haven't reproduced yet."

The elimination of the four fish daily limit sounded to me like a step backward in properly managing the halibut fishery, until Bartlett explained the rationale. "When DMR set a fifty fish season limit, it wasn't enforceable. The only way they were collecting information about how many fish were being caught was from the fishermen's own landing reports, [which weren't reliable]. So DMR decided to strengthen enforcement. Now fishermen have to put a tag on the tail of every halibut they catch, and they can only get fifty tags a season. And that tag stays on the fish all the way until it's cut up. By making the fifty fish limit enforceable, there's no need for a daily catch limit."

The new regulations, however, don't address the fact that little is known about the health of the halibut stock and why it hasn't recovered since it was first depleted 100 years ago. Kanwit said that halibut were placed on the federal government's list of species of concern based entirely on the results of trawl surveys, and halibut are not susceptible to being caught by trawlers. "Their burst swimming speed is really quite fast," she said, so they are able to out-swim and avoid trawl nets. "They catch the odd fish occasionally, but the Canadians have done some research on hook surveys versus trawl surveys, and there was something like a tenfold difference between the abundance estimates they got from the trawl survey versus the hook survey. And not only did they get more with their hooks, but they also got a more complete size range. Because of the burst speed of the adults, the trawls only catch small fish for the most part. It's rare that they get big fish."

Does that mean the population is much healthier than the government claims? No one really knows. Or as Bartlett said, "I can't even fathom how the stocks are doing." But he and Kanwit believe that the research they are doing will help answer that question. Fishermen claim to be seeing more small halibut than they have in a long time, so that's a good sign, but years of underreporting large fish and capturing undersize fish may mean there's still a long way to go to restoring a healthy population of halibut.

Bartlett described it this way: "When we started the experimental fishery in 2000, I called a guy from NOAA Fisheries, and he said that halibut are primarily a 'shack fish,' a money fish that the guys were selling on the side. The larger halibut weren't coming through the traditional markets so they weren't being reported. The smaller fish were also being disguised mixed in with other flatfish, a lot of which included halibut that were only two to four pounds. Until the feds put the thirty-six-inch limit, small halibut weren't being sold as halibut."

The struggle to recover Atlantic halibut is the opposite of the experience in the Pacific, where halibut are abundant and the fishery is strong and sustainable. The Pacific halibut is nearly identical to the Atlantic species, and some argue that they are the same species, but that's where the similarities end. Commercial fishing of Pacific halibut began in the 1880s, and the population has been monitored by the International Pacific Halibut Commission for 80 years. During that time, about 55,000 pounds of halibut have been caught each year on a consistent basis, with a total value today of about $126 million.

"The difference is that they stepped in with management at a really early stage," Kanwit said. "They've been really proactive, they've done tons of research and tons of surveys. They do quotas there, so it's a totally different management style, but I don't think the population was ever as low as it got here, so they didn't need to have the recovery that we need to have a viable fishing population. They got down to the point where they were having twenty-four-hour openings for fishing . . . They went from that derby style insanity to quotas and other systems of management. They have a whole agency devoted to one species. They've got twenty-five biologists who do nothing but halibut, so they know the life stage as well as you can for a species. Here in Maine, the feds have one person assigned to do an assessment, but it's mostly off the radar screen. Maine is the only state that pays attention to it at all, so it's just a real different management scenario."

An additional challenge to managing the halibut fishery in the Atlantic is the limited interaction between U.S. and Canadian policymakers. While the scientists from both countries have a close working relationship, and the Canadian fishermen played an important role in Maine's experimental fishery by sending tags from captured fish to Kanwit, a similar relationship doesn't exist between the two country's fishery managers. Rules, regulations, and policy decisions regarding Atlantic halibut in Canadian waters differ markedly from those in U.S. waters, despite the fact that the fish themselves ignore the political boundaries and appear to mix freely.

When Alley gave a tug on our third set of hooks after hauling in the anchors holding the line to the bottom, he said it wasn't promising. He didn't feel the weight of a fish on the line, and as he began to pull it in, every hook was barren of bait or fish. So as Alley finished hauling, Kanwit and I talked about the greater and sooty shearwaters, Wilson's storm petrels and fulmars that continued to swarm around the boat looking for a handout. All four species are part of a group of seabirds that spend ten months of the year far out to sea and are often collectively referred to as tubenoses—they have external tubular nostrils on the upper portion of their hooked beaks which may help them locate airborne odors indicating the location of food on the open ocean. The unique tubes also enable them to eject excess accumulated salt from a special gland located above the eyes.

As Kanwit and I continued to watch the birds, Alley called out for our assistance. Glancing into the water, we saw a huge halibut just ten feet below the surface, its bright white underside looking like a blurry silvery mass as it was pulled toward us. Alley knew all along that he had a fish on the line, but he wanted to surprise us, and he certainly succeeded. They both then jumped into action.

Using a large square net with a long handle, they scooped up the massive fish and, with my help, hauled it on board, where it landed at our feet with a thud. It was a thick, muscular creature with large lips and a vaguely patterned chocolate coloration on the upper side. Most notable to me were its oddly positioned eyes, which were clearly not symmetrically placed on its face. As Alley and Kanwit grabbed their tags and tools, I watched as the fish thrashed several times, simultaneously lifting its head and tail aggressively and slapping them back down on deck. It opened its mouth several times as if it were straining at a bit, then flared its gills, which were colored deep blood red.

While Alley quickly placed a thin yellow numbered tag through the edge of its upper gill, Kanwit grabbed a tape measure and extended it from lips to tail—56 inches. They both then weighed the fish while it was still in the net, and later subtracted the weight of the net to learn it was a 60-pounder, the second biggest fish of the year for Alley. Kanwit then pierced two pins through its flesh just below the dorsal fin and attached an inch-long tubular data storage tag, which would record information about water temperature and depth wherever it goes. They had intended to place a satellite tag on the fish as well—which collects even more information and after 3 months pops off, floats to the surface, and transmits the data to Kanwit's computer via satellite—but much to their disappointment they were missing a part that was needed to attach the device to the fish. And then the fish was laboriously tossed back overboard, where it disappeared into the depths so quickly that it was gone before the bubbles made by its splash had cleared.

The whole process took less than 5 minutes, which was the target time Kanwit aims for so the fish is stressed as little as possible. But the excitement of the catch and the rush to process the fish made us exhausted, particularly since the boat was crowded with equipment, making it somewhat difficult to maneuver around such a large creature. Once we caught our breath, I asked them what they had noticed about the fish that a beginner like me would have missed. Kanwit said she saw a slight blistering on its underside—I don't even remember seeing its underside—which likely was caused by scraping across the hard, rocky bottom. Alley pointed out that it had been hooked in the upper jaw, which is an atypical location. And both noticed one sea louse, a whitish inch-long worm-like thing that I saw but didn't recognize as a louse, located in the center of its body on the upper side.

"Otherwise, it was a really nice fish," Kanwit said with a smile.

"That's a good fish," added Alley. "Not a giant, but anyone would be happy about that fish. I'm pretty proud of that one."

So was I, and I had nothing to do with catching it.

When the adrenaline wore off and the gear was stashed, we turned west for Jonesport. As we did, I realized that we didn't have any bycatch, despite having 300 hooks in the water for more than 5 hours. Alley said that wasn't unusual. Sometimes he'll catch a cusk or dogfish, and even less frequently a skate may get hooked, but more often than not his only catch is a halibut. Not that he was complaining.

On our way back, dark clouds rolled in and we were hit by a brief but strong shower, but it didn't dim the excitement from a successful day. Alley unexpectedly stopped the boat just west of Cutler, grabbed a buoy from the water, and started to haul in another set of hooks. Those weren't part of the research project, but rather they were his usual set in state waters. He was using it as his ace in the hole, giving me an extra chance to see a halibut in case the sets in federal waters near Machias Seal Island came up empty. But his two sets in state waters came up empty instead.

As he was working, Alley glanced around at a fishing boat that passed nearby and nodded toward Cutler harbor. He said that many fishermen are territorial about their fishing locations, especially halibut fishermen from Cutler, who have been known to cut the buoy lines of fishermen from other communities who they think should not be working in "their" waters. Alley knows several fishermen who have lost their gear to such petty vandalism, but it hasn't stopped him from fishing where he thinks he has the best chance of catching halibut. He occasionally takes precautions, however, including disguising his halibut buoys as lobster buoys and working quickly to get out of the area as soon as he can.

After the last haul, he baited the hooks again and strategically dropped them back into the water. As he did so, he talked about one of his favorite subjects—bait.

"Bait is really key. You need good, fresh bait to catch halibut. Fresh or frozen mackerel is good. Fresh herring is a good bait, but it's hard to get. We use alewives sometimes, but they're only available for a short time. Before this project came up, I wasn't convinced that mackerel was going to catch any halibut, but I'll definitely use it again next year."

"Don't forget suckers," Kanwit added. "Halibut like suckers. Some of these halibut fishermen will chase bait all over the state. They'll take day trips to Millinocket [160 miles inland] just for suckers."

The local fishermen—who have made it clear to Kanwit that the proper pronunciation of the word halibut is actually HAWLibut—are also pretty proud of their boats, so much so that they've even created a series of lobster boat races up and down the coast that takes the lawn mower races at the state fair to the next level. But Alley seldom participates except informally with his brother. He knows his boat doesn't have a chance against most of the competitors. "It's not my favorite boat," he said. "It's a traditional lobster boat, and when I bought it, it was perfectly average—average in size and horsepower and equipment and electronics. Ten years later it's the bottom of the barrel. The other boats you see are bigger, have more power, better electronics. Everybody else has made a lot of money lobstering and has upgraded, and I haven't. But it's still able to be out here, and it's perfectly fine. It's just on the smaller side of the spectrum now." To Alley, size doesn't matter except when it comes to halibut.

As we neared Jonesport after 14 hours on the water, two adult bald eagles were perched regally on a channel marker at the entrance to the harbor. Despite our close approach, they didn't move, which caused me to ask Alley whether they were even real. They were. And it got me thinking. The eagles were removed from the federal endangered species list in 2007 after a remarkable recovery from near extinction. Perhaps the strength, confidence, and determination exhibited by those two birds in Jonesport could be interpreted as a hopeful sign for the future of the Atlantic halibut, too.

3

Harbor Porpoise

When I was a kid, my father used to eat sardines out of a tin while watching television, though it was a taste I never grew to appreciate, just like his proclivity for serving lamb kidneys for breakfast. Sardines never caught on as a popular snack food with my generation, nor with the generations after mine, yet they're still a big business. Sardines are the juvenile form of Atlantic herring, a plankton-eating fish that lives in coastal and continental shelf waters from Labrador to Virginia and that usually occurs in huge schools. Frozen and salted herring are a valuable commodity in overseas markets, and herring are an effective bait fish for the crab, lobster, and tuna fisheries. They're also an important food for a wide variety of marine mammals, from whales and seals to porpoises and dolphins, as well as for seabirds and many species of fish. In fact, the Atlantic States Marine Fisheries Commission suggests that Atlantic herring "may be the most important fish in the Northeast United States because of its vast role in the ecosystem and its importance to the fishing industry." That's why the commission and the New England Fishery Management Council regulate fishing of the species even though herring are considered somewhat abundant and overfishing is not currently occurring.

That's not to say, however, that overfishing of Atlantic herring hasn't happened in the past. A fishery for herring developed in New England in the late nineteenth century when the canning industry first became established. At the same time, the lobster fishing industry was taking shape and herring immediately became the most popular lobster bait. In the late 1800s and early 1900s, and then again in the 1940s and 1950s, annual landings of Atlantic herring were about 60,000 metric tons. That number grew sevenfold in the late 1960s, however, when foreign fishermen arrived on Georges Bank and took advantage of the unregulated fishery, leading to the collapse of the offshore herring stock. By 1976, the foreign herring fleet was gone, and since 2000, landings of herring have averaged 90,000 metric tons per year, mostly from the Gulf of Maine.

Unlike river herring, which migrate each year to spawn in freshwater, Atlantic herring spend their entire life at sea. Adults migrate from their spawning grounds on Georges Bank and the Gulf of Maine to spend the winter in the waters off southern New England and the Mid-Atlantic States. Juveniles—those under 3 years of age—migrate seasonally from offshore to inshore waters, where they are abundant in shallow coastal embayments in the summer. Spawning on gravel or sandy bottoms from Nova Scotia to the Nantucket Shoals at depths of 50 to 150 feet, each female produces 30,000 to 200,000 eggs. Some large schools produce so many eggs that they sometimes carpet the seafloor in dense piles, with each egg taking 10 to 12 days to hatch. At the end of their first year, the young herring may be 3 to 5 inches long, growing to 10 inches by the fourth year and up to a maximum of 15 inches and 1½ pounds at the end of their life span, which is usually 15 to 18 years.

Today, herring are usually caught from commercial fishing vessels using trawl nets or purse seines, though up until the 1940s the predominant gear was a weir, a net affixed in one location in shallow water. Weirs are still the way that herring are caught in some traditional fishing communities, like on Grand Manan Island, New Brunswick. Located just six miles from Campobello Island at the easternmost point of Maine, Grand Manan is a popular vacation destination for Canadians seeking a refuge from crowded tourist hotspots. The nutrient-rich waters of the Bay of Fundy make it an excellent base for whale- and seabird-watching excursions, including one of the region's only whale-watching sailboats, and its soaring cliffs, classic lighthouses, and rich wildflowers make it an enjoyable site for a relaxing weekend. First settled in 1784, the island had long been a prosperous fishing village, thanks to the abundance of herring, but as herring stocks declined in the 1880s, so did the island's population, which peaked at 2,600. While fishing remains the primary occupation on Grand Manan, tourism and boat building are increasing in importance.

Notwithstanding a handful of lighthouses, the dominant man-made feature on Grand Manan is the scattered weir nets that line the many coves at the island's north end. To the uninitiated, a weir is an architectural wonder that can't possibly do what it is designed to do—capture and contain tens of thousands of herring. From shore they look like a massive abstract art installation made of netting and wooden poles, but from above they appear like a heart-shaped locket on a chain. Called the fence by weir fishermen, the "chain" is a line of netting perpendicular to the coast stretched between wooden posts made of hardwood saplings 70 feet long pounded into the seafloor. The "heart," also made of netting strung between hardwood saplings, is open 22 to 30 feet wide at the point—called the mouth—where a chain would connect to a heart locket. At night, herring swim close to shore, following the coastline. When they approach the fence net, they turn and follow it straight into the mouth of the heart-shaped weir. Instead of reversing course to exit the mouth, they swim in continuous figure-eights around the inner edge of the net, with the curves of the weir continually directing them away from the exit. Every morning at dawn, the fishermen check their weirs to see if a school of herring has stumbled into their nets, and if so, they "pull up the drop" to close the mouth of the weir to keep the fish from escaping until the fishermen are ready to retrieve the fish.

Herbie Lambert is a 78-year-old herring fisherman on Grand Manan who has maintained a weir for more than 60 years. "Most fishermen have just one weir at a time," he said. "In my life I've had about twelve weirs, but never more than one or two at once. On a good day it's not unusual to bring in a hundred tons of herring in one weir."

When the weir is full, the fishermen deploy a seine net inside the weir to pull in the fish, and then a boat with a vacuum pump sucks the fish onboard for delivery to the processor. Herring quantities are calculated using a unit of measure called a hogshead. "Many years ago there used to be a wooden container built like a barrel that could hold as much as five regular barrels, and that was called a hogshead," Lambert explained. "A hogshead of herring holds about twelve hundred and fifty pounds."

Almost all of the herring caught in the region is sold to Connors Brothers, the largest sardine cannery in the world and the majority owner of Bumble Bee Seafoods, located in Blacks Harbour, New Brunswick, right next to the dock where the Grand Manan ferry arrives and departs every day. Since Connors Brothers has a virtual monopoly, it controls how much herring it buys from each fisherman and when. As soon as a fisherman calls the cannery to say they have fish to sell, Connors Brothers decides how much it wants and sends the carrier boat with the vacuum pump. It's important for the fishermen to stay in the good graces of the Connors Brothers executives, since they could play favorites if they chose to and make life difficult for uncooperative fishermen, but most fishermen say the company is quite fair to everyone. The only other option the fishermen have is to sell to a much smaller cannery in Maine, but if they sell too much to the competitor, they risk being denied future sales to Connors Brothers.

"Ever since I can remember, we always sold to Connors Brothers," Lambert said. "In the old days there were a lot more fish here, and we sold them all there. The fish aren't so plentiful now, but the price is still good."

The only real down side to the weirs, like almost every other form of commercial fishing, is by-catch. A wide variety of nontarget species sometimes ends up in the nets as well, especially in August when herring landings peak. According to Lambert, it isn't uncommon to find squid, mackerel, sharks, porpoises, and all kinds of predatory fish in the nets, and when the nets were pulled in to collect the herring, most of the by-catch would get smothered and die. "They were mostly considered trash fish," Lambert said, "because there was no market for them."

While there still isn't a market for most of the species considered by-catch, a team of biologists spends every summer monitoring the weirs and helping the fishermen remove the harbor porpoises that follow the herring into the nets. Launched in 1991 by Dave Gaskin of the University of Guelph and the Grand Manan Whale and Seabird Research Station and now led by Andrew Westgate and Heather Koopman of the University of North Carolina at Wilmington, the Harbor Porpoise Release Program has developed a system to help fishermen remove porpoises from weir nets without affecting their herring catch.

"When Heather first came here, we didn't know where she came from or why she was here, so we didn't know whether to accept her or not," said Lambert. "We were afraid that she was from some government agency, but she won over everybody. We originally thought that if she was going to protect the porpoise, it would be bad luck for us because there are porpoises in the weir all the time. We just didn't know what was going to happen. But she seemed to get along with the fishermen, and it all went along fine. All the fishermen are participating now, and I don't hear anything bad about it."

Harbor porpoises (*Phocoena phocoena*) are one of the smallest cetaceans on Earth and the smallest by far of those found in the North Atlantic, reaching a maximum length of just 5 feet and growing to only 150 pounds. In the National Audubon Society's *Guide to Marine Mammals of the World*, harbor porpoises are described as having a "robust body and a short, poorly demarcated beak . . . The color pattern is subtle but complex. A simple dark gray cape is overlaid on a much lighter gray dorsal field, with variable dark gray flecking in the light gray area. The throat and belly are white, and there may be gray streaking on the throat. There are often a dark chin patch, a dark eye ring, and a dark stripe (sometimes several) from the corner of the mouth to the flipper." While marine mammalogists say that harbor porpoises are difficult to mistake for any other species, the experts also recognize that most people don't know the obvious differences between porpoises and dolphins.

"Everyone always says 'porpoise-dolphin, same thing.' They're not," said biologist Heather Koopman. "There are a couple of diagnostic features that allow you to distinguish dolphins and porpoises. One of them is the shape of their teeth, which is not very useful in the field. You know, you're not going to get them to open their mouths for you. Dolphins have cone-shaped teeth and porpoises have spade-shaped teeth like little shovels. The dorsal fin shape is also different—dolphins have falcate, sickle-shaped dorsal fins while porpoises have squat little triangular dorsal fins. And the other thing is their noses. Dolphins have long pronounced rostrums and porpoises look like they've run into a brick wall."

Harbor porpoises are found throughout the temperate waters of the Northern Hemisphere, including western North Africa, the North, Baltic, and Black Seas—but not the Mediterranean—and the northern Pacific Rim from the Sea of Japan north to Alaska's Aleutian Island chain and south again to northern California. In the North Atlantic, they roam the waters around Europe and Iceland as well as from southern Greenland and the Gulf of St. Lawrence south to Cape Hatteras. In total, there are believed to be several hundred thousand harbor porpoises in numerous distinct populations, with about 75,000 found in the eastern North America population, which is centered in the coastal waters of the Gulf of Maine and the Bay of Fundy. "Most of them shift between Cape Cod in the winter and up here [Grand Manan] in the summer to feed," Koopman explained. "They typically show up here in greater numbers in May and June, peaking in August and September, and then they start to dwindle down into the fall . . . Mostly they go south a fair distance but not much beyond Long Island, though you do find them off New Jersey, too, in the winter. Wherever they go, they're always coastal, never pelagic."

Koopman invited me to join her on Grand Manan Island in early September 2007 to learn about harbor porpoises and to get a firsthand look at her project to release them from weir nets. So I climbed aboard the ferry out of Blacks Harbour early one morning and received an immediate lesson about the famous Bay of Fundy tides. While tides rise and fall around the world from the gravitational forces of the sun and moon, the unique funnel shape of the Bay of Fundy causes dramatic tide changes there and gives the region the right to claim the highest tides in the world. At its mouth near Grand Manan Island, the tides rise and recede more than 20 feet twice each day, while at the eastern end where the bay is at its most narrow, the tides rush in and out dangerously quickly to heights of 45 feet and more, leaving long stretches of exposed shoreline during low tides and then quickly engulfing inattentive beachcombers on the rising tide.

When I arrived in Blacks Harbour, I didn't realize at first how large the ferry was, as the vessel's departure time corresponded with the day's low tide and nearly the entire ship sat below the level of the dock, making it barely noticeable from the parking lot. During the first 20 minutes of the trip, we slowly exited the harbor and skirted several small islands as we headed toward open water, passing shorelines showing a high tide line well above the water line and exposing tremendous quantities of seaweed-covered rocks, with many harboring herring gulls exploring for their breakfast. The water was placid at first, with few birds in evidence save for an occasional small flock of common eiders hidden in coves, three black guillemots barely visible behind the tip of a small island, and a common loon that hardly bothered to get out of the way of the ferry. The skies were gray and cool, but on the western horizon a tiny line of blue sky and sunlight suggested that the weather would soon improve. During the crossing, occasional mats of floating seaweed were visible—difficult to identify from the top of the ferry but probably a species of rockweed, likely dislodged from the rocks by the fast-moving tides.

Thirty minutes out, the wildlife activity started. Sooty and greater shearwaters began to show up in large numbers, first mostly sitting on the water and then circling low in flocks of twenty to thirty birds in areas where there must have been abundant quantities of food. Two fin whales momentarily showed their massive backs and proportionately tiny dorsal fins, then disappeared for good. And then I saw my first porpoises, mostly in ones and twos but later a pod of four. They were frustratingly difficult to get a good look at, despite my high-powered binoculars. They appeared above the water line very briefly, taking three or four quick breaths before submerging again and disappearing for several minutes. They arc their bodies out of the water much less than do dolphins and whales, so seldom did I see much more than a gray-black triangular fin. By the time I got my binoculars up to my eyes, they were gone. Then, three solitary Atlantic puffins made a brief appearance, followed by a large flock of northern gannets, their white bodies reflecting the tiny bit of sunlight available.

As the ferry approached Grand Manan's north end, officially called

Long Eddy Point but referred to by locals as The Whistle, the incoming tide made the water appear to boil with turbulence and wildlife activity. A minke whale breached alongside several porpoises, while gannets dove into the water from high in the air and hundreds of gulls swarmed like bees to a hive. A little further from shore, a humpback whale spouted several times and then showed its flukes before diving deeply. Two more minke whales and a fin whale cavorted in the distance. When the activity at The Whistle was too far away to see well, I walked to the opposite side of the ferry just in time to see nine porpoises make an appearance, swimming straight toward the ship, then veering off and coming up alongside us. I learned later that this was an unusual behavior, as harbor porpoises seldom exhibit curiosity toward vessels, especially noisy ones—and the ferry was certainly noisy. The pod of nine animals I counted was also unusual, as harbor porpoises are considered among the least social of the dolphins and porpoises, seldom traveling in groups larger than four or five unless actively feeding. They also seemed to arc out of the water more than was typical, even showing off their pale undersides on occasion, making me think for a moment that they were Atlantic white-sided dolphins. And then, as I had expected, they simply disappeared.

It was a great way to start the day.

As the ferry rounded the last point before arriving at the dock, I saw my first weir nets and was reminded of why I was there. After docking, I walked up to the Grand Manan Whale and Seabird Research Center, an old house across the street from the ferry landing, and entered the front door where a tiny museum and gift shop raised funds for the porpoise release program. I perused the exhibits with great interest, including a prepared specimen of a young harp seal, numerous local seabirds, and several full marine mammal skeletons—a white-sided dolphin, a minke whale, two harbor porpoises, and a gray seal. The museum also displayed the massive skull and flipper of a humpback whale and numerous other artifacts, including a bizarre-looking tuna skull. When I introduced myself to the gift shop worker, she directed me through a doorway to the research station, which consisted of a kitchen, a makeshift lab, and several crowded bedrooms. Most of the researchers were still asleep when I arrived, recovering from their annual end-of-the-year party the night before, though several awoke on time to check the weirs at dawn. In the kitchen, which seemed to be the general meeting place for all the researchers, were lists tacked up indicating who was scheduled to cook dinner, who was responsible for the "weir check" the next morning, and a tabulation of how much beer each individual had drank during the summer, less as a way to boast than as an indication of how much to charge each member for their consumption. Judging by the tally, graduate students Zach Swaim and Hilary Lane owed a lot.

When Koopman arrived, she announced that a harbor porpoise had been found the previous day in one of the weirs, but before I had a chance to get excited, she also said that she had been unable to track down the fisherman who owned the weir because it was a holiday weekend and he was probably out of town. This meant that we probably would not have a chance to release the porpoise before I had to leave. But she offered to take me out to see it anyway, and at 11 A.M. we climbed into the research station's 16-foot skiff and, with Swaim at the controls, headed out to get a close-up look at a porpoise. Ten minutes later we arrived at a weir that looked nothing like the others—a 100-foot-diameter circle of black plastic tubing sitting at the surface with the unseen netting hanging beneath it. A long white buoy line punctuated with larger pink buoys marked the fence line that directs the herring into the weir. And the whole contraption was anchored by four eight-ton concrete blocks on the seafloor. Several gulls sat on the tube, loafing or perhaps hoping a herring would make itself available for an easy meal.

This was the modern version of a herring weir, which fisherman Herbie Lambert said he and his son first designed about 15 years ago. "They don't work as well," Lambert told me later. "It's a tough job to keep them in place with the tides. They do catch fish, but then again when it's rough weather it's quite a job to take the fish out of it because there's nothing to hang onto like the poles on the old weirs."

The porpoise in the weir wasn't readily visible, but as we watched we eventually caught a brief glimpse of a small dorsal fin and a hint of the back of a small porpoise. While in the weir, Koopman said, the porpoises are not entangled—they can swim, feed, and breathe normally, but like the herring, they just don't swim out on their own. She thought this one was a one- or two-year-old, given its small size, but it seemed to be doing just fine. The water was a bit choppy, so when it surfaced to breathe, it raised itself out of the water slightly more than it typically would in calmer water. "He's really hopping around in there," Koopman said somewhat excitedly. "Now he's surfing. Cool!" We watched the weir for about 15 minutes, but the porpoise only came to the surface briefly to breathe four or five times, mostly seeming to enjoy the anonymity of swimming beneath the surface. As we returned to the dock, we stopped at a traditional weir for a close-up look. The posts supporting the net were the thickness of my arm, and the net—called a twine—consisted of 1-inch mesh tailor-made for the weir. The top of the netting 15 feet above our heads was draped in seaweed, showing how high the tide gets each day.

As we were about to leave, Koopman pointed out a harbor seal that had popped its head up inside the weir. As I was about to ask if she removes seals from the net as well as porpoises, she said that the seals are the only animals seemingly able to easily get out by either swimming under the net or exiting from the open mouth of the weir. She also talked about how herring fishermen are able to determine with great accuracy how much fish they have in the weir by "feeling" for it—dropping a weighted line down to the bottom and feeling how many fish bump into it. Some claim they can even tell how big the fish are by the strength of the strikes. "It's a dying art," Koopman said, "since most of the younger fishermen now use sonar on their lobster boats to tell how much fish they have."

Back at the research station, activity levels were high as various researchers were immersed in their individual projects. When not chasing harbor porpoises, each member of the team had his or her own research to conduct on a wide variety of topics. Swaim, a graduate student at the University of North Carolina at Wilmington, was studying how North Atlantic right whales digest the usually undigestible lipids in copepods, the whales' primary food source, by comparing the lipids in the copepods to the lipids in the whales' fecal material. Rob Ronconi, a doctoral student at the University of Victoria who has been working at the research station since 1996, was using satellite tracking devices to follow the daily movements and migratory patterns of greater and sooty shearwaters, seabirds that breed in remote islands in the South Atlantic and feed in the summer in the North Atlantic. And Hilary Lane, another grad student at the University of North Carolina but originally from Chicago, was examining the lipid content of herring to see how it varies from season to season and from place to place.

The fishermen in the area claim that the herring they catch are quite different from the herring caught by other fishermen elsewhere, so Lane was testing that hypothesis. "Herring are the most common fish in the Atlantic," she said, "so understanding them will help us understand those things that eat herring: marine mammals, fish, gulls, shearwaters." Lane invited me into a screened tent in the backyard of the research center where she used a Cuisinart food processor to grind up herring every day. Later, at her North Carolina lab, she would use a gas chromatograph to determine their fatty acid composition. But in the tent, she put a whole eight-inch fish in the food processor, turned the machine on, and after the table stopped vibrating she scooped out a mushy paste that looked like paté but smelled like old fish. She then took a small quantity of the fish paste and pushed it into a thumb-sized vial, capped it, and stored the vial in a cooler before starting again with another herring. During the summer of 2007 she processed 1,700 individual fish in that way.

The two students' lipid-related projects are an offshoot of Koopman's primary research focus. She describes herself as a lipid biologist whose interest in protecting porpoises is primarily a sidelight. A native of Burlington, Ontario, an hour from Toronto, she followed her passion for marine life to the University of Guelph, which had a reputation for its marine biology program and an active group of researchers studying marine mammals. She soon found herself working for Dave Gaskin, the founder of the research station on Grand Manan, which led to a master's degree project on porpoise blubber. She then followed one of Gaskin's doctoral students to Duke University, and after earning her Ph.D., she took a faculty position at the University of North Carolina at Wilmington and soon took over responsibility for the porpoise release program with colleague Andrew Westgate.

"When we picked up the reins for the porpoise release program, we had to do all the fund raising as well as the day-to-day logistics," she explained. "Andrew coordinates what goes on with people on boats and equipment and our field plans for the day, and I would be the one who would go and talk to the fishermen. We initially decided that they would be less threatened if a woman talked to them, and it was a good decision. The relationship [with the fishermen] is now pretty solidified, we're all happy and we understand each other, and I really like hanging out with them. I go out of my way to talk to these guys because they're interesting and interested and they have that long-term local knowledge that isn't published in any scientific paper. So you get things from them just by their experience of years and years and years of working on the water in the bay. It's like a whole valuable source of information that never gets tapped into. It's good for the fishermen, it's good for the research station, and it's good for us.

"It's so easy to live in a vacuum when you're a scientist. You live in your own little bubble and you never really think about anything beyond your lab work or the scope of your project. [Talking with the fishermen] opens up your eyes a little bit and sometimes lets you see something from another perspective. 'Have you ever really thought about this, Heather,' they ask me sometimes. 'You're the doctor; you're supposed to know this stuff.' "

For the most part, she has the answers, even to some of their more complicated questions about reproductive behaviors. "Mature females are pregnant and lactating simultaneously for most of their adult lives as far as we can tell," Koopman explained. "She'll become reproductively mature probably on her third or fourth birthday, mate in June and become pregnant, and then she will give birth to that calf in May. Then a month later she will mate again, so she'll be pregnant with the next one and she's still got the first one. We think weaning happens sometime around February or March, so she's then got a couple months to get herself together to give birth to her calf in May and then get pregnant again. It is very energetically demanding for them. Harbor porpoise milk is somewhere between 25 and 40 percent fat, depending on where you are in the lactation stage, which is an incredible amount of lipid that she has to glean from her diet in order to produce that for the calf. So we think that female harbor porpoises have this incredible need to eat a lot . . . She's going to have to feed on whatever she might encounter, including hagfish, which are kind of gross. We've never found hagfish in male stomachs."

But there is still a great deal that is unknown about harbor porpoises. Like, what makes a porpoise swim into a weir and where did they all go in 2007? "It's weird," Koopman said. "This summer normally we should have seen a lot more porpoises around, so I'm not sure if we're experiencing some kind of a shift where not as many of them came into the bay this year and they're going elsewhere. I don't know why that would be because there's tons of prey here for them. Herring are everywhere. It's been a really odd year for us, though last year was a slow year, too."

Some of the unanswered questions are being examined thanks in large part to the porpoise release program. It's the only current project that allows biologists to get their hands on wild, living porpoises, which has allowed Koopman's team to study a wide range of unknowns, from porpoise diving behavior and movement patterns to their blood chemistry. Other marine mammalogists have also taken advantage of this ready access to live porpoises as well. For instance, Woods Hole Oceanographic Institution graduate student Stacey De-Ruiter is studying porpoise acoustics in order to estimate the range at which they can detect fish and communicate with one another. So before Koopman's team releases a harbor porpoise from a weir, they use a hydrophone to record the sounds that the animal makes, which they then send to DeRuiter. Equally important, the live porpoises also allow the researchers to collect a wide range of data that may play a critical role in understanding any future problems the porpoises are faced with.

But first the animals have to be removed from the net alive, which is a massive undertaking that must be coordinated by fishermen in two boats, two divers in the weir, and the team of biologists in a skiff. The fishermen begin by deploying a conventional herring seine net around the inner circumference of the weir and then gradually cinch it up from the bottom like pulling the drawstring on a sweatshirt hood. This slowly concentrates the herring and the porpoise in a smaller and smaller area of water. It is a particularly dangerous process because the porpoise can easily get caught beneath the pile of herring and become trapped, unable to reach the surface to breathe, or it could become disoriented and become entangled in the net. But it is also dangerous for the divers in the water—graduate students Rob Ronconi and Zach Swaim.

"It's a lot of watching and waiting at first," explained Ronconi, "and then your adrenaline kicks in as things get exciting. People are constantly calling out and pointing to where the porpoise is, or they're telling you that it's been three minutes and the porpoise hasn't surfaced yet [so you have to go look for it]. Then the porpoise might swim right at you, and you think you can catch it, but then it turns on a dime. You almost never catch them until they bumble into the net. You have to constantly patrol the net and look for spots where it's sagging. Our job is to spot the porpoises when they're caught in the net and get them out. You have to make a lot of quick decisions. It's pretty stressful."

"You also have to keep in mind your own safety," added Swaim, "since it could be easy to get yourself entangled, too. By the time I've finally got the porpoise in my arms, I've usually burned out all my energy, so I try to roll on my back until I calm down again. All porpoises act differently in your arms—some go limp and some kick and thrash and kick. Sometimes I just point the porpoise in the right direction and let its tail kick us toward the boat. When the porpoise is in the boat and the net has been pulled tight and it's full of fish, you can almost walk across them. That's when I like to stay in it just for the fun."

For the biologists in the boat, however, it's still quite stressful. Koopman pulled out a large yellow tackle box containing all of the tools used during the process to show me exactly what they do with each porpoise. She called the box the Roto-tag kit, named for the plastic tags that ranchers attach to the ear of cattle. When the porpoise is removed from the net by the divers, it is placed upright on a soft mat on the bottom of the skiff. In the boat are Koopman, two helpers, and a videographer who documents the entire process for later review. The porpoises generally sit upright, though they sometimes need gentle restraining if they flop their tail around. The helpers must constantly sponge water on the animal's tail, flippers, and dorsal fin, which can quickly get overheated.

Once the porpoise is secure and calm on the floor of the boat, the biologists determine its gender by turning it on its side—the male genital slit is directly under its dorsal fin, while the female's slit is closer to its tail. A Roto-tag is then inserted into the rear of the dorsal fin, with the tag on males placed high on the fin and those on females placed low. The set of pliers used to attach the tag also removes a small plug of skin that is retained for DNA analysis. Next, the animal's length and girth are measured. "The girth measurement tells us how healthy they are," Koopman said. "Fat is good. That means they have a lot of resources available to them. You never want to be a skinny animal. Harbor porpoises don't carry a lot of blubber around; just enough to last them about a week. It's not like a large whale that can go months and months and months fasting and living on its blubber reserves. We don't get many skinny porpoises. Most of the animals look really healthy."

Next, a fecal swab is taken for a study of bacteria in the gut, and a blood sample is taken from the top of its tail fluke. Then the porpoise is placed on a stretcher, weighed, and placed in the water for release. The total process once the animal is in the boat should take less than 15 minutes. Since 1991, more than 700 harbor porpoises have been safely removed from herring weirs in this way—including one day when thirteen were released at once from one weir.

Occasionally difficulties arise, like when an animal is over-stressed and stops breathing or arches its back excessively, which indicates a problem. In that case, the porpoise must immediately be placed back in the water—while the biologists continue holding it—to allow it to breathe more comfortably. Calves, especially, find it hard to breathe in the boat, as it is likely the first time they have ever felt the full weight of their body. Infrequently, a porpoise doesn't survive the removal process, usually due to a problem that occurred before it made it as far as the skiff. That's why Koopman tries to get the fishermen to use what she calls a mammal seine during this process, rather than the typical herring seine. The mesh of the mammal seine is considerably larger, allowing the herring to swim through the net and back into the weir, while the porpoise remains safely in the seine, no longer facing the prospect of suffocating beneath 50 tons of herring. When the mammal seine is used, just 2 percent of the trapped porpoises die, while the herring seine has a mortality rate of 11 percent.

The tissue and blood samples collected prior to releasing the porpoises from the weirs are another element crucial to understanding the animals and being prepared to answer future questions about them. The release team includes veterinary pathologist Aleksija Neimanis, who has been conducting long-term health studies of the porpoises, including an examination of diseases transmitted from pilot whales and other animals, as well as the potential effect of run-off from pesticides and sewage.

Andrew Westgate, Koopman's co-director on the porpoise release project, said that the blood samples, in particular, have been archived in a massive database for future analysis in case of a significant change in the health of the population. "A few years ago in England, over half of the harbor seals died from a distemper epidemic that swept through the population," he explained. "Harbor seals were dying left, right, and center. If that were to happen here to harbor porpoises—and it could well happen here—we would be able to use our database to understand it. Part of the problem is that, in most populations, you can't go back and look at what their blood chemistry was like before the epidemic. We have the ability to do that. It's kind of a sentinel approach. We now have the data that may or may not ever be useful, but if it is, it's going to be really, really useful."

Thanks to the porpoise release program, few porpoises die in weir nets any longer. Koopman calls the weir fishery "one of the most environmentally friendly fisheries you can have. First, it's a fixed gear fishery, so your weir isn't going anywhere, it's just sitting there, it's passive, so you're not causing any habitat problems from dragging up the bottom. It's also passive in the sense that you wait for the fish to come to you. You're sort of limited by how many are going to swim into shore and get caught, so in that way it's very sustainable. And the product is always fresh. It stays in the weir until the market wants it or the fish plant wants it or the bait market wants it, so you just collect it when you need it and it gets processed immediately. And on a community level, it's a local, smaller scale kind of fishery that's largely still family operated. You don't see that very much anymore. So for a lot of reasons it's a very green kind of fishery."

But the weirs aren't the only kind of fishing gear that entraps harbor porpoises. The gillnet fishery is a continuing problem for harbor porpoises, representing the greatest current threat to the species. Gillnets are long mesh nets anchored to the seafloor or attached to floats at the surface and designed to intercept fish during their normal movement patterns. Several of these nets are typically linked together to form a barrier that can be a mile long or more. According to Amanda Johnson, a fisheries biologist with the National Marine Fisheries Service, fishermen using gillnets in New England waters typically set their nets on the bottom like a fence to target groundfish like cod, haddock, and flounder, as well as monkfish and dogfish. Because harbor porpoises can dive more than 250 feet deep and will often chase their prey near the seafloor, it is not uncommon for porpoises to become entangled in gillnets and die. Between 1990 and 2005, more than 16,000 harbor porpoises died this way in the Gulf of Maine and adjacent waters, with annual deaths ranging from 1,200 to 2,900 during the first 6 years of the period and declining to between 53 and 782 since 1997, according to the 2007 harbor porpoise stock assessment report.

The high number of deaths in the early 1990s triggered a mechanism in the Marine Mammal Protection Act to create a Harbor Porpoise Take Reduction Plan. Johnson, the coordinator of the plan, said that the mortality level in the gillnets exceeded what is called the level of "potential biological removal," a conservative estimate of the number of human-caused deaths that a population can withstand annually without impairing the animal's ability to remain viable and sustainable. Essentially, too many porpoises were dying in gillnets for the porpoises to maintain a healthy population. So a plan was implemented in 1999 to reduce the number of porpoises entangled in gillnets through a variety of restrictions. Six distinct fishing areas—those where harbor porpoises are found in abundance at particular times of the year—were targeted for restrictions, including all of the coastal waters from the Maine/New Brunswick border to Massachusetts Bay, as well as an area south of Rhode Island and an offshore area called Cashes Ledge. Each area has its own set of restrictions consisting of a period of time each year when gillnetting is prohibited and/or when pingers are required on all gillnets.

"Pingers are acoustic deterrents that beep every four seconds within the hearing range of porpoises—ten kilohertz," explained Johnson. "Pingers must be placed at each end of a net and one at every bridle connecting net panels together. Timing and locations for using the pingers coincides with the harbor porpoise distribution. So, for example, off Boston pingers are required from December through May, but the area is closed entirely to gillnets in March because there has been a high take of porpoises in March. We know that even if you have pingers it's not going to completely eliminate the take, but having no gillnets in the water during peak abundance will."

As soon as the Take Reduction Plan took affect, porpoise deaths declined dramatically, but in the last few years the numbers have slowly climbed again. So fishery managers, researchers, environmental groups, and fishermen reconvened in 2008 to revisit the plan and see what needs to be done to bring the numbers down again. One reason for the recent increase could be what Joseph DeAlteris calls "the dinner bell effect." The professor of fisheries at the University of Rhode Island and member of the harbor porpoise take reduction team speculated that "harbor porpoises might have learned that if the net is there, there's food there, too, and they might then get entangled. They might also have become habituated to them. After a while they may think the ocean is filled with pingers and they just ignore them and get tangled up again." DeAlteris also wonders if the fishermen are maintaining the pingers. "Maybe they're just not working," he said. "It's not something that is easy for a human to hear, particularly over the drone of a diesel engine." Regardless of the reason for the decline, he believes that keeping harbor porpoises out of gillnets will take a combination of better management, more closed areas, use of new technologies, and getting the fishermen to continue to pay attention to the problem.

Enforcement of the regulations is also a major issue. "We have observers who go out on the boats, and they regularly observe fishermen going into closed areas or not using pingers in areas where they're supposed to," DeAlteris said. "The fishermen are often blatant about it because they know the observer can't issue them a ticket. We don't want to get in the business of having observers being enforcement guys, because the observer program is supposed to be science based. But we're at the point now where it's so blatant that we're looking at observer data to generate a summons. The observer isn't doing the enforcement; we're just taking the data [collected by the observer] and using it for enforcement later."

Assuming that the problem of porpoise entanglements in gillnets can be satisfactorily addressed, biologists are cautiously optimistic that the outlook for the population is good. While the International Union for the Conservation of Nature classifies harbor porpoises as vulnerable and they are somewhat protected under the Species At Risk Act in Canada, they are not included on the U.S. endangered species list. Besides fishing gear entanglement and capture as by-catch, the species appears to face few serious threats in New England waters. Few porpoises are found to strand themselves on beaches, especially in northern New England, which has few long sandy beaches where they could easily strand. There is no evidence that environmental pollution or global warming is affecting them, though they may shift their distribution as sea temperatures rise. And other than an occasional shark, they are not limited by predation.

Yet Heather Koopman still worries about them.

"Everything could change next year. You just never know," she said. "There's not much gillnet fishing now because there's less groundfish around, but if the groundfish rebound and gillnet fishing increases, then we would see an increase in porpoise mortality. Or if next year something happens to the herring, or if there's a new kind of fishery that comes in that's damaging to them, then the porpoises are going to be in trouble. You can't really rest on your laurels because they are vulnerable to whatever is going on around them."

Historically, what was going on around them in many places in its range was a fishery targeting the harbor porpoises themselves. Beginning in the 1830s, harbor porpoises were hunted for more than 100 years by Danish fishermen, who typically caught about a thousand animals per year. Between 100,000 and 300,000 porpoises and dolphins were killed each year in the Black Sea before World War II, and Turkish fishermen continued catching 34,000 to 44,000 animals annually until the hunt was suspended in 1983. Today the Black Sea population is considered threatened and unlikely to recover fully due to ecological collapse, while in the Baltic Sea they are doing even worse. Surveys conducted there in the early 2000s suggested that the population was so low that the annual by-catch of just seven porpoises was considered unsustainable. The only area where harbor porpoises are still hunted for food is in West Greenland, where approximately 1,000 porpoises are shot annually for food.

The day I was scheduled to leave Grand Manan Island, I got up early to join Caitlin McKinstry and Sarah Wong, two more members of the porpoise release team, to check the weirs. At seven o'clock, we climbed into what looked like a miniature lobster boat for a bumpy ride to visit the thirteen weirs at the north end of the island. At the weirs—each of which is named by its owner—we waited for the required four minutes to determine if a harbor porpoise had swum inside during the previous evening.

The first weir, named Doo Little, was just 200 yards from our starting point in the harbor. After gazing expectantly at the water's surface within the weir hoping to see a porpoise, we left disappointed. We did the same at Iron Lady, the weir owned by Herbie Lambert, who named it for the nickname the Russians gave to British Prime Minister Margaret Thatcher. At Cora Belle, a seal surprised us when it popped its head up briefly, but there were no porpoises there and apparently no fish either.

Approaching the weir named Intruder, Wong said she could tell it was filled with fish because of the large number of gulls swarming around it, mostly immature herring gulls. The birds cried out constantly as they flew from the top rim of the weir to the water's surface and back, sometimes bumping into the net, but mostly just paddling around on either side of the net. It was easy to get distracted by the gulls and forget to watch the water for surfacing porpoises, so we stayed an extra minute or two to be sure it was porpoise free.

It was a rough five-minute ride to the next weir, Bulls Eddy, which also was surrounded by gulls, and then on to First Venture, Jubilee, Star, Winner, and Mystery, none of which had fish, gulls, or porpoises. We then reversed course and headed to the weirs just south of the harbor. Half Acre was the floating weir that had a porpoise in it the day before, and as we arrived, Wong said she hoped it had escaped on its own, because that would have meant that it was certain to get out safely. We stayed only long enough to verify that the animal was still there.

At Pipe Dream, another of the floating weirs, the owner arrived in a tiny blue skiff at the same moment we did. With a brief glance and a smile, he steered his boat into the weir and around the inner edge, continuously watching his depth finder. In less than a minute, he turned to leave, having seen that the weir was absent of fish. Our last stop was Roma, and it, too, was empty.

We arrived back at the research center just as many of the rest of the team were strolling into the kitchen to feast on blueberry buckles, a delicious muffin-like meal that clearly made the researchers happy. The pastries were made by Koopman, who everyone credits for the excellent baked goods they ate all summer long. "If I weren't a marine biologist, I'd be a pastry chef," she told me after we ate. "It's very therapeutic." Later, when the museum manager's husband arrived with two gallon-sized buckets of blackberries he just finished picking himself, I could see Koopman's mind racing with ideas for what to make with them.

For Koopman, that's not all that races during the summer on Grand Manan. "When you're seining a porpoise, your adrenaline is racing. But it's so rewarding on a very intimate, personal level to pick up that porpoise and release it back into the ocean. You just feel fantastic!" Koopman said. "You get really attached to the little guys, and it's great to let them go. You also feel good about conservation as a whole. You're doing your little part on a local level to serve in some conservation fashion, and you're doing it cooperatively with the fishing industry, which is also great."

Perhaps the greatest continuing challenge for the porpoise release team is finding enough funding to keep the program going. Koopman and Westgate spend every winter writing grants to pay the cost of gas for the boats, food for the team, and a tiny bit of compensation for the fishermen to make it worth their while to cooperate. The fish processing company, Connors Brothers, has supported the project for years, as have the Britain-based Whale and Dolphin Conservation Society and the International Fund for Animal Welfare. Small grants have come from a wide range of other agencies, but there is never enough to be confident that the project will survive for even a couple more years.

The ultimate goal is for the fishermen to eventually consider porpoise removal a regular part of their job. There is no legislation in Canada that requires fishermen to make an effort to release the porpoises unharmed, so they would have to be self-motivated to do so. Thankfully, Koopman said that many of the fishermen are coming around to that perspective. "They tell me that we've changed their minds and they think differently about porpoises now," she said. "Some of them have said to me, 'you have my word that nothing will ever happen to a porpoise in my weir.' Even Herbie said that his attitude has changed. The fishermen have become curious about the porpoises, too. Like, they say 'tell me about porpoise biology' or 'where do they go in the winter' or 'what are those tags telling you.' I think porpoises have gone from being something that either wasn't on their radar or was just a kind of a nuisance to something where they actually see porpoises as individuals. We've come a long way."

4

American Horseshoe Crab

The windswept beaches of Tierra del Fuego in extreme southern Argentina are about as far as a New Englander could go in winter to find birds that are later seen on their own local beaches and mudflats. It's easy to find sanderlings there, the common shorebirds that feed at the waterline by comically racing out in search of marine invertebrates as each wave recedes, then race-walk back shoreward moments later as the next wave approaches. Less common shorebirds like Baird's sandpipers, white-rumped sandpipers, and American golden plovers are also found around Tierra del Fuego in winter and along the New England coastline during migration in spring and fall. But it is the red knot that is perhaps the most famous—and most imperiled—of the migrant shorebirds that make the trip.

The red knot is named for the beautiful cinnamon coloring on its face, breast, and belly, though that characteristic disappears during non-breeding months, when it is more easily distinguished from similar-looking birds by its chunky, rounded shape, straight black beak, and somewhat greenish legs. Most of the knots that breed in the Canadian

Arctic in the summer feed in similar habitats at the opposite end of the world. In early spring they begin their long northward journey from Tierra del Fuego, leapfrogging up the coast to Brazil, where they stop for a month to bulk up for the next leg of their trip. In May, they take off over the Atlantic and fly for as long as a week straight, with almost the entire population landing along the shores of Delaware Bay, which separates the states of New Jersey and Delaware. Their arrival there coincides with the breeding cycle of the world's largest population of horseshoe crabs, which crawl out of the water and deposit billions of eggs in the sand. On one day in 1990, there were an estimated 1.24 million horseshoe crabs spawning on the beaches of Delaware Bay.

As William Sargent wrote in *Crab Wars: A Tale of Horseshoe Crabs, Bioterrorism and Human Health,* each red knot "eats 135,000 horseshoe crab eggs; together they gorge down 248 tons of fat and protein. Each square meter of the beach contains over a million eggs, totaling more than a pound. But the birds can reach the eggs only in the top 6 inches of sand. They must rely on there being so many horseshoe crabs that late-arriving crabs dig up the eggs laid by earlier-arriving crabs. And there still must be another million eggs buried 8 inches below the surface to ensure the continuation of the crabs. It is superabundance on a staggering scale. The horseshoe crab eggs give the red knots the fuel they need to fly directly to the Arctic and start laying eggs. The horseshoe crab eggs are critical to the birds' survival. When they arrive above the Arctic Circle, there is no food. The ground is still frozen and covered with snow. They may not eat for two more weeks."

But the crabs are being overharvested by fishermen who use them as bait for the eel and whelk fisheries, dramatically reducing the food available to the knots. According to a 2007 assessment by the U.S. Fish and Wildlife Service, knot numbers in Delaware Bay plummeted from more than 100,000 birds in the 1980s to fewer than 13,000 today. Yet the Fish and Wildlife Service has repeatedly rejected petitions to protect the shorebirds under the Endangered Species Act.

Delaware Bay isn't the only place where red knots stop to refuel on their northbound migration. Small numbers also turn up every year along sandy beaches and mudflats in New England. I've seen them at Napatree Point and the Charlestown Breachway in Rhode Island and at Monomoy National Wildlife Refuge and Parker River National

Wildlife Refuge in Massachusetts. The birds there also feed upon horseshoe crab eggs, among other things, but crab numbers in New England appear to be declining as well, though they were probably never as abundant in New England as in Delaware Bay. Several horseshoe crab abundance indices in Rhode Island have shown dramatic population declines from their peak in the mid-1970s. And since few biologists have paid much attention to them until very recently, decisions about how to manage, monitor, and restore their populations are based on little but speculation.

Everyone who has spent even a little time walking beaches, exploring tide pools and salt marshes, or fishing or boating along the Atlantic coast is acquainted with the American horseshoe crab (*Limulus polyphemus*). Its distinctive appearance is unmistakable—a hard, curved brownish shell resembling a helmet or a horse's hoof (hence its common name), a long spiked tail, five pairs of legs, and ten eyes. While the crabs are seemingly well known to the casual observer, many of whom fear them out of a mistaken belief that the tail is dangerous, it is not generally recognized that horseshoe crab populations are in any danger.

Horseshoe crabs are among the most ancient creatures on Earth, having evolved more than 350 million years ago, long before the dinosaurs and flowering plants and almost as far back as the earliest visible life forms. They are most closely related to trilobites—next to dinosaurs, one of the most familiar of the fossil groups—which appeared during the early periods of the Paleozoic Era 540 million years ago and disappeared during the mass extinction at the end of that era 250 million years later, when 95 percent of all marine species became extinct. But horseshoe crabs survived. As arthropods, which have segmented bodies and limbs, they are also kin to spiders, scorpions, and crustaceans, but they belong to their own class, Merostomata, meaning "legs attached to the mouth." This class includes just four very similar horseshoe crab species, two of which are found in the Indian Ocean and one in the western Pacific Ocean, the latter of which is on the verge of extinction due to pollution in its major nesting area, Japan's Inland Sea.

The American horseshoe crab ranges from Maine to the Gulf of Mexico, though it is most abundant from New Jersey to Virginia. The crabs are bottom-dwelling scavengers that feed on worms, clams, and other small creatures living on or in the sediments on the seafloor. Adult crabs are, in turn, preyed upon by sharks and loggerhead turtles in the water and by scavengers like gulls on the beach. What is perhaps most remarkable about them is their spawning behavior. According to Mary-Jane James-Pirri, a marine ecologist at the University of Rhode Island who has studied horseshoe crabs in southern New England waters, spawning occurs en masse from May to July on the highest tides of the month, which typically correspond with the new and full moon. "If you have a really windy night or if it's cold, they will spawn on other tides," she said, "but their spawning is basically linked to the lunar phases of the tide. The males hang out waiting in the lower intertidal zone for the females to arrive, and the males grab onto the female as she comes up." While females are usually much larger than males, one sure way to distinguish them is by the front pair of legs, which in adult males look like tiny boxing gloves that are adapted to grasp onto the shell of spawning females.

Typically, one male attaches itself to a female, though sometimes as many as fifteen males—called satellite males—may congregate around a lone female and try to attach. The females follow the tide up, dig a hole, and lay their eggs in the sand, anywhere from the surface to 6 or 7 inches deep, and the male then fertilizes them. During the spawning season, each female may lay up to 80,000 eggs in as many as 20 separate nests by digging four to five nests per high tide and depositing about 4,000 eggs in each nest. Nests are typically found in a band between the low-tide and high-tide line, with those laid higher on the beach where they are exposed to more warmth from the sun—but not too high where the sand is too dry—developing most rapidly. The eggs hatch in about 14 days, and the larval horseshoe crab begins the only period in its life cycle that is not spent on the seafloor. James-Pirri calls larval horseshoe crabs "little miniature versions of themselves," because they already have their first shell and look exactly like tailless adults. She also refers to them as "planktonic trilobites. Planktonic means they swim in the water, but they do so for a very short period of time, just for a few days or a week. That's very short when you compare them to lobsters that spend maybe the whole summer in the plankton before they go down to the benthos again," she said.

Twenty days after emerging from their eggs and still living in the intertidal zone near the beaches where they began their life, juvenile horseshoe crabs molt their shell for the first time, something they must do in order to grow. They typically molt up to six times during their first year—after which they will still only be about half an inch across in size— three times in their second year, and twice more during the third, followed by annual molts until they are age 10. Although little is known about the lives of juvenile horseshoe crabs, it is believed that they spend their first summer or two on the intertidal flats, feeding for short periods and burrowing into the sand for most of the day. Eventually they move off into deeper water for up to 10 years before migrating back to the intertidal zone to spawn for the first time. "Where they go offshore to mature is a big black box that we don't know much about," noted James-Pirri. "We believe they return when they reach maturity at somewhere around ten or eleven years, which is a long time to mature."

Biologists speculate that horseshoe crabs spend those years maturing on the continental shelf, which extends about 200 miles offshore from the coastal zone before the seafloor slopes gently downward to the abyssal plain. Geologically part of the North American continent, the shelf is found in water about 600 feet deep and is made up mostly of bedrock on which can still be seen the long, narrow ditches created by glaciers scouring the seabed during the last Ice Age. The bedrock is covered with a thick blanket of terrigenous sediment—deposits of eroded terrestrial material—where fossilized marine organisms are regularly unearthed. It is there on the muddy sediment, usually less than 50 miles from shore but occasionally 100 miles or more, that horseshoe crabs spend their adolescent years.

Little is known about how many horseshoe crabs live in New England waters today, and even less is known about what those numbers were a decade ago or more. In the nineteenth century they were so abundant in Delaware Bay that 4 million were harvested annually during the 1870s for use as fertilizer and to feed to pigs, though the latter was discontinued because it was believed that the crabs made the pigs taste bad. More than 1.5 million horseshoe crabs were captured each year from the 1880s to the 1920s, but by the 1960s the annual catch was down to 42,000 crabs. Little attention was paid to the species during the twentieth century because commercial fishing activity focused on more popular and lucrative target species.

To help understand the health of the horseshoe crab population in New England waters, tagging studies have been undertaken throughout Cape Cod, beginning in 2000 by James-Pirri and by staff and volunteers of the Massachusetts Audubon Society and Monomoy National Wildlife Refuge. In June 2007, I was invited to join U.S. Fish and Wildlife Service biologist Monica Williams and a team of volunteers as they captured, tagged, and released horseshoe crabs on North Monomoy Island on a gray and windy day when tidal conditions ensured that spawning horseshoe crabs would be in abundance. The refuge, which is home to endangered piping plovers and least terns and is a major stopover point for shorebirds during migration, is an 8-mile-long sandy peninsula that extends southward from the town of Chatham at the elbow of Cape Cod and is accessible only by a short boat ride from the mainland. The size and shape of North and South Monomoy Islands change regularly, sometimes quite dramatically, depending on the impact of major storms. In recent years, storms have shifted sand from North and South Monomoy to form a small, new island some are calling Minimoy.

After a brief orientation, Williams and her ten volunteers made the 5-minute crossing to the north tip of North Monomoy and then walked for 10 minutes around to the west side of the island to an area of mudflats where many of the horseshoe crabs in the region spawn. Along the way, there were numerous dead crabs in the wrack line, probably flipped over and eaten by the abundant herring and great black backed gulls that nest on the island. Laughing gulls, the small gull with an attractive black hood, floated by occasionally in the brisk breeze, and willets—a large, drab-looking shorebird with a noisy call and distinctive black-and-white wing pattern visible only in flight—made frequent appearances. My favorite shorebird, the fanciful American oystercatcher, mostly stayed far away from us, though occasionally a pair flew by in the distance, calling as usual. Dressed in black above and white below with a yellow eye, they slide their fluorescent orange beaks in between the shells of mollusks and snip the adductor muscle so the shellfish can be easily opened and eaten. Common and least terns, and probably a few endangered roseate terns as well, constantly whirled around us in the air as they fished for minnows in the shallows.

Williams set down her pack to establish a processing station in a barely dry patch of sand where salt-marsh cordgrass grew at the edge of the water and was regularly inundated during high tides. Closer to the dunes where the salt water seldom reached, the vegetation changed— American beach grass was predominant, with scattered bayberry bushes and salt spray rose providing nesting habitat for salt-marsh sharptailed sparrows. From her pack, Williams removed the few tools needed for the day—an electric drill, some bright pink numbered tags, a couple of rulers, and some forms to record data. Then she sent the volunteers to wade into the knee-deep water to collect horseshoe crabs. The animals were easy to find at first. Many seemed to be wandering aimlessly around the edge of the cordgrass, probably males searching for an available mate. The larger females looked like they had a plan and knew exactly where they were going, crawling in a straight line toward the beach. Within minutes, more than a dozen horseshoe crabs were placed upside down in the sand for processing. Since most of the team seemed to only want to collect the crabs in the beginning, I volunteered for the first shift of tagging and measuring them.

The process involved drilling a hole in the left corner of the carapace and inserting a 3-inch-long plastic tag into the hole. When done correctly, the tag extended outward like a highly visible antennae. We then measured across the widest point of their shells, determined their gender and age, and assessed whether the crabs had any physical damage or missing limbs. Aging a horseshoe crab was a somewhat subjective determination—those with dark shells are judged to be old and light shells are young. Crabs with numerous barnacles and slipper shells attached to them were also considered to be old.

I was quite tentative the first time I drilled a hole into the shell of a live and squirming horseshoe crab, but the animal didn't seem to mind as long as the drill bit didn't strike any of its soft parts, which I succeeded in avoiding. I worked as fast as I could for 30 minutes, but the volunteers continued to stack up the crabs beside me and I had difficulty keeping up with them. In the early going it seemed like for every crab that was processed and returned to the water, two more appeared beside me. When I saw that my knees were red and sore from kneeling in the sand and my fingertips were tender from the most challenging job—poking the pink tag through the newly drilled hole—I called for some reinforcements.

After stretching my legs for a few minutes, I joined the rest of the volunteers who were still wading in search of more crabs. By then, most of the crabs we saw had already been tagged, so we had to walk farther afield to find new ones. The water was quite shallow for about 100 yards in every direction from the processing station, and the light sandy bottom made it easy to see the dark-shelled horseshoe crabs 10 or 20 yards ahead as we walked around. Most of them swam casually, almost at a plodding pace, so they were easy to catch up to and grab. But once they were lifted from the water they immediately struggled, flailing their legs and pulling their abdomen and tail forward, perhaps to protect their gills. Their appendages struggled forcefully to push me away. When I finally collected my first one, the long walk back to the processing station allowed me to examine the crab more closely than I ever had before.

The bodies of horseshoe crabs are divided into three parts, the cephalothorax, the abdomen, and the tail, though they are sometimes called the prosoma, opisthosoma, and telson. The cephalothorax contains a bulbous brain, a tubular heart, and a large intestinal tract, and it is connected by a hinge to the abdomen, where its gills and most of its 750 individual muscles are found. But held upside down in the hand, mostly what one notices of the cephalothorax is six sets of appendages, all of which have what appear to be pinchers at the ends but which surprisingly don't pinch at all. The first pair is the smallest and is used exclusively for putting food into its mouth, while the remainder are used for locomotion. Behind the legs are the book gills, which are used both for propulsion when swimming and for collecting oxygen for respiration.

Perhaps most remarkable of all are the eyes, which often go unnoticed because so many barnacles and shells cover the animal. But by looking closely at the top of the shell, I found the two oval compound eyes that are used mostly for finding mates and can magnify sunlight up to ten times. Early research by H. Keffer Hartline in the 1930s and 1940s led to discoveries about sensory cells in the retina of horseshoe crabs that earned the researcher the Nobel Prize in physiology in 1967. Several additional simple eyes are located on the forward portion of the shell and can sense ultraviolet light from the moon, enabling the crab to see as well at night as in the daylight. These forward eyes give it a cyclops-like appearance and account for its species name, *polyphemus*, the mythical one-eyed giant who was blinded by Odysseus. More eyes are found on the underside and on the tail and may be used when the crabs swim upside down, which they do on occasion. The tail, while appearing potentially dangerous at first glance, is easily broken and is simply used as a rudder to help change directions when the crab is walking or swimming. Crabs also use it to right themselves if they become flipped upside down.

Their hard shell and unusual shape make adult horseshoe crabs a prey item that few creatures will feed upon. While some sharks will occasionally eat them, only the loggerhead turtle makes a habit of it. In fact, horseshoe crabs are the most abundant food item found in the stomachs of loggerheads, which range up and down the East Coast in summer, preferring river mouths and turbid estuaries where crabs are often abundant. Sea turtle researcher John Keinath, in *The American Horseshoe Crab*, wrote that "loggerhead turtles are well adapted for foraging on horseshoe crabs. Their thick beak, a keratinous jaw sheath up to three centimeters thick, along with very large jaw muscles account for their name. These jaws are ideal for eating hard-bodied organisms. When a crab is encountered, the turtle turns the crab upside down and uses its beak and claws to scoop out the legs, gills, eggs and underlying structures."

When I returned to the processing station with two horseshoe crabs, my arms tired from the surprisingly heavy creatures, the novice processors were a bit backlogged, just as I had been when I started out. A dozen or so crabs lay calmly upside down in the sand, though occasionally some would use their tails as a lever to flip themselves right side up and try to crawl away. Many of the crabs collected that day were in pairs, with the males latched onto the female's shell. As the volunteers carried the crabs to be processed, the male typically re-

leased the female, but Williams insisted that they be processed together and released together in hopes that they would connect again
and spawn. One pair of horseshoe crabs that I returned to the water
immediately swam off in opposite directions despite my best efforts to
retrieve them and bring them together again. As with humans, the in-
terruption apparently killed the mood. Others that were returned to
the water were observed to immediately bury themselves in the sand,
which is partly a defense mechanism—they could probably sense that
the tide was going out and they didn't want to be stranded where gulls
could easily flip them over and eat them. Once I even saw an orange
tag that appeared to have dropped off a crab in shin-deep water, so I
bent down to retrieve it and found that it was attached to a horseshoe
crab submerged in the sand.

After two hours, the team of volunteers had collected and processed 141 horseshoe crabs on the west side of North Monomoy Island, ranging in size from 16 to 24 centimeters across at the widest
point of their shells. We then returned to the northernmost tip of the
island to start the process over again. We quickly found 40 crabs, but
the darker colored sand and the deeper water made it difficult to find
more. The wind had also picked up again, whipping up white caps
and waves and making the work far less enjoyable. So we headed for
the boat. As we did, we watched a crowd of at least forty herring and
laughing gulls feeding in the wet sand. The boatman, another Fish and
Wildlife Service biologist, called us over as he picked up a handful of
sand. Mixed among colorful grains of sand, sediment, and detritus
were several tiny opaque gray eggs that looked like pinhead-sized ball
bearings. Those eggs, and the nutrients they provide migrating shorebirds, were the reason for our efforts that day to monitor and protect
Cape Cod's horseshoe crab population.

When Mary-Jane James-Pirri shifted her research focus to the study
of horseshoe crabs, she assumed she would have reams of scientific papers to refer to from past research projects. She was wrong. Until recently, very little research had been conducted on the species. "I was
coming from the study of lobsters, where everything is known about

them and there are a lot of people working on it and there's loads and loads of information available," she said. "So I went through a library and was surprised at the limited amount of research done on the species, and what there was had primarily been done by just a few people. Not a lot is known about horseshoe crabs, perhaps because it hasn't been commercially important, and maybe just because it's not a species that has been on everyone's radar."

It is now. In 2007, the first International Symposium on the Science and Conservation of Horseshoe Crabs brought together dozens of scientists from around the world to share the results of their research. Some are studying horseshoe crab population dynamics, habitat, spawning, food preferences, mortality, and other ecological factors, while others are examining their physiology, including their vision, evolution, embryonic development, and the role of pheromones in mate selection. Still other researchers are using the tools of biotechnology to examine horseshoe crabs at a molecular level, in part to study human diseases. For instance, Robert Jacobs of the University of California at Santa Barbara is using horseshoe crab blood cells to investigate the biochemical processes that cause allergic responses in humans, while Daniel Gibson at Worcester Polytechnic Institute is examining the role of amino acid neurotransmitters in horseshoe crab muscle twitches, which he hopes will provide insight into how these amino acids contribute to strokes in the human brain.

James-Pirri's research was aimed at providing the National Park Service with baseline information about the horseshoe crab population on Cape Cod. "They knew they had crabs in the park," she said, "but they didn't know anything about where they were, what they were doing, or how many there were. When I started, Massachusetts Audubon and Monomoy National Wildlife Refuge were gearing up to do similar studies, so we all standardized our methodology. We weren't really testing anything, but we found that there were certain hotspots on Cape Cod where there seem to be high spawning densities of crabs, particularly in Pleasant Bay and at Monomoy, whereas Cape Cod Bay always tended to have much lower densities." Not only were there a great many crabs spawning in Pleasant Bay, but unlike Monomoy to the south and Nauset estuary to the north, Pleasant Bay had an unusual gender ratio among its spawning population. For every female found in the bay, James-Pirri found between six and nine males, whereas the ratio elsewhere was closer to one to two or one to three.

Pleasant Bay, located just north of the elbow of Cape Cod and bordering the towns of Chatham, Harwich, and Orleans, may be the center of abundance of horseshoe crab spawning in New England. The largest bay contiguous to the Cape Cod National Seashore, it contains 7,285 acres of saltwater at high tide and is a popular location for boating, fishing, bird-watching, and beachcombing. Due to the popularity of the bay, a group that calls itself the Friends of Pleasant Bay was formed in 1985 to protect it, and the group played a significant role in helping to protect its horseshoe crab population as well. While James-Pirri did the initial studies to assess the population of crabs in the bay, the Friends group paid for a follow-up study by students from the marine program at Boston University. In 2003 they reported that there were approximately 13.5 million juvenile horseshoe crabs in Pleasant Bay in 2001 and 500,000 adults, including those that were buried in the sediments and nonspawning adults, which are often missed in other surveys. They also found that of the thousands and thousands of eggs each adult crab lays, just one egg in a thousand survives its first year, and just 78 percent of those yearlings reach adulthood. Though seemingly alarming, those are typical survival rates for lobsters, crabs, and other crustaceans in New England waters.

The greater threat comes from the overharvesting of adult horseshoe crabs by commercial fishermen for use as bait in the eel and whelk fishery. American eels are captured in eelpots baited with female horseshoe crabs, preferably those with eggs. Commercial landings of eels reached 4 million pounds during some years in the 1970s and declined to approximately 1 million pounds in the late 1990s and 2000s. The majority are exported to support a significant demand for "glass" eels—juvenile eels up to four inches long—in Europe and Asia. Whelks, also called conchs, are large sea snails found in shallow coastal waters off the New England and Mid-Atlantic states from spring through fall. The channeled whelk and the knobbed whelk are harvested for sale to Southeast Asia and the Caribbean islands in large numbers. The peak of whelk landings occurred in 1994, when 5 million pounds were caught, though typical harvest numbers in recent decades are closer to 3 million pounds annually. Channeled whelks are typically caught in traps baited with horseshoe crabs, while knobbed whelks, which are too large to climb into most traps, are harvested using trawls and dredges.

Millions of horseshoe crabs are collected during spawning season to support these fisheries. According to data from the Atlantic States Marine Fisheries Council, nearly 3 million horseshoe crabs were harvested annually from 1995 to 1997. Due to concerns about a decline in crab numbers and the resulting impact on shorebirds, a fishery management plan for horseshoe crabs was approved in 1998, and an addendum implemented in 2000 capped the harvest at 25 percent below the 1995–1997 level. Additional addenda in 2001, 2004, and 2006 placed further restrictions on the horseshoe crab harvest in Maryland, Delaware, Virginia, and New Jersey, which reduced the annual landings to about 500,000 animals.

In an effort to reduce the demand for horseshoe crabs without impacting the eel and whelk fisheries, researchers have been studying alternative bait and trap designs. Experiments have been conducted using herring, crushed blue mussels, blue crabs, shrimp heads, and surf clams as an alternative live bait, but horseshoe crabs have been found to be the most effective bait for both fisheries. An artificial bait is also in the works for the eel fishery, based on the chemical cue in horseshoe crab eggs that is seemingly an attractant to eels. Researchers are also trying to develop a "bait extender" by mixing ground horseshoe crabs with a surf clam by-product to increase the amount of bait that can be obtained from one crab. The most promising research, however, is the development of a polyethylene bait bag that protects the bait from scavengers to extend the useful life of the bait. A bait bag developed by a commercial fisherman in Delaware and adopted by fishermen in Virginia has reduced the number of horseshoe crabs used in the whelk fishery by 25 to 50 percent. The same bag is now being used by fishermen harvesting horseshoe crabs in Massachusetts.

While the eel and whelk fishery continues to be the greatest threat to the horseshoe crab population on the East Coast, it is by no means the only concern. Recreational vehicle traffic on beaches can destroy their habitat and crush their shells; an oil spill at the wrong time and in the wrong place could have devastating effects; coastal erosion and sea level rise due to global warming could wipe out critical areas of spawning habitat; and channel dredging, seawall construction, and shoreline stabilization structures could further degrade habitat. In addition, natural strandings take their toll as well. Crabs that are flipped upside down on the beach from wave action can quickly die if their gills dry out or if gulls eat them. As a result, a horseshoe crab conservation organization in the Delaware Bay area, the Ecological Research and Development Group, launched a program called Just Flip 'Em, which its web site says is "designed to bring attention to the hundreds of thousands of horseshoe crabs who die each year from stranding during their yearly spawning ritual and to encourage individuals, through a simple act of compassion, to take the time to assist and appreciate these remarkable creatures, who will not survive public indifference." In 2007, an unrelated citizens group in Pleasant Bay launched a similar effort, including a regular survey of the bay's uninhabited islands to assess how many horseshoe crabs are found upside down and dead on the shoreline. The following year, another Cape Cod-based group, the Committee for the Conservation of Horseshoe Crabs, partnered with the Massachusetts Audubon Society and others to initiate a 3-year horseshoe crab survey on the Cape to try to get an accurate count of how many crabs live in the region.

While compassionately righting upside-down horseshoe crabs will not likely have a noticeable impact on their population numbers, it's a good way of engaging the public in a wildlife conservation effort. And it's the least we can do for them. Strange as it may seem, horseshoe crabs play a critical role in human health care. Without even knowing it, many of us have probably had our lives saved by the ancient creature.

Horseshoe crab advocate and author William Sargent described the health care connection at a lecture I attended in 2006. "If we have a wound, we have a whole system of antibodies that go to the area and coagulate and they fight the infection. We have about sixteen proteins that are all involved with doing that. Instead of blood cells, horseshoe crabs have amebocyte cells, which migrate to the area and coagulate and keep the infection out. It's a very primitive system, but a very elegant system. It was probably the first immune system to evolve in the animal kingdom. The bottom line is that scientists are able to extract [the horseshoe crab's] blood, separate out the amebocyte cells, and make what's called *Limulus* amebocyte lysate (LAL), and this is used as a test for gram-negative bacteria. So whenever you go to a hospital, anything that's going to come in contact with your blood system, whether it's a flu shot or a scalpel or anything like that, has to be tested to make sure that it is pathogen free, that it's free of gram-negative bacteria. And the way that they do that is with horseshoe crab blood."

LAL was discovered by scientists at the Marine Biological Laboratory in Woods Hole, Massachusetts, in the 1960s. Researcher Frederik Bang found that clotting occurred when common bacteria were injected into horseshoe crabs, and the clotting was due to an endotoxin in the bacteria. By demonstrating the clotting reaction in a test tube, he was able to develop a reagent so he could further study the process. Later, a scientist at the Woods Hole Oceanographic Institute, Stanley Watson, used the reagent in his research and set up a procedure for producing it for his own use. When demand for his reagent increased from other scientists and pharmaceutical companies, he established a company, Associates of Cape Cod, and received approval from the Food and Drug Administration to license and manufacture it commercially. Since then, the test has become the accepted replacement for a test using rabbits, and two more U.S. companies, as well as others in Japan and China, have formed to manufacture LAL.

The harvesting of horseshoe crabs for their blood is a sustainable practice. Regulations in states where the animals are captured for the biomedical industry require that the crabs be returned to the waters where they were caught within 72 hours after the bleeding process. Not only is that requirement the most appropriate step for the long-term conservation of the crabs, but it is also ensures that the crabs contribute their greatest economic value to society. According to Sargent, horseshoe crabs are one of the most valuable marine animals in New England waters. When used exclusively for the production of LAL, each horseshoe crab is worth about $2,500 over its lifetime—one quart of processed blood is valued at about $15,000—whereas they are worth about 30 cents per pound as bait. However, the unsustainable practice of harvesting horseshoe crabs for bait is a growing concern, and the regulations are confusing.

In Massachusetts, for example, fishermen can either hold a bait permit for collecting horseshoe crabs or a biomedical permit, not both. Biomedical permit holders can only sell to the biomedical industry, but bait permit holders can double dip—sell their crabs to the biomedical industry for bleeding and then sell the same crab as bait. Alison Leschen of the Massachusetts Division of Marine Fisheries calls it the rent-a-crab program and sees it as a positive twist to the regulations. "If the crabs are going to die as bait, they might as well bleed them once first," she said. "And if the bait market is terrible, which it is sometimes, the dealers have the option of releasing them."

Despite the state's somewhat confusing regulations, the fact that regulations and quotas are in place at all seems to be having the desired effect. When the federal horseshoe crab management plan was implemented in 1999, nearly 200 fishermen reported harvesting almost 550,000 crabs for both bait and biomedical uses in Massachusetts. However, since that year's harvest figures were to be the basis for a quota system, the state assumed the fishermen over-reported their harvest and that the actual figure was closer to 440,000. The Massachusetts annual quota was set at 330,000 crabs, and reported harvest numbers have never come close to that figure, declining from 272,000 in 2000 to 69,000 in 2004. In the following years, horseshoe crab landings in Massachusetts increased slightly and officials worried the harvest was going to continue to grow, so the quota was cut in half to 165,000 in 2008.

"Part of the reason for the cut was from a concern about the population, because we have little information about how many crabs are out there," Leschen said. "All of the Delaware Bay states have moratoria or big restrictions on the harvest, and last year New York absorbed a lot of that market because they hadn't changed their regulations yet. This year [2008] New York put in strict regs, which left Massachusetts crabs vulnerable to out of state pressure."

In Rhode Island, which established its own quota system considerably more restrictive than the federal plan, the quota is 14,655 (an additional 34,194 can be captured for the biomedical industry and returned to the water). According to Scott Olszewski, marine fisheries biologist for the state of Rhode Island, the annual harvest for bait has ranged from a low of 6,000 crabs in 2004 to a high of 15,500 in 2006.

In years when the harvest exceeds the quota, he said the quota for the next year is reduced by the number of crabs captured above the quota.

The timing of the horseshoe crab harvest is also a key element to ensuring that the fishery is sustainable. For example, during a day of counting horseshoe crabs in 2000, volunteers from the Rhode Island environmental group Save the Bay found just twenty crabs at the peak of spawning season at a site where they previously were abundant. And no sooner had the volunteers made their count when a fisherman picked up all twenty animals and tossed them into his boat for bait. None of the crabs had even had a chance to lay its eggs. In response to that event, and the fact that the state had no regulations in place at that time, the state banned crab harvesting 48 hours before and after the new and full moon in May, June, and July, the peak of spawning season. No such regulation is in effect in Massachusetts or Connecticut, however.

In the Delaware Bay area, where horseshoe crab abundance was believed to have declined precipitously and where their eggs are so very important to migrating shorebirds, especially the endangered red knot, a 1,500-square-mile horseshoe crab sanctuary in federal waters was established in 2001. But regulations limiting the crab harvest have been met with stiff resistance. To protect the birds in Delaware Bay, the states of Delaware and New Jersey enacted a 2-year ban on the horseshoe crab harvest in 2006. But a judge struck down the Delaware ban after just 1 year when a fisherman and a Virginia seafood company sued the state. While the New Jersey ban remained in effect, the ruling immediately opened Delaware Bay to the harvest of 100,000 crabs annually. And while the harvest of that relatively small number of crabs probably won't have a significant impact on the future of horseshoe crabs in the region, it may have a devastating impact on the red knots, which some computer models suggest could be extinct by 2010.

5

Leach's Storm Petrel

The ferry crossing to Grand Manan Island in late June 2008 was far different from my trip 9 months earlier, when I visited the island to learn about harbor porpoises. Due to the thick fog, I saw no whales, no porpoises, and just a few scattered seabirds. Instead, I spent the trip repeatedly drying my eyeglasses from the incessant mist, attempting to block out the annoying blast of the ship's foghorn, and squinting hard into the opaque air searching for life, eventually being rewarded with a muddied view of an Atlantic puffin. The 30-minute ride south from Grand Manan to tiny Kent Island the next morning was under similar conditions, with visibility less than 100 yards as calculated by Marko Murray, captain of the 23-foot Novi boat *Ernest Joy* that transported me and the island's cook. By the time I got my first glimpse of Kent Island, we were nearly alongside the dock, where a dozen people greeted us to help unload a week's worth of groceries and other supplies. Most of those in the group were students at Bowdoin and Kenyon colleges, who were there with their professors to conduct research on birds, plants, beetles, and other wildlife.

Situated at the dividing line between the Gulf of Maine and the Bay of Fundy, Kent Island is a stunningly beautiful place, though it is usually so fogged in that it's difficult to appreciate its interesting variety of fields and scattered small mixed forests. Long and narrow, the island's South Field is littered with numerous tree swallow nest boxes and divided by mowed lines delineating research quadrats for savannah sparrow studies. Herring gulls nest in the tall grasses at the edge of the field closest to the shoreline, and the aggressive adults sometimes attack while researchers are walking the paths. From before dawn until well after dark, the gulls constantly call and cry and bicker. The fields were formerly cultivated and now contain mostly timothy grass, red fescue, raspberries, blueberries, and scattered wildflowers, including goldenrod, hawkweed, sheep sorrel, and starflower.

The island has a rich and unusual history. Used for centuries by indigenous people for seal hunting, it was named for its first European settler, John Kent, who arrived in the late 1700s and died in 1828. In 1913, Grand Manan fisherman Ernest Joy shot a yellow-nosed albatross in the waters nearby—just the second time the species had been seen in North America—and gave it to his friend Allan Moses, a taxidermist. Some years later, Moses traded the specimen to the American Museum of Natural History in exchange for a chance to join the museum's expedition to Central Africa in 1929. Funded by wealthy sportsman J. Sterling Rockefeller, the trip was considered a great success after Moses shot a tiny green bird called a Grauer's broadbill. Rockefeller was so pleased that he offered to reward Moses, who requested that Rockefeller purchase Kent Island to protect the seabirds living there from egg collectors. The philanthropist agreed, and the island was donated to Bowdoin College for use as a scientific research station in 1935. Students and researchers have conducted a wide range of studies of its flora and fauna every year ever since.

The facilities on the island are somewhat primitive but functional— a two-seat outhouse, a solar shower that is seldom warm enough for comfort, little running water or electricity, and a dozen small, unfinished buildings with names like the Rat Shack, the Cow Barn, the Warden's House, and Fog Heaven, the latter of which is a six-foot square structure that doubles as a laboratory and contains little more than a small makeshift bed. I was assigned a room on the second floor of the largest building on the island, known simply as The Dorm, which had a large kitchen and long table for group dinners on the first floor, a small library and game room called the Dingleberry where everyone gathered after dinner, and four bedrooms upstairs.

After dumping my duffel bag in my room, I was immediately put to work helping students Priscilla Erickson and Sami Nichols, who were collecting blood samples from recently hatched savannah sparrows. We visited several nests that the students had already staked out, collected week-old nestlings, and processed the birds in Fog Heaven. The students' aim was to study the development of the chicks by examining their diet and testing if an enzyme added to their food provided a boost to their immune system. After weighing and banding the first batch of nestlings and collecting blood from a vein beneath one wing, Erickson said, "It's time for these guys to go home," and she carefully delivered them back to their nest.

An hour later I was finished recording sparrow data and was invited by Bob Mauck, the director of the research station, for a walk in the Shire, a small woodlot near the western edge of the island. It's the site of several research projects involving Leach's storm petrels, a robin-sized seabird that nests in underground burrows and was the reason for my visit to Kent Island. Named by Mauck's daughter several years ago, the Shire is a three-acre mound dominated by balsam fir, white spruce, and heart-leaved birch trees with an understory of spinulose wood-fern, whorled wood aster, and scattered masses of beautiful blooming bunchberry. Most of the tree branches were covered in old man's beard lichens, giving it the feel of an old growth forest, which it sort of is. There are no young trees or saplings on the island, the result of snowshoe hares introduced 50 years previously—finally eradicated in 2007—that ate all of the new growth. They also ate the bark of many old trees, causing an abundance of dead and decaying trunks lying around the forest covered in moss.

A maze of trails leading through the hip-high ferns allows researchers access to the Shire's 300 storm petrel burrows, many of which had fern stems placed across their entrances like jail cells to determine the comings and goings of the unusual birds. Each burrow was labeled with a metal stake and a blue numbered tag, some of which also had lavender yarn or orange or pink surveyor's tape tied on by the researchers. The burrows were somewhat narrower than I expected, and because most are long and angled, a hidden man-made entrance has been dug and covered by a wooden board to provide easier access to the nest chamber. After finding an empty burrow that wasn't part of anyone's research, Mauck told me to stick my arm in. Despite every instinct telling me not to, I did. It's quite disconcerting to reach into a hole in the ground up to your shoulder, uncertain what's inside and what might bite you, but it's required of anyone who wants to study Leach's storm petrels. The good news is that the island has no snakes or mice—though plenty of beetles and other bugs—and the only mammals are muskrats (which do live in burrows, but thankfully not in the Shire) and bats.

I reached in slowly and immediately found that it was going to be a tight squeeze. The hole bent to the right slightly, and just past my elbow it opened up and I felt a pile of soft leaves where an adult storm petrel would be sitting on its egg. But there was no bird, no egg, and thankfully no bugs or anything else creepy. When I removed my arm, it was covered in soft dirt and scratches, which I noted later was a clear indication of who on the island was studying storm petrels and who was not. So we moved a few yards away to another burrow, and Mauck reached inside. I could tell by his reaction that he detected a bird, and he soon pulled out a faintly speckled and slightly dirty white egg and handed it to me. It was quite warm. Despite the petrels being about the same size as a robin, the egg was more than twice the size of a robin's egg. Mauck said that when the egg is laid, it weighs about one quarter of the body weight of the female petrel, and all I could imagine was a human mother giving birth to a child one quarter her weight. Ouch! He then struggled for two or three minutes to remove the bird, at one point blurting out, "Come on bird, bite me." The process for removing a storm petrel from its burrow is to entice it into biting you, then grasp its bill and carefully pull the bird out head first by the beak. Removing it in reverse may damage the bird's feathers or injure its wings. Eventually Mauck pulled out the petrel and handed it to me.

It was a soft, gray-brown bird that at some angles may even seem to have a hint of steel blue in its feathers, with a slightly forked tail and a white rump patch. It had a dark eye, a smallish head, and a bizarre curved, grooved and crooked beak with a short tube on top for ejecting salt, making it look somewhat like a caricature of a witch's nose. Its feet were webbed and its legs were somewhat short—a characteristic that separates the birds from their closest relative, Wilson's storm petrel. The bird had a steel alloy band around its leg—aluminum bands typically placed on most other species of birds aren't sturdy enough to last the 35-year life span of a storm petrel. Holding that bird in my hand was a special moment for me, as Leach's storm petrel was the only bird that breeds in the Northeast that I had never before seen. As I sat there savoring the moment, Mauck told me not to hold the bird facing either of us, since petrels are notorious for projectile vomiting without warning. Thankfully, this one just sat calmly in my hand.

Leach's storm petrels (*Oceanodroma leucorhoa*) are one of a family of small seabirds that spend most of their lives far out to sea, where they pitter-patter across the waves and hover on long, pointed wings as they search for small marine organisms on which to feed. Sometimes called Mother Carey's chickens, a nickname given by eighteenth-century sailors to several types of storm petrels, Leach's come to shore only to breed, primarily on uninhabited islands far enough offshore to be free of mammalian predators. They nest in abundance around the Canadian Maritimes and north and west to southern Labrador, southern Greenland, Iceland, Scotland, and Norway. Their southernmost breeding colony in the Atlantic is on Penikese Island in Buzzards Bay, Massachusetts, where fewer than 10 pairs nest each year, a site nearly 200 miles south of the next nearest colony. The birds also nest on a few dozen islands off the coast of Maine, as well as around the Pacific Rim from California to Alaska and southwest to Russia and Japan.

Despite their wide distribution and relative abundance, few people ever see them, even during the breeding season, because of their remote breeding locations and the fact that they forage great distances from land, traveling between their nest and feeding grounds exclusively at night. Almost invariably when a storm petrel is sighted flying around New England waters, the species seen is Wilson's storm petrel, which breeds in the Southern Hemisphere and spends the austral winter in the North Pacific and North Atlantic.

To Bob Mauck, the most intriguing feature of Leach's storm petrels is their odor. "The smell is what always captures me first," he told me. "Anybody who studies petrels, their clothes have a smell that stays with them for the rest of their existence." Mauck and the students I met on Kent Island agreed that the birds smell like a combination of musty attic and fish—the attic smell likely derived from the odor of their burrows and the fish smell from their food. Everyone always noted, however, that it wasn't necessarily a bad smell, and when I got my first whiff of a petrel in the hand, I had to agree. To me, it smelled more like hay than attic, and I didn't notice the fish smell at all, though the students told me that the fishy smell would be quite obvious the first time one vomited on me. I couldn't wait.

The marine organisms that the storm petrels feed upon are mostly euphausiids, a group of pelagic, shrimp-like crustaceans up to an inch long that are often found just beneath the surface of the water. The birds will also eat almost any other marine organism of a manageable size that they can reach, from copepods to tiny squid and juvenile cod. "Storm petrels aren't diving birds, so they just eat what food they can reach by sticking their heads under the water," said Mauck. "They'll eat almost anything they can get a hold of. They have a pretty wide range of things that have been found in their stomachs. If you want to find out what, just point a petrel at somebody and there's a good chance it will vomit it out for you."

Where they find their food is a question Mauck can't answer with any certainty. During the breeding season, they likely forage as much as 100 miles offshore, and studies have shown that they can easily travel that distance and find their way back to their nests without difficulty. "Apparently the food they're looking for isn't available locally, otherwise you would expect to see them when you see a Wilson's. So we're figuring that they're going out into Georges Bank, but we don't know for sure. We do know a little bit about where they go the rest of the year. Just like Wilson's are coming up from the Southern Hemisphere, these Northern Hemisphere breeders are heading down to the Southern Hemisphere for the winter. We don't have a good sense of their migratory route, but some band returns indicate they're taking a circle route. They may be going over to Europe and then down to Africa and then back to the Caribbean and up. But we don't know that for sure."

What Mauck does know for sure is a great deal about the life cycle of the petrels. He said they show up on Kent Island in mid May, mate in a burrow—often the same burrow they nested in previously, or one quite close by—and lay their one egg in early or mid June. Incubation takes about 44 days on average, but varies from 35 to 55 days. The parents share incubation duties, with one sitting on the egg for several days while the other is feeding at sea. "We know that the males tend to do more of the incubation of the egg than the females, which is a little surprising, because usually we think that males are slackers, but we know that the males tend to do a little bit more. You might consider that to be a function of the female just having invested all that energy into producing a big egg, so the male may be in a better position to do the incubation," he said.

The variation in the length of incubation is particularly notable among storm petrels. The more time the birds spend incubating their egg, the quicker it will hatch. But because of the uncertainty of weather conditions and the challenges of finding food in the ocean, one parent may be away from the nest for as long as a week. During that time, its mate goes without food in the burrow while keeping the egg warm. Eventually, however, the incubating bird loses so much weight that it must abandon the nest—even if its mate hasn't yet returned—to find food for itself. As a result, incubation is highly variable, and there may be days at a time when the egg is alone and cold. According to Mauck, the egg can withstand long periods of chilling and neglect and still hatch. "It's a whole system made for the uncertainty of life at sea. There's no predicting with certainty where the food is going to be. So the parents are looking for food, and if they don't find it they don't have enough energy to come back and incubate. But the eggs are made for it to happen that way."

When the chick hatches, it generally takes 65 days before it fledges, but that, too, is variable for the same reason—food availability and the energy needs of the foraging parents. With the exception of the first week or two, the parents seldom spend any time in the burrow with the chick. They simply fly in to deliver food, usually between midnight and 3 A.M., and leave to go find more.

Unlike the chicks of most land birds, which are fed regularly all day long and put on weight at an even and continuous rate, storm petrel chicks grow with fits and starts depending on when the parents arrive to feed it. Because the chick may be in its burrow alone for several days between feedings, its weight fluctuates up and down regularly. "I've had a fifteen-gram chick double its weight overnight, but then two days later it's lost five or six grams," Mauck said. "It all depends on when the parents come to give it food, and they don't come at any regular interval at all. They seem to be completely uncoordinated. Each parent is doing its own thing, and it doesn't matter whether the chick is even hungry or not. The parent just brings food, dumps it and leaves. That's what makes for this really erratic growth rate."

Eventually, the chicks reach a maximum weight, which may be twice that of their parents, and some intrinsic signal tells them to stop eating. At that point, they are too heavy to take their first flight, so they fast for a few days until they become light enough to fly. Then they leave the burrow, sometimes returning for a few days before be-ginning their southbound migration, and other times immediately disappearing and spending their next 4 or 5 years out of sight of land before breeding for the first time themselves.

Much of what is known about Leach's storm petrel nesting and chick development is based on the work of Chuck Huntington, the dean of Leach's storm petrel researchers, who spent 50 years mon-itoring the burrows on Kent Island. A retired biology professor at Bowdoin College, Huntington visited Kent for the first time in 1947 while still a graduate student at Yale. When he earned his Ph.D. in 1952, he took a job at Bowdoin teaching physiology—a subject he was barely familiar with himself—in part as a way of getting to spend time at Kent. A year later, he took over as director of the research sta-tion, a role he continued until 1988.

"I banded a few storm petrels my first summer there, and it was then that I realized that there were a lot of unanswered questions about them," Huntington said. "How long is their incubation period? How old are they when they first breed? Did they come back to the same burrow year after year? There were a lot of fundamental ques-tions, so I started out to answer some of those questions, and I was quickly captivated by the birds."

Beginning in 1955, Huntington numbered all the burrows in sev-eral sections of the island, and he collected data about the petrels that

nested in each one. He was the first to confirm that petrels usually returned to the same burrow year after year, and the first to conclude
that the chicks almost never return to the island where they were
hatched. "We've had returns of chicks only one-and-a-half percent of
the time," he said. "It's a mechanism for dispersal, I guess."

Among the most notable things he discovered was one pair of
storm petrels that returned to the island 33 years in a row—a record
that may be broken in 2009 if another long-term pair returns to
Kent—and a bird that had a German band on its leg indicating that it
had been previously captured on a research ship in the North Atlantic.
But his favorite memory is of taking "a lovely girl from Radcliffe that
I met at a biological meeting" to visit Kent Island and marrying her
the following December. When we spoke in 2008, Huntington reported that they had been married for 51 years.

The island hasn't changed much since Huntington first started
studying storm petrels there, but what is known about the birds has
increased dramatically thanks to his meticulous studies.

"It takes a special kind of person to do that for 50 years," Mauck
said. "It takes someone with a deep fascination with the natural world
to keep doing the same sort of study for that long. Chuck is remarkable in that way. Fifty years of data is incredibly useful for analysis, for
helping to figure out some bigger questions that we're just now beginning to ask . . . Age makes a big difference with a lot of different
things, so it's really important if you want to get a really good picture
of what's going on to have some idea of how old these individuals are.
The beauty of the Kent Island system is that Chuck had covered his
study area exhaustively for fifty years, so we have every bird in there
with a known breeding history."

My first full morning on Kent Island was spent with Lisa Harn, one
of Mauck's students at Kenyon College, who described her storm
petrel research project as an examination of the parent–offspring conflict. It's an issue that Mauck says makes storm petrels particularly interesting to study. "It's a question of the trade-offs between reproduction and survival among short-lived and long-lived animals," he
explained. "For short-lived savannah sparrows, for instance, it's a flip

of a coin whether they make it back next year to breed, so they put all the energy they can into raising their chicks. But for the Leach's storm petrel, which is going to be around for as long as thirty-five or forty years possibly, the trade-offs they face are an extreme solution." The conflict, added Harn, is "between using your energy to maintain your own well-being or using your energy to raise your chick. In long-lived species like storm petrels, any single year's chick is not nearly as important as the health of the adult bird so it can live to breed for many years into the future."

With guidance from Mauck, Harn was testing this conflict by increasing the energy demands on a group of storm petrels by trimming off a tiny bit at the tip of their wing feathers, slightly increasing the energy they must exert to fly. She wanted to know whether this added burden resulted in less time incubating their eggs and feeding their chicks and more time spent in self-maintenance. One way of assessing the rate of self-maintenance is through examining how long it takes for the birds to grow their feathers, something Mauck's mentor Tom Grubb dubbed ptilochronology—the study of feather growth as an index of nutritional health. It's all part of Mauck's effort to further understand the variability in the length of the incubation period.

So we walked through the Shire to check on the birds in a number of burrows. At burrow 704, the first stop of the day, Harn reached in and removed a cold and dirty egg, indicating that it hadn't been incubated recently. She noted that the lattice covering the burrow entrance had been knocked down for several days in a row, which suggested to her that the birds nesting there may be what the researchers call "loser birds," those that come to the burrow every day but don't stay long enough to incubate.

At burrow 826, the lattice was up. Checking her notes, Harn said that an adult bird was incubating the day before, so since it hadn't knocked down the lattice, it must have still been in the burrow. So we left it alone.

Harn reached into burrow 670 and quickly pulled out a storm petrel and carried it carefully to a tiny tent to process it. Using a thin metal ruler, she measured its wing length at 151 millimeters, then switched to calipers to measure its tarsus—a segment of its leg—at 24.3 millimeters. She then subjected the bird to what most people would consider a gross indignity: She weighed it by inserting it head-first into what scientists call a gravimetric restraining device but what was really a toilet paper tube and set it down vertically on a scale, its hidden head pointing down and its kicking feet and twitching tail sticking out the top. It weighed 45.1 grams. Harn then trimmed 1.5 centimeters from its wing tips, collected a small blood sample, and removed a tail feather for the ptilochronology project. I then followed her back to burrow 670, where she pointed the bird toward the burrow entrance and it quickly crawled back inside.

The weight of breeding Leach's storm petrels varies considerably from day to day, from about 43 grams to 60 grams. The heavy ones had probably just arrived at their burrow with full bellies after several days of feeding at sea and were likely just beginning a turn at incubating their egg. The lightweights, on the other hand, had probably been incubating for a while and hadn't eaten in days, so they were due to leave the burrow soon to find food.

The next two burrows we visited had their lattices up with incubating adult birds still inside. At burrow 502, Harn removed a petrel through the roof board, measured its wing at 160 centimeters, its tarsus at 22.5 centimeters, and its weight at 49.4 grams. As she called out the numbers to me to record in a notebook, I noticed a northern parula warbler in the trees overhead, its ascending song barely breaking through the constant din of calling gulls. When Harn completed processing the petrel, she pointed out that its foot was missing its claws and parts of its toes and webbing. That's not an uncommon injury, she said, and is probably the result of fish nibbling on its feet while it sits on the surface of the ocean.

Harn offered to let me remove the storm petrel from the next burrow on her list. She reached in first to verify that it was there and pulled out a warm egg so I didn't break it. I stuck my arm in through the roof board opening, and I immediately knew it was going to be a struggle. A root crossed the top of the burrow, and I almost couldn't get passed it, but I kept pushing. I felt nothing at first, so I forced my arm even deeper and, with my ear almost on the ground, I heard a little shuffling noise in the burrow. And then the petrel bit me! I knew it was going to happen, but I was concentrating so much on getting my arm inside that I was unprepared when it did. While it was quite a surprise and somewhat startling, in no way was it painful. I tried to grasp the bird's beak, but it felt like it had turned around after biting me because I think I felt its tail or wing. So I gave it a little nudge with my finger tips and eventually grabbed onto what I think was a leg. And then it bit me again. This time I was prepared, and I was able to briefly grasp its beak between two fingers, but when I tried to pull it toward me, I lost my grip. With Harn providing suggestions and encouragement behind me, and after another minute of poking the bird with my fingers, it finally bit me again and I held on to its beak firmly between my thumb and forefinger. By then, my arm was wedged into the hole pretty well, so it took some effort to extricate myself without harming the bird. Slightly raw from scraping the root, my arm was rather sore when it finally emerged, but the storm petrel was unharmed, though clearly agitated. After Harn processed it, I released it back to its burrow, but the petrel struggled to get in. I worried briefly that my effort to remove the bird had clogged the entrance, but in about ten seconds it squeezed its way in and disappeared.

I left Harn to continue her research, and I made it back to the dorm just as the sun forced its way through the fog for the one and only hour of my three-day visit. Butterflies seemed to take advantage of the warmth, flitting about and visiting the suddenly wide-open flowers scattered throughout the island. A short walk across the South Field turned up a bevy of painted ladies, a red admiral, common ringlets, cabbage whites, lots of American coppers, and one tiger swallowtail.

Bowdoin student Meredith Steck decided to take advantage of the sunshine, too. She was conducting a census of the island's beetles, and I invited myself along to help. An initial survey had been conducted in the 1970s, so Steck was attempting to replicate the survey to determine whether any new species had arrived or whether others had disappeared. We placed a sheet beneath a large spruce branch and struck the branch repeatedly with a stick, hoping to knock any beetles onto the sheet below. After sorting through the detritus and finding nothing but spiders and other non-beetle insects, we switched habitats and tried again amid the low vegetation at West Beach. There, Steck aggressively swept an insect net through a mass of beach pea and other shrubbery. After ten sweeps, she carefully opened the net, first allowing tiny moths and flies to escape, and then staring intently just inches from the net as she used a tiny paintbrush to sort through the remaining bugs. She quickly and excitedly announced every beetle she found, brushing each into a tiny collecting jar—click beetles, weevils, rove beetles, lightning bugs, lily beetles, and more. Most were so small that I couldn't imagine the challenge she had ahead of her, identifying them to species under a microscope.

Steck became interested in insects as a result of a college project, which led her to the beetle survey on Kent Island. She said the pinning process used in insect collections is a challenging art, which helps to appreciate the classification system and the evolution of insects. To pin insects appropriately, she said, it's necessary to understand their anatomy and movement so the pin doesn't damage the specimen. It's exacting work, which Steck believes is respectful to the insects because it forces you to pay close attention to each specimen. "Beetles are purposeful, beautiful, and elegant creatures," she said. When asked whether she ever felt that bugs were creepy, as many girls do, she looked at me with amazement that anyone could possibly consider insects in that way. She didn't know what to say, but her expression clearly indicated that her answer was no.

Far from being rare or endangered, the worldwide population of Leach's storm petrels numbers more than 8 million breeding pairs and an unknown number of non-breeders plying the oceans. But in New England, the numbers are relatively small. Brad Allen, a wildlife biologist for the Maine Department of Inland Fisheries and Wildlife and the state's group leader for bird conservation, said that thirty-five islands in the state are home to 10,366 breeding pairs of petrels, though 90 percent of them nest on just two islands—Great Duck Island and Little Duck Island, near Acadia National Park. Two-thirds of Maine's petrel nesting islands have fewer than fifty pairs of the birds, and only six have more than 200 pairs.

The good news, according to Allen, is that twenty-eight of the nesting islands are owned by state, federal, or private conservation agencies, and most of those that are in private hands have conscientious owners who are doing a good job of protecting the birds and the habitat. The petrels on those islands are also protected by regulatory provisions designed to ensure the health of seabird colonies in the state.

"When we imply to the private owners of the islands that the birds would be better protected if the islands were in state control, they often aren't too pleased with us," Allen said. "They tell us that the islands have been in their families for two hundred years and they think they've done a pretty good job of protecting them. Which they have."

John Anderson of the College of the Atlantic has spent the last 10 years monitoring the Leach's storm petrel population on Great Duck Island, which he said has about 5,000 breeding pairs of the birds. He believes, however, that with 6,000 islands in Maine, storm petrels probably nest on many more than the thirty-five islands the state confirmed.

Anderson is taking a close look at the habitat on Great Duck and other breeding islands to try to come up with a way of predicting where else the birds may be found and how many there may be. "How do you conserve something when you can't count it?" he asked. "How can you tell whether or not an island has petrels? Back in the nineteenth century, all these islands had people or livestock on them. Now we're in a new state where the Maine coast is an important tourist destination. We've had people camping on islands and found in the middle of the night that they were sleeping over a petrel burrow. We need to come up with a predictive model that says that one island is more likely to have petrels than another. We're trying to relate it to the macro-vegetation characteristics that you can get from an aerial photograph. Ideally we should be able to say that this island is worth censusing for petrels and this one is not."

He believes that part of the answer lies in the height of the vegetation on the island. Great Duck Island has relatively short vegetation, with a thin understory in its forests, which Anderson thinks makes it easier for the storm petrels to move around after dark. "We find a lot of birds using old farm roads on the island as transit routes," he said. "So if an island has vegetation that's too dense, it's probably not great to be a petrel there." He notes, for example, that Schoodic Island, which has vegetation very similar to Great Duck, has no petrels. The primary difference between the islands is that Schoodic has taller vegetation.

While the birds are in no danger of becoming extinct, Anderson and Allen are worried about the wide variety of threats facing Maine's breeding Leach's storm petrels. The fact that only a small handful of islands are home to the large majority of petrel nests in the state is cause for concern, he said. If the colonies on just one or two of these islands were to fail, it could result in a sudden and dramatic decline in petrel numbers statewide. A big oil spill at the wrong time and in the wrong place could also be devastating.

They are equally concerned—as is Bob Mauck—about the potential for predators finding their way to the islands. "We live in constant fear of someone letting loose cats or a pet ferret," Anderson said. "It wouldn't necessarily be noticed very quickly, but we could lose most of the birds on the island. It's the sort of thing that someone might do out of the kindness of their heart to give [an unwanted pet] a happy home on that pretty island across the way, but it could lead to enormous carnage on the petrels."

Mink and great black-backed gulls are occasionally a problem on some islands, and great horned owls are a potential threat, as well. A researcher in 1977 found the remains of fourteen Leach's storm petrels in the pellets regurgitated by owls on Franklin Island, Maine. And Mauck noted that ravens occasionally dig up a burrow and kill a petrel on Kent Island. But he worries most about rats. "If rats got loose here, the petrels would be in trouble. They don't have a great defense against predators."

Most troubling to Anderson and Mauck, however, are potential impacts to the storm petrel's food base. Might global warming affect the dynamics of the marine organisms upon which they feed, perhaps moving them too far from their breeding islands for them to access conveniently, or pushing the organisms too deep below the surface to reach? Will ocean acidification resulting from the buildup of carbon dioxide in the atmosphere dissolve the shells of the euphausiids they feed upon? What will happen as the temperature of the seawater changes? Are toxic substances affecting the food chain and building up in the petrels?

The answer to the last question is an unqualified yes. Wing Goodale, senior research biologist at the Maine-based Biodiversity Research Institute, has assessed twenty-three different bird species for a broad variety of contaminants, and the results are alarming. Leach's storm petrels were chosen for inclusion in the study because they feed where few other birds in the study are found. "If you collect a blood sample from a cormorant or a black guillemot, for example, the mercury in their blood represents what they've eaten in the last week or two, and those birds forage close to the coast," he said. "But a blood sample from a petrel that feeds beyond the continental shelf will have a mercury signal that is representing much more of a global influence rather than the local influence from coastal species."

In addition to mercury, the study evaluated the presence of flame retardants, banned pesticides, polychlorinated biphenyls (PCBs), industrial repellants, and other toxic compounds in bird eggs, and every compound they looked for was found in Leach's storm petrels and all of the other birds studied. "There are so many challenges that a young bird faces, from hatching and fledging to getting through their first year, yet these contaminants that they're born with and fed are making them a little less fit, a little less strong, maybe just enough to push them over the edge," said Goodale, who was particularly surprised at the contaminant levels found in the petrel eggs.

Of the twenty-three species studied, Leach's storm petrels were found to have the fourth highest level of mercury and fifth highest of the banned pesticide DDT. The bird was in the lower third for levels of flame retardants and industrial repellents, and overall it fell in the middle of the pack. The greatest concern is over the petrel's mercury levels, which were well above the threshold at which negative effects are produced. While "effects thresholds" are being debated among the scientific community and "sublethal effects" are particularly difficult to measure, it is clear that mercury can have devastating results, from behavioral changes and neurological disorders to chronic fatigue and, in a developing embryo, molecular changes and immune problems.

"When we began the study, I expected that our top predators like eagles and osprey would probably have these contaminants in high levels, but many species would be below detection limits," Goodale said. "But we found that none were below detection limits. If there was going to be a bird with low levels or no levels, I expected it would have been the petrel because it isn't affected by local inputs of pollutants. [With the petrel results], we can definitely say that we are seeing a global impact."

· · ·

After playing games, singing songs, and sitting around a campfire until nightfall at Kent Island, Lisa Harn led me and six students on a midnight petrel walk to listen for their unusual calls. Since the birds only come and go from their burrows under cover of darkness—probably to avoid gulls and other predatory birds—that's the only time to glimpse one in flight. As soon as we walked out the door of the dorm, storm petrels could be heard from behind the outhouse chattering and cackling like excited chickens. Using headlamps for illumination, we walked slowly for 10 minutes northward on Petrel Path, along the edge of the North Field and through various small woodlots toward the area where Chuck Huntington had conducted his 50 years of research. The whole way out, storm petrels were calling from every direction, some very close by in the brush, some sounding like they were in the trees, and others overhead. The birds have a bizarre call, what one student described perfectly as sounding like "mischievous gremlins mocking you."

Occasionally we stopped and flashed our lights into the sky above us, hoping to see a storm petrel fly by. Eventually a petrel fluttered through the light, looking more like a large, fast bat than a bird. With the fog still heavy in the air, the next one caught in a beam of light was a fleeting ghost-like blur, an apparition, until it followed the light and crash-landed in a shrub five feet from me. One of the students immediately dove to the ground to catch it, but the bird disappeared out of view by running beneath the vegetation. So we continued walking and, in time, had several brief glimpses of petrels overhead while their calls rang out in loud, continuous bursts.

At one point I asked everyone to turn off their lights so we could focus our entire attention on listening. When they did, I noted for the first time that gulls were still screaming far off in the distance, a foghorn sounded equidistant in the opposite direction, and the bell on the Cannon Ledge buoy clanged once and then went silent. And yet the storm petrels kept yapping away. In the darkness, Ross Mauck, Bob's teenage son and the youngest person on the island, quietly said, "If I didn't know what a storm petrel was, I'd be scared out of my wits." I smiled at his words, but agreed wholeheartedly with the sentiment. The petrels' call could easily be interpreted as ghoulish and wicked, especially if you're alone on the island for the first time.

We turned around and began to retrace our steps when the line of students ahead of me stopped short. A petrel had been found walking along the path, and one student casually bent down and picked it up. He passed it to Harn, who noted that it was unbanded, and she wished aloud that she had brought her banding kit. Harn then opened her hand and the bird fluttered away and landed in a pile on the ground. It then slowly waddled down the path without even attempting to fly or hide in the vegetation. We left it to be and continued walking back to the dorm. As we did, I tried again to focus on the birds. It was extremely difficult to tell exactly from what direction the calls were coming. While the rhythm of the notes was almost always the same, the tone and pitch seemed to vary somewhat from bird to bird, and Mauck told me later that there is a one-note difference between the songs of males and females. While it's clearly some sort of communication, no one really knows what they are saying.

Near the end of the walk, Harn pointed out the unusual purring call made by a few individuals. It didn't sound nearly as soft or sweet as the purr of a kitten; rather it was a bit more mechanical. She was hoping to hear a pair of storm petrels purring in duet, which Mauck said was a mating call most often heard when two adults are together in one burrow. Harn eventually heard a duet somewhere in the distance, with one bird picking up the purr when the other stopped, overlapping only slightly, but I'm not really sure I heard it. At the end of the walk, as I stood outside the dorm preparing to retire for the night, I counted seven storm petrels calling repeatedly nearby. Despite my having become accustomed to their calls during the previous hour, they all still sounded like mischievous gremlins to me.

The next morning I visited the Shire one last time with Harn, who shared her favorite storm petrel story about getting her arm caught in a burrow while all alone one morning and wondering whether anyone would notice if she didn't show up for dinner that night. While we chatted, she opened the roof board to burrow 818 and was surprised to find a storm petrel and egg clearly visible. As she reached to grab the bird, it cackled loudly and startled us. That close, it sounded more like the Woody Woodpecker cartoon call than the maniacal or frightening call I remembered from the previous night.

Later, we were met by Don Dearborn, a biology professor at Buck-

nell University, who has studied seabirds in Hawaii, Alaska, and elsewhere in the Pacific and was beginning his first Leach's storm petrel
study on Kent Island. He planned to test the coordination of parental
care to learn whether storm petrel chicks develop better if they are fed
at regular intervals. He planned to manipulate when food was delivered to chicks in different burrows to determine whether those on a
regular feeding schedule grow faster and more evenly than those fed
at irregular intervals. While I was there, he was doing preliminary
work checking burrows to see when eggs were being laid so he would
know when the chicks were going to hatch, triggering the beginning
of his experiment.

The results of the various storm petrel research projects on Kent Island, in combination with Chuck Huntington's long-term data set,
are providing an increasingly clear picture of the natural history of
what one biologist called "this utterly spectacular bird." They are
even uncovering clues to the complex question of what makes some
individual petrels better than others. In addition, researchers in Maine
and Newfoundland and elsewhere are examining equally revealing
questions.

At Bon Portage Island, Nova Scotia, where 50,000 pairs of Leach's
storm petrels nest, Acadia University biologist Dave Shutler is trying
to get a handle on why they have such robust immune systems. He
found no blood parasites in the birds he has studied, and very few ec-
toparasites in their plumage. "They seem to be investing a great deal
in their immune system, but they don't seem to need it," Shutler told
me. He is also conducting a genetic analysis to try to understand how
the petrels select a mate. Curiously, he believes that smell might play
a role. Scientists have already demonstrated that Leach's storm petrels
use their sense of smell to find food and even to navigate around the
oceans and to find their burrows, so perhaps it shouldn't be unexpected to suspect that it may also help them find a compatible mate.

But why bother doing all of this detailed research in the first place,
since it's not likely to be of much benefit to people? That's a question
that Bob Mauck thinks about often, and he insists that his students
think about it, too. Mauck took a tremendously roundabout route to
becoming a scientist. He studied classical civilizations in college, became a smoke jumper to fight fires in Alaska, wrote for the *Anchorage*

Daily News, coached professional football in Italy, and started a software company in Ohio before turning to biology in his late thirties. While in graduate school at Ohio State, he finally became excited about science.

"The way I had understood it, science was about answers," he explained. "But I learned there that science is really about questions, and that's what makes it so interesting and exciting. It's about saying, 'Hey, we don't know the answer to this, so let's find out. How do we design an experiment that will let us find out?' Those are tremendously creative and exhilarating pursuits."

Mauck is proud of the research being conducted under his leadership at Kent Island, and proud of how a couple of months on Kent has changed the lives of so many students. While he is somewhat of a father figure to the students working on the island, he is mostly their mentor, encouraging them to think in ways that they aren't used to, guiding their daily progress, and providing encouragement in their continuing growth as budding scientists.

And yet, he said, it's difficult to convince people that science for the sake of science is worthwhile. They still want to know how it relates to humans.

"The reason it's worthwhile to me," Mauck said, "is because we're trying to figure out how the world works. It may not help humans, but it will help us understand the order in the world. It's very important to me to try to understand how the world works. That's enchanting, fascinating, and profoundly satisfying . . . And you can certainly make the argument, especially in these days of man's influence on global climate, that the more we understand these things, the more we might be able to manage things in the future so that even with those changes we don't have quite as severe an effect. But that is not my primary objective."

That's a good enough answer for me.

Euthora cristata   Gary Saunders

6

Seaweeds

Security is tight at the Millstone Nuclear Power Station in Waterford, Connecticut, as it should be. The plant's two units are pressurized to 2,250 pounds per square inch and operate at 596 degrees using a combined total of 414,645 pounds of uranium fuel at any one time. A third unit, which ceased operation in 1998, is being decommissioned. Although the federal government was supposed to have built a permanent storage facility decades ago for spent fuel and other radioactive materials from all of the country's nuclear power plants, it hasn't, so all of the fuel used at Millstone since the first unit opened in 1970 is still there. The most recently used fuel rods are stored in a spent fuel pool, while older fuel is contained in waterproof steel canisters that are then stored in steel-reinforced concrete bunkers.

I used to work in the electric utility industry and have toured the inner workings of a number of nuclear plants, so I'm not concerned about the safety of their operation. My brother is a nuclear engineer and was a former safety officer at Millstone, and we've discussed the redundant safety features at the plant. The reactor at Unit 3, for instance, is surrounded by a 5⅜-inch steel wall that is further encompassed by a steel-lined, 4½-foot-thick concrete containment wall.

Despite being designed to withstand significant catastrophes, the plant is not totally invulnerable. A bomb or plane crash could inflict considerable damage and potentially cause radiation to leak from the facility, so other security features are in place as well. Multiple gates, fences, and checkpoints limit access, and only official vehicles are allowed to pass. My visit to the site in June 2007 was official, but it had nothing to do with electricity or nuclear power. I was there to learn about seaweed.

Staff at Millstone's environmental lab discovered an invasive species of seaweed, *Grateloupia turuturu*, in 2004, and I joined researchers from the University of Connecticut to learn how far it was expanding and how it was impacting the ecology of the Long Island Sound coastline. The long purplish seaweed with a wide flat blade was first discovered at Beavertail State Park at the southern tip of Conanicut Island, Rhode Island, in 1994, and since then it has colonized a number of other locations throughout Narragansett Bay and spread eastward to Cape Cod and west to the Millstone site and to Montauk Point on Long Island. As the seaweed is native to the shorelines of Japan, experts speculate that it arrived in New England in the ballast of a ship or hitched a ride on shellfish transported to the region.

"It's got a pretty long range in its native environment, and it has the capacity of a huge temperature tolerance—it's eurythermal," explained Charles Yarish, professor of ecology at UConn and one of the region's leading experts on algae. "It showed up in Europe in the English Channel in the early 1980s, then spread to Normandy and moved to Spain. [In 2006] it showed up in Portugal on the Iberian Peninsula. It's a prolific spore producer, so where there's space, it moves in."

That it took 10 years to travel the 40 miles from Beavertail to Millstone suggests that it doesn't travel fast, but once an organism becomes established in the marine environment, it is virtually impossible to eradicate. So Yarish and his students are keeping a close eye on it.

Our escort through Millstone security required us to change vehicles twice as we drove by enormous transmission towers carrying high-voltage power lines, past a tall red-and-white striped smokestack, and alongside several smaller buildings before getting a clear view of the two massive square structures that house the nuclear components of the plant. Two vocal families of osprey were perched on raised platforms near the reactors, seemingly oblivious to the complicated structures that served as their neighbors. After changing vehicles one more time at the environmental lab, we crossed the canal where warm water is released from the plant into Long Island Sound, past an old sign for the former employee recreation area that consisted of a solitary decaying volleyball net, and out to Millstone Point.

The view from the point was quite spectacular, with a dozen recreational fishing boats jostling for position near the outflow where they were aiming to catch striped bass lingering in the warm water. To the west is the heavily developed coastline of Niantic Bay and the Niantic River, while to the east, just past the outflow canal, is a less developed bay with a somewhat deserted sandy beach and a few exposed rocky islands where double-crested cormorants and Canada geese rested. The water was dead calm, and at low tide we could see Two Tree Island about a mile offshore, which, despite its name, is a treeless rocky mass that is submerged at high tide and which Yarish said is surrounded by wonderful kelp forests beneath the water's surface.

The research site at Millstone Point consists of two distinct habitats adjacent to each other—a steep cobble beach of football-size rocks that are challenging to walk on and that clearly get tossed around during major storms, and a flat rocky platform that is partially submerged at high tide. These two habitats allow for an interesting comparison of the seaweeds that easily attach to the rocky platform but that get scraped off of the constantly moving cobbles.

According to Yarish, *Grateloupia* established itself at Millstone Point because it is an area that meets with a great deal of natural turmoil. "Cobble beaches are notorious for having disturbance, and so it's an open surface. If the spores land at the right time and the right place, it grows. If it landed in the late spring or early summer, which it probably did, it's a quiet time in [Long Island] Sound, so it established itself. That first year it probably spread on to other cobbles. Then the disturbance of the winter made the cobbles move around and wiped out the plant. But *Grateloupia* has basal crusts that are a little more tolerant of the rocks rubbing around."

During the summer and fall, *Grateloupia* typically grows 1 to 2 feet in length—occasionally as long as 9 feet—in shallow water down to about 6 feet below the low tide line. In the late fall, however, it reduces down to a crust-like form to live out the winter months. When the water warms and days get longer, its blades grow again in what is sometimes called its upright phase. It reproduces by releasing thousands of spores into the environment, and those spores are at the mercy of the currents. Eventually the spores settle down and attach to a rock, produce a tiny disk the size of a pinhead, and from that disk grow its long blades. Even if the fragile blades are scraped off the rock, the disk remains and can produce additional blades.

The major concern about the appearance and expansion of *Grateloupia* in the area is its unknown effects on native species. It already appears to be outcompeting a native seaweed, *Chondrus crispus*, particularly in disturbed areas.

"But so what?" asked Yarish. "The big 'so what' is that there is an animal community that has developed over the last twenty to thirty thousand years that feeds and associates with *Chondrus*. We're not seeing some of our local snails grazing on the *Grateloupia*. They may not like it. So the food value is not there [for our snails]. It's also got different morphology so the habitat value may be different. It may take longer for our grazing organisms to adapt to this particular plant. *Grateloupia* is a plant with a long blade, whereas *Chondrus* is bushy, and that bushy structure has a lot of microhabitats within it for a lot of different organisms. *Grateloupia* is changing the habitat there. Seaweeds are a critical habitat species, so if you have these invaders come in, they start to change the ecosystem of the near-shore environment of the Sound."

To understand these impacts, Yarish and colleague Bob Whitlach have several teams of graduate students studying various aspects of the *Grateloupia* invasion, including spore dispersal, food-chain relationships, and colonization differences between the cobble beach and the rocky platform. On the day of my visit, the latter project found Becky Gladych and her team of three fellow students wearing a mix of wetsuits, chest waders, and hip boots as they scrambled around on hands and knees at the water's edge. They used a quarter-meter-square grid made of white PVC pipe—subdivided with intersecting strings into smaller sections—to assess the diversity and abundance of seaweed species. Well up the rocks from where the students were working, the uppermost layer of abundant seaweed was rockweed (*Fucus vesiculosus*), a thick brown mat that is likely familiar to anyone visiting rocky beaches and tide pools. Inches below the rockweed was a separate layer of fluorescent green sea lettuce (*Ulva linza*), which has a beautiful wavy blade when examined individually but in a large pile looks somewhat like a field of artificial turf.

Right where the water meets the rock and the calm sea lapped 2-inch-high waves across the seaweeds, was a mass of *Chondrus*—its densely forked flat branches looking browner than I expected—mixed with *Leathesia difformis*, which grows on other seaweeds and looks like a golden plastic sac, somewhat like a tiny frog egg mass but slightly firmer. *Leathesia* is only visible for 6 weeks—my visit coincided with the peak of its active season—before it withdraws and becomes a tiny crust hidden amid the rest of the seaweeds.

Kneeling half in and half out of the water and setting the grid down in a predetermined location, Gladych ran her hands through the seaweeds within the gridlines, identifying each species she saw while calculating in her head the percentage of each. She then called out a long list of Latin names, which an assistant carefully recorded: *Grateloupia* 5%, *Chondrus crispus* 20%, *Neosiphonia* 5%, *Ulva linza* 10%, *Fucus vesiculosus* 30%, *Codium fragile* (another invasive species) 10%, *Corallina officinalis* 5%, *Ectocarpus siliculosus* 5%, *Scytosiphon lomentaria* 5%, and *Leathesia difformis* 5%. Then she crawled out further into the water, found another permanent marker (a plastic golf ball nailed into the rocks) that signified the corner of the next quadrat, and began the process again. As she moved to deeper water, it became more challenging to identify the species, so she put on her dive mask and snorkel and placed her face in the water to get a better view.

Over at the cobble beach, Noreen Blaschik was in charge of the field work for the study of food-chain relationships. She watched as a wetsuit-clad student used an odd contraption akin to an underwater vacuum cleaner to suck up designated patches of *Grateloupia* and *Chondrus*. Every few minutes, the student surfaced with a tiny mesh bag made from a window screen that contained the samples he collected, tossed it to Blaschik, then put another bag on the suction device and sank back underwater. In one bag there were pieces of *Grateloupia*,

Neosiphonia, Ulva, Chondrus, and a wide variety of very tiny snails, crabs, and amphipods. It was my first look at *Grateloupia,* and out of the water it looked like a dark purplish-brown lump, though true to its reputation it certainly felt slimy, which, much to my surprise, is not true of all seaweeds. The grazers in the sample looked simply like tiny specks on Blaschik's hand. She pointed out several juvenile blue mussels, a nearly invisible crab, and a skeleton shrimp, which she said are found abundantly in most of the samples and appeared to me like the mosquito larvae I occasionally find in my bird bath.

As I stood on the cobbles at the water's edge admiring a beautiful mass of sea lettuce undulating with the waves and struggled to distinguish between murky patches of *Chondrus* and *Grateloupia* beneath the surface, Gladych arrived and waded out into the water to collect measurements of the light levels in the water. She used a sensor that looked like an old light bulb to measure what she called photosynthetically active radiation—the light spectrum that plants can "see" and use in photosynthesis. Gladych explained that the sensor uses a unit of measure called micro-einsteins, which she said is the same thing as micromole photons per meter per second, neither of which means anything to me. The part I did understand, however, was her description of how light levels diminish as water gets deeper, and how each species of seaweed requires a certain amount of light to thrive. So the measurements are an indication of which species can survive at Millstone Point. Clearly, *Grateloupia* loves it there.

Staring out at Long Island Sound as his students continued to collect data, Charlie Yarish talked in is thick Brooklyn accent about how a city kid developed a passion for seaweed. He said he was contemplating medical school when a professor at Brooklyn College—"a little bit of a lady, but very dynamic"—suggested he take a summer course in Nova Scotia taught by a who's who of marine botanists. When he got back, "this boy from Brooklyn who walked on the shores of Jamaica Bay just got so interested in the seaweeds that I went crazy and stayed at the shore learning as much as I could," he said. "I did a survey of the seaweeds of the New York metropolitan area and decided this is the career I want."

Since then he has studied the ecology and physiology of seaweeds on four continents and developed an expertise in seaweed cultivation that has led to widespread efforts to farm seaweed around the world. While many people complain about seaweed marring shorelines and beaches, what they don't know is that they rely on seaweed every day of their lives, and farming it has become a big business. The species used in the most commercial products is the same one that *Grateloupia* is displacing in Long Island Sound, *Chondrus crispus,* one of the few seaweeds with a common name (Irish moss).

A variety of extracts from seaweeds are used as thickening agents in a wide range of food products. The carageenan from *Chondrus* is responsible for making many products smooth and creamy, from ice cream and toothpaste to Jell-O, laxatives, yogurt, and cottage cheese. Even McDonald's used it in the 1990s in its "fat-free" hamburger McLean DeLuxe. Another seaweed extract, alginate, is used in such diverse products as syrup, dental impressions, and coatings for paper, film, medications, and fabric. A third extract, agar, is used in fruit pie fillings as well as in biotechnology labs as a medium in which to grow bacterial cultures. Some seaweeds are also eaten directly as a salad ingredient, vegetable, or as the wrappings for sushi.

To me, the most interesting use of *Chondrus*, however, is for blancmange, a gelatin dessert popular in the 1800s and early 1900s along the coast of northern New England and Western Europe. Most recipes suggest boiling fresh or dried *Chondrus* until it is gelatinous, then flavoring it with sugar, vanilla, honey, nutmeg, brandy, or fruit to taste. I'm not very adventurous when it comes to food, so I passed on the opportunity to try it, especially when I learned that it contains a high proportion of indigestible carbohydrates. Yet as late as the 1930s it was still included in the Fannie Farmer cookbooks.

Considering how many other kinds of plants provide food for human consumption, it shouldn't be surprising that some varieties of seaweed are edible. But while seaweeds are indeed plants, they are very different from the plants living on land. To get a better understanding of the natural history of seaweed, I visited Carol Thornber, a biology professor at the University of Rhode Island, for an introductory lesson. To start with, she said that seaweeds are officially called algae, which are then divided into the microalgae—single cells or small chains of cells that generally require a microscope to see—and macroalgae that are the large, familiar organisms found in both fresh and salt water. The earliest types of algae were cyanobacteria, which Thornber noted have been found on Earth for 3½ billion years and are still highly successful. Algae are further divided into green, red, and brown groupings. While all contain chlorophyll, which makes them green, the red and brown seaweeds also contain pigments that mask the green coloration from the chlorophyll.

Seaweeds typically have three main parts. The holdfast anchors the plant onto a rock, shell, or other hard object, but unlike the roots that secure plants in place on land, the holdfast does not absorb and transport nutrients. The stem that grows up from the holdfast of some species of brown seaweed is called a stipe, and some species also have a part that looks like a leaf but is instead called a blade or frond. "Fronds are not called leaves because they're structurally very dissimilar from leaves," Thornber said. "And sometimes the distinction between the stipe and the fronds is less clear, so those terms can be flexible." Some also have floats—little air sacs that allow them to remain upright in the water and get closer to the surface and closer to the sunlight.

The life cycle of seaweeds is very complex and variable. Thornber said that when she teaches her undergraduate students about seaweed life cycles, they often go away perplexed. I did, too. "Some algae have a life cycle that is vaguely similar to an animal life cycle: The thing you pick up and see is diploid and it produces gametes when it goes to reproduce that are haploid, essentially equivalent to sperm and eggs. Those will fuse, form a zygote that settles to the bottom, and create a new diploid individual. But that happens in only a small fraction of the species. Most have a much more complicated life cycle. If we start off from a diploid organism, instead of producing haploid gametes it will produce haploid spores, and those spores will then land and settle and grow into a haploid individual, and depending on the species, the diploid and haploid may look nothing alike. And then when those haploid individuals are ready to reproduce, they will produce gametes that are haploid, they will fuse, form a zygote that will settle, and then grow into a new diploid organism. It's called a biphasic life cycle—essentially two different stages in its life cycle. Some algae will have a third stage, too. So it can get very complex very quickly." Right. And that's the simple explanation.

Several hundred species of seaweed live along the eastern shoreline of the United States, and several thousand species are known worldwide. Since they all grow by photosynthesis, they only grow as deep in the water as sunlight can penetrate. In the murky waters of the Northeast they can be found down to 50 or 60 feet, while in the clear waters of the Tropics they can grow more than 10 times deeper. The greatest diversity, however, is usually found in the intertidal zone—the area that is submerged at high tide and exposed at low tide.

What may be most impressive about intertidal zone seaweeds like *Chondrus* and *Grateloupia* is that they can survive at all. Crashing waves impart tremendous forces on living organisms along the windswept shore, even in calm weather. But according to Emily Carrington, a University of Washington biologist who has studied the biomechanics of creatures living in the intertidal zone in southern New England and elsewhere, the forces that seaweeds and their associated animals must withstand during hurricane season are the equivalent of a person standing on the wing of an airplane going 600 miles per hour.

"Water is a thousand times more dense than air, so even standing up in water that's moving at one meter per second (2.2 miles per hour) is really hard," she said. "During hurricanes, flows of ten meters per second would not be uncommon. The record is thirty-five meters per second. What is most interesting for seaweeds is that summertime is when there is a lot of light so many species grow faster and get bigger. Then they are particularly at risk in September and October when we get big storms that bring big waves and high velocities [that can break or dislodge seaweed]. That's why the beach wrack is so large in the fall."

While mussels grow strong bissal threads to hold themselves in place and barnacles produce a strong, natural adhesive to do the same, Carrington said that the secret to the survival of *Chondrus* and other intertidal seaweeds is that they grow in tight aggregations to buffer themselves from the physical pounding they take from the waves. Nonetheless, many individual plants don't survive.

The life expectancy of seaweeds varies tremendously. Microscopic species may live for just a day or two, while some macroalgae can live for several years. One species, *Ascophyllum nodosum*—a type of rock-weed—grows a new float every year, so its age can be determined simply by counting the floats, sort of like counting the rings on a tree. Seaweed mortality occurs primarily from being dislodged by wave action, scouring by ice in northern regions, and herbivory by invertebrates and fish, especially in the Tropics.

"Some also die from wild fluctuations in temperature," Thornber explained. "Say you have some really hot temperatures that correspond with low tide in the middle of the day. When the water goes way out and there are some species down at that lower edge that aren't used to being out of the water, they might get bleached white and can die."

Some species of seaweed also face human-caused threats. Roadway runoff, sewage discharges, and other pollutants released into bays and waterways can have a negative effect on many species, though others may thrive in nutrient-rich environments, particularly the weedy varieties that grow quickly. Invasive species like *Grateloupia* can have a major impact, not only on other seaweeds but on the entire ecosystem. And increasing water temperatures from global warming can shift species northward out of areas they have long inhabited. That's exactly what is already happening to the waters of Long Island Sound.

The Sound is an urban estuary that contains 18 trillion gallons of water covering an area of 1,320 square miles to an average depth of 64 feet and drains a watershed totaling 16,820 square miles. Six hundred miles of coastline surrounds the Sound, and 20 million people live within 50 miles of it. Although the Sound's estimated value to the local economy tops $5.5 billion annually, it hasn't received the respect it deserves.

In addition to teaching at UConn, Charlie Yarish is also the science co-chair of the U.S. Environmental Protection Agency's Long Island Sound Study, a partnership of researchers, regulators, user groups, and others working to restore and protect the Sound by implementing a conservation and management plan that was released in 1994. Yarish calls the Sound "a very dynamic place, a system that's constantly changing. For a couple of hundred years, it was the dominant dump for all the people who lived around its watershed. For the last twenty-five, thirty years, with all the people living in the states of Connecticut and New York finally realizing that it's a jewel and a valuable resource, they've worked very hard . . . trying to manage the Sound, primarily nitrogen management, and that has had some impact. The history of the Sound is in the sediments, and if you get a good storm, [that history] moves up from the sediments and back into the water column."

The history of Long Island Sound can be traced back to the advance of the Wisconsinan glacier, which reached Connecticut 26,000 years ago, and stopped on what is now Long Island about 21,000 years ago, where it left piles of glacial debris. In the *Geologic History of Long Island Sound*, geologist Ralph Lewis of the Connecticut Geological and Natural History Survey wrote that "when the Wisconsinan glacier was at its maximum, sea level was about 91 meters (300 feet) lower than it is today, and the shoreline was 80 to 110 kilometers (50–70 miles) south of Long Island. By about 20,000 years ago, the glacier could no longer maintain itself at its terminal position because it was melting faster than new ice was being pushed south. As the ice front receded from its southernmost position, it stuttered and paused several times. At each of these pauses (recessional positions), it left a pile of glacial debris known as a recessional moraine . . . .

"Because this moraine stood high on the southern margin of the Long Island Sound basin, it made an ideal dam for meltwater from the glacier. As the ice continued to retreat northward, glacial Lake Connecticut formed north of the moraine dam . . . .The expanding glacial lake eventually grew to be about the same size as present-day Long Island Sound, and may have been connected with similar freshwater lakes in Block Island Sound and Buzzards Bay." Eventually the freshwater drained out of Lake Connecticut into the sea, and then rising sea levels filled it back in with seawater. The rate of the rising sea levels slowed about 4,000 years ago, which allowed coastal wetlands to form. Since then, the water levels have risen another 20 feet.

But that's not the history of the Sound that Yarish was talking about. The history found in the sediments that he referred to is the result of toxic chemicals like mercury and other contaminants dumped into the Sound by a wide range of industries for more than a century.

He was also talking about the leaks and overflows from some of the 105 sewage treatment plants that line the Sound and raise bacteria levels, making swimming and eating shellfish unhealthy and causing such low oxygen levels that fish and other organisms struggle to survive. And while conditions are slowly getting better, populations of some species still occasionally crash, like the major lobster die-off in 1999 triggered by high water temperatures and low oxygen levels that left the animals vulnerable to a parasite.

Today, increasing water temperatures from global warming—not pollutants—is the big concern. According to Yarish, summer water temperatures in the Sound have changed little in recent decades, but winter temperatures are up about 3 or 4 degrees Centigrade compared to the 1970s, which means the Sound no longer reaches the freezing point. Without that annual cold snap, warm-water-adapted species are invading northward, making the Sound more like Chesapeake Bay. And species adapted to cooler water are retreating northward. Yarish said that there are about twenty species of seaweed that are starting to show this migration north, and one of the first of these species to disappear from Long Island Sound is lacy red weed, better known to scientists as *Euthora cristata*.

I first heard about *Euthora* from Peg Van Patten, the communications director for the Connecticut Sea Grant program, which funded much of the invasive seaweed research at Millstone Point and which published a slim volume of the *Seaweeds of Long Island Sound* that Van Patten wrote in 2006. It's easy to get caught up in her enthusiasm for seaweeds, and after a short conversation about collecting and pressing seaweed, it's impossible to understand why everyone else in the world isn't as excited about it as she is. While *Euthora* is included in her book, the book notes that finding it is the "equivalent of finding a four-leaf clover." Yarish is even more dire when discussing the species, claiming that it has disappeared from the Sound entirely.

"*Euthora* is a cold temperate species," he explained. "It survived in the Sound because the Sound had cold temperate properties up until recently. Thermally elevated temperatures are going to affect the organisms that had their southern distribution in the Sound, and they're going to migrate north to colder waters." Since it's most often found in 30 to 40 feet of water, I asked him if it could still be somewhere in the middle of the Sound where scientists haven't checked yet. He wasn't optimistic. "The problem is that as you go into deeper water you have less light penetration, and you're not going to have seaweeds there because of turbidity in the water."

Bob Wilce isn't yet convinced that *Euthora* is gone from the Sound, but he is pretty certain that if it hasn't disappeared yet, it probably will soon. Wilce is the dean of seaweed experts in New England, having been one of the founding members of the Northeast Algal Society in 1960. At age 84, the professor emeritus at the University of Massachusetts was still making discoveries about seaweeds, especially species found in the Arctic, about which he is the world's leading expert.

On a rainy spring day, I visited Wilce in his office in Clark Hall on the Amherst campus, where new buildings were springing up in almost every direction. Clark Hall is the former home of the botany department, but the faculty relocated when a new building was constructed a while back, though Wilce soon returned to Clark with a few other mostly retired professors who now share the quiet, brick structure with an art studio. Wilce has commandeered the former chairman's office—two rooms with hardwood floors and 14-foot ceilings lined with stacks of files and old journals, a dusty microscope, and ancient-looking bottles of chemicals. The only thing that looked somewhat new in the office was his computer, where I found him typing away upon my arrival.

Wilce is a kindly gentleman who seemed genuinely pleased to share some of his half century of knowledge of seaweeds with a beginner. He said he was a graduate student studying the structure of wood when he followed his advisor's suggestion to take a summer course about seaweeds at the Marine Biological Laboratory in Woods Hole, Massachusetts. "Three other phycologists were there," he recalled, "and they posed questions that were unanswered about algae. They gave me an appreciation of diversity that was not known, and the beauty of the algae just blew my mind." After first studying under a professor whose specialty was tropical algae, Wilce turned his attention to the Arctic. "I subsequently have, over the last forty-five years, essentially worked further and further north and around the polar sea. From the nineteen-sixties on, diving under sea ice, to find out what the Arctic flora is and how it adapts to dark and cold. Those are the two big questions I have. How does benthic alga flora adapt to its environment." He claims that the most exciting discovery of his long career came when, at age 82, he discovered a new reproductive strategy exhibited by a brown alga.

Wilce described *Euthora* as "a fleshy, erect, highly branched, dissected red structure that looks plant-like, but it isn't. Bright red, it's got chlorophyll, but a red pigment masks the chlorophyll. It has a discoidal (disk-shaped) holdfast. The structure is delicate by comparison to [related species] on the West Coast, but still similar in morphology . . . It is a lovely alga, and it has an aesthetic quality." Seldom growing larger than two inches, Wilce said it likes shade so it is never found in shallow water where it could be exposed to full sunlight, preferring instead to attach itself to the base of kelp or other structures that may shield it from the penetrating sun. He said he remembers seeing it growing no more than a centimeter tall in Long Island Sound many years ago in about 35 feet of water.

"You might not find it there today," he said, "because of the temperature increase. It only takes a degree or two of temperature and it's gone. But as you go further north, at ten meters you still have cold water. Nothing compared to zero to five degrees [Centigrade] in the Arctic, but as you go north, say off the Labrador coast, it's very abundant. This, like many many other species, increases in population number as you go north from Long Island Sound to Labrador. But then as you go [further north] to Baffin Island, Devon Island, and Ellesmere, the population numbers drop, the algal size drops, and the species becomes less abundant. In Labrador, it reaches a peak of abundance and size."

To demonstrate the variability of *Euthora*, Wilce opened up one of several tall gray cabinets that line the walls in his office and are scattered about in the hallway. Those cabinets contain his life's work: shelf after shelf of 11- by 17-inch folders, each containing numerous pages of dried and pressed seaweed samples; most he collected himself decades ago, but some of the more recent samples came from his graduate students. The cabinets and shelves are divided by genus, and they are further divided by the location where the samples were collected. He said there is no other collection like it in the world, primarily because his is the only one with so many Arctic species represented. Flipping through some of the pages of *Euthora* samples—each page containing up to three dozen individual specimens haphazardly arranged—he points out specimens collected at Halibut Point off Cape Ann, Tinker Island off Marblehead, East Point, Nahant, and Manomet Point, Plymouth, all in Massachusetts. All looked quite beautiful and delicate. But then he turned to another folder of samples collected much further north where the water is colder, and the specimens looked more robust. He explained that *Euthora* is found in shallower water the further north it is found, where it has adapted to the turbulent conditions in such waters by growing smaller and with sturdier branches. Samples collected in the high Arctic in waters just 10 feet deep were only half an inch tall.

Next Wilce turned to pages of samples of closely related species found in the Pacific, all of which are considerably larger than their North Atlantic cousin. He said that the West Coast has 12 to 15 species in the genus *Euthora*, while the Atlantic has only one. The difference, he explained, is that the Atlantic is relatively young while the Pacific is old. Not enough time has elapsed in the Atlantic—compared to the Pacific—for the ancestors of *Euthora* to have evolved into more species. And that's not just true of *Euthora*. The Pacific is home to three times as many seaweed species as the Atlantic. Similarly, just 150 species of seaweed are found in the Arctic Ocean, compared to 350 in the waters of the much older Antarctic region.

Euthora cristata was first described by Carl Linnaeus, the Swedish naturalist who was the first to attempt to classify organisms into related groupings, which ultimately led to modern taxonomy. Born in 1707, Linnaeus is described by some as an egoist who once declared that "God creates, Linnaeus arranges." He also could be called spiteful for naming smelly and ugly plants after those who criticized his method. Yet his classification system has outlasted his critics, even though some of his classifications have not. Bob Wilce said that the beauty of *Euthora*—which Linnaeus would have found in abundance along the coasts of Sweden and Norway—probably caught the taxonomist's eye. Unfortunately, Linnaeus categorized the species incorrectly. One hundred years later, another Swede, C. A. Agardh, along with his son, tried to correct the error.

"Agardh and his son are the fathers of systematic phycology. They set the stage for understanding systematics, especially of the red algae," Wilce explained. "They came from a place called Lund, Sweden. The father was a mathematician and the head of the Swedish church at the time, a bishop at Lund, and he got interested in biology and phycology, and he promulgated this with his son. Between the two of them they set the stage for all red algal understanding of systematics." The Agardhs placed the species in the genus *Euthora*, where it remained until the German phycologist F. T. Kützing reclassified it as *Callophyllis cristata*, though molecular analysis by Gary Saunders at the University of New Brunswick in 2000 reclassified it back to *Euthora*.

When I left Bob Wilce's office, he suggested that I search for *Euthora cristata* in the waters north and east of Long Island Sound. I started at King's Beach, which is hardly a beach at all. Instead it is a small fishing access site along a rocky section of Ocean Drive in Newport, Rhode Island, surrounded by the monstrous summer homes of the rich and somewhat famous perched precariously near eroding cobble beaches and crashing waves. It's a popular area for scuba divers in Rhode Island, and many scuba students like me went on their first ocean dive there. It's an easy walk into the water, and several small rocky islets less than 200 yards off shore provide excellent subsurface habitat to explore. On the first warm day in late May 2007, the water was still just 54 degrees at the surface and 49 degrees at 25 feet below, yet several small groups of divers took the plunge anyway.

Soon after sinking beneath the surface of the water and breathing from an air tank in the ocean for my first time, I came upon a beautiful forest of golden seaweeds of a dozen varieties—some appearing fern-like, others like lettuce, and many others reminding me of ostrich plumes, goose down, coarse hair, and dense bushes. Never before had I seen so many shades of soft gold and amber, all swaying with the ever-changing pulse of the tidal current. It looked so delicate that I worried that if I accidentally touched it with my flippers it would break off and die. Yet I also felt the urge to run my gloved fingers through it, and found it both soft and strong.

Occasionally, amid the golden hues, was a single unnatural-looking fluorescent yellow species, somewhat like the color of the translucent marker I used to highlight my college textbooks. Its leaves were thicker than the predominant species in the area, and it moved less than the others. Dancing in and out among the vegetation were small fish I couldn't identify, perfectly camouflaged with streaks of gold and orange. They allowed close inspection, but remained just out of reach. Upon turning to explore another direction, I startled a 15-inch tautog from its resting place, its thick chocolate-smeared body and angry face looking somewhat out of place amid its well-dressed brethren. A sandy patch of the seafloor I approached was strewn with kelp—not the tall Pacific variety that stands vertically like redwood forests, but a similar Atlantic species that in this location lay twisted across the sand.

My group of five divers—three first-timers like me, our teacher, and a dive master in training who followed behind while dragging a rope attached to a dive flag at the surface—moved slowly around the tiny islands, whose giant walls of vegetation led to the surface. It was there, in perhaps 20 feet of water, that I noticed scattered patches of a small, dark red alga with multiple branches that I'm convinced was *Euthora*. We were far enough away from Long Island Sound that the species could have been expected, but it wouldn't be considered common like it still is further north. Unfortunately, my scuba class kept on moving, and my efforts to stop and take a closer look were met with curious hand signals from the dive master behind me urging me to keep up with the rest of the group. I made a mental note to return for a closer look, but I never made it back.

As we exited the water that day, I couldn't help but be puzzled by how *Euthora cristata*, which is seemingly quite common north of Cape Cod, could completely disappear from the southern part of its range in Long Island Sound. All it took was an increase in water temperature of just a few degrees in winter. While the species isn't in danger of extinction, it certainly makes me wonder how many more varieties of marine life—seaweeds, snails, fish, worms, and more—are going to disappear from the Sound as global warming raises water temperatures even further in the coming decades. And how many more invasive species like *Grateloupia* will be introduced to the marine environment and further disturb these delicate ecosystems? Bob Wilce said that there's little interest and even less funding available to study the north-ward retreat of *Euthora* and those species facing similar fates. What will their disappearance mean to the health of the ecosystem? Sadly, we will soon find out.

7

Leatherback Turtle

The quality about plastic that makes it so useful and popular is also what makes it so troublesome. It doesn't degrade, so it persists in the environment—primarily as trash—for decades and decades and probably longer. Since it is derived from oil, it should break down eventually into carbon dioxide and water from exposure to the sun. But if it finds its way into the ocean, as massive quantities do every year, it remains cool and is mostly protected from the sun's ultraviolet rays by algae and other marine organisms.

According to *Altered Oceans*, an award-winning series of stories in the *Los Angeles Times* in 2006, nearly 90 percent of floating marine litter is plastic, and about four-fifths of it comes from land, "swept by wind or washed by rain off highways and city streets, down streams and rivers, and out to sea. The rest comes from ships. Much of it consists of synthetic floats and other gear that is jettisoned illegally to avoid the cost of proper disposal in port. In addition, thousands of cargo containers fall overboard in stormy seas each year, spilling their contents."

The floating debris may travel for thousands of miles, sometimes getting caught up in any number of naturally occurring swirling vortexes that hold it for a while before it shoots off on an ocean current that takes it elsewhere. Some of it sinks, some of it washes ashore, but much of it remains on a seemingly never-ending tour of the world's oceans. The United Nations Environment Program estimates that in every square mile of ocean can be found 46,000 pieces of plastic litter. Not only is that figure appalling, it is also quite dangerous to marine life. Forty percent of albatross chicks die from ingesting plastics brought to their nests by their parents after foraging for food in the ocean, and more than twenty-five species of whales, dolphins, and seals found dead have had quantities of plastic debris lining their stomach cavities and intestines.

One animal that is particularly susceptible to ingesting plastics is the leatherback turtle (*Dermochelys coriacea*). The largest turtle in the world, it feeds almost exclusively on jellyfish, and it often mistakes floating transparent bags and other plastic for its favorite food, sometimes with deadly results. Once it takes a bite, the numerous spike-like papillae that line its esophagus, which are great for ensuring that jellyfish don't slip out, prohibit the turtle from ejecting the unwanted plastic.

Bob Prescott, director of the Massachusetts Audubon Society's Wellfleet Bay Wildlife Sanctuary and the Massachusetts state coordinator for the Sea Turtle Stranding and Salvage Network, who has conducted necropsies on dozens of leatherbacks in the last 20 years, said that the most significant change he has seen in the turtle carcasses he has studied is the increasing amount of plastic found in their system.

"Colleagues in New Jersey and Long Island were seeing plastic in leatherbacks regularly years ago, but not here in Massachusetts," he said. "But now it's in almost every turtle we see. We believe that's the primary cause of death now."

Despite the occasional outcry over the mass release of helium balloons into the air, many of which end up in the ocean and are thought to be mistaken by leatherbacks for jellyfish, Prescott has never found a balloon in a turtle stomach. Mostly he finds plastic sandwich bags and plastic grocery bags, but he also recalls finding labels from prescription bottles, packaging from cookies, and even a 4-foot-square piece of construction-grade plastic. "They're just slurping everything down and they're not able to digest it," he said. "We also almost always find a nodule of undigestable plastic material that builds up in a pouch near their large intestine. Twenty years ago we found that mass in less than half of them. Clearly they're picking up more and more debris in the marine environment."

The marine environment off coastal New England is an increasingly dangerous place for sea turtles to search for food, and not only because of the abundance of plastics in the water. Prescott notes that more and more leatherbacks are being struck by ships in the region, especially in Buzzard's Bay and Nantucket Sound, a factor that he said was never an issue in the early part of his career. And leatherbacks are also being found entangled in fishing gear at a greater rate than ever before, though numbers fluctuate dramatically from year to year.

"Usually when we necropsy a turtle, it's so decomposed that it's hard to say exactly what the cause of death was," Prescott said. "The turtles' tissues are so soupy by then that it's hard to quantify. Internally, there's always plastic, and externally you usually find scarring around the front flippers that is consistent with entanglement."

Despite these challenges, leatherback turtle populations in the Atlantic are doing surprisingly well. The population seems stable, or perhaps even trending upward, at about 25,000 nesting females, which is in large part due to the protections at their nesting beaches. For instance, on St. Croix in the Virgin Islands, where researchers have been monitoring leatherback nesting for 25 years, the number of nesting females increased from 30 to 186 and hatchling production rose from 2,000 per year to 49,000. Breeding numbers on beaches in the northern Caribbean and Florida are increasing dramatically, too, while they remain healthy and stable in the northern South American countries of Guyana and Suriname. For the first time in 70 years, a leatherback nest was discovered in Texas in 2008. In the eastern Atlantic, on the west coast of Africa, leatherback numbers in Gabon and Congo are estimated at 10,000, the second largest nesting population in the world.

That contrasts sharply with the Pacific population, which is critically endangered and has declined by more than 97 percent, from more than 90,000 to fewer than 3,000 during the last 20 years of the twentieth century. The genetically distinct nesting population in the

Indian Ocean—India, Sri Lanka, Australia, and elsewhere—is considered extinct, and those that nest in Malaysia, formerly considered a stronghold, are down to a handful. The only place in all of the Pacific where leatherbacks continue to nest in any substantial numbers is on the northwest tip of New Guinea, where perhaps 500 to 1,000 turtles nest annually. Considering that the worldwide population was once between 1 and 5 million, the leatherback situation in the Pacific is worse than dire.

In his wonderful book about leatherbacks, *Voyage of the Turtle: In Pursuit of the Earth's Last Dinosaur*, Carl Safina writes that "superlatives abound" about this remarkable creature:

"Leatherbacks are the fastest-growing and heaviest reptile in nature, the fastest-swimming turtle, the most widely distributed and highly migratory reptile, and the only one that can be called 'warm-blooded.' In this and other respects, they seem halfway to mammals. As a species, the leatherback ranges more widely than any animal except a few of the great whales. As individuals, probably no whales range farther. How could they? Leatherbacks cross entire ocean basins, and then crawl ashore to nest. No whale can do that. And leatherbacks dive deeper than whales. Certainly no land animal, including humans, can call so much of the world their native habitat and home. Leatherbacks range through tropical and temperate seas to the boundary realms of Arctic and Antarctic regions. That wide range, and their multiplicity of nesting sites, should make them extinction-proof. But they have their vulnerabilities."

It's easy to get excited about the tremendous feats of leatherback turtles, but there is also so much that isn't known about them, like how long they live, how and where they mate, where juveniles spend their growing up years, and how they find their transparent prey in the dark depths of the ocean. Skeletal remains suggest that they have been around for more than 100 million years, yet it seems almost certain that the Pacific Ocean population won't last another half century. With a shell length of up to 6 feet, a flipper "wing-span" of 9 feet, and weighing up to 1,500 pounds, they are about the size of the original Volkswagen beetle. As University of New Hampshire leatherback researcher Kara Dodge can attest, the first thing that comes to mind when you see one is how large they are.

"Until you've actually seen one you can't really appreciate their size," she said. "They are just absolutely huge animals. How something that eats jellyfish can grow to be so large is really cool. It's interesting that we have this enormous animal that's eating a really nutrient-poor diet. And they are very prehistoric looking, so it's like going back in time when you see one. They're just magnificent animals. There's nothing like them."

Unlike all other sea turtles and most terrestrial turtles, leatherbacks do not have a hard shell. Instead, their carapace is made up of hundreds of tiny interlocking puzzle pieces of bone embedded in oily connective tissue and covered by a thin black skin that has a somewhat leathery feel to it. This mosaic of bones makes the shell very flexible at high pressure, allowing the turtles to dive to extraordinary depths without it cracking. They have been recorded undertaking dives as deep as 4,200 feet, several hundred feet deeper than the deepest dive of the deepest diving cetacean, the sperm whale, and remaining under water for as long as an hour. To do so, they have evolved several physiological adaptations to ensure a healthy return to the surface—the largest heart of any turtle, lungs designed to collapse at about 300 feet to protect them from the bends, a mechanism to pre-dissolve oxygen reserves into their blood, and the highest density of red blood cells of any reptile.

Not only do they dive to great depths, but they appear to be constantly swimming somewhere. In fact, Carl Safina writes that they "cannot stop traveling. If captured and placed in an aquarium, a leatherback won't stop swimming. And eventually, against the wet glass, it'll abraid itself to death. They don't recognize barriers. They never realize there are limits. In the ocean, they just go and go." As a result, adult leatherbacks have never survived long in captivity, despite numerous efforts to rehabilitate injured or entangled turtles. The only place that hatchling leatherbacks have been successfully reared in captivity for more than a year is at the University of British Columbia, where doctoral student Todd Jones devised a deceptively simple solution. He custom-designed tiny turtle harnesses made of soft rubber hoses and attached them to the pool with fishing line. Placed in what he calls an "infinity pool," the turtles can swim continuously as if they are swimming freely in the ocean.

Wild leatherbacks repeatedly circle the oceans for years, though as far as anyone knows, they don't follow the same migratory path. After breeding on beaches on the coast of Florida or Mexico, on Caribbean islands or along northern South America, female leatherbacks have been tracked following the Gulf Stream north to New England, or straight through the center of the Atlantic to the Grand Banks off Newfoundland, or heading eastward to West Africa and then north to the waters off Portugal, Spain, and France, or on any number of other routes. More often than not they take a different track back southward again. Since males never come to nesting beaches, few have been tagged so even less is known about their migratory routes, though even that is more than is known about where hatchlings go between their first dip in the water and the day they are found on their breeding beaches 10 years later. Wherever they go, they almost certainly never stop swimming.

Leatherbacks found in New England waters in the summer and early fall probably take a wide variety of routes from as many different places. "We don't really know where they're coming from," said Kara Dodge, "since no one has really done many studies of leatherbacks here. What's been happening in New England over the last twenty-five or thirty years has been mostly noting sightings, entanglements, and dead stranded turtles. What we know about leatherbacks here comes from those turtles. In terms of a dedicated research effort to try to find out where they're coming from, that really hasn't happened yet.

"What we do know is that they have few thermal or geographic barriers in the Atlantic. They go as far north as Newfoundland and they forage off of eastern Canada and the northeast United States for the large portion of the summer and fall . . . Toward the mid to late fall they start a southerly migration, but that migration could be coastal or right through the middle of the ocean or over to the other side of the Atlantic. There are no migratory corridors."

While it is uncertain exactly where most of New England's leatherbacks come from, Dodge knows of two leatherbacks found stranded in Massachusetts and Rhode Island that had been tagged on nesting beaches in Trinidad and Costa Rica. Some almost certainly arrive from the central coast of Florida, where I was invited by Kelly Stewart of the Duke University Marine Lab in May 2008 to watch the hulking turtles come ashore to lay their eggs.

It was Memorial Day 2008 when my wife Renay and I met up with Stewart at 10 P.M. on Juno Beach, the middle of a 12-mile stretch of sandy beach between Lake Worth Inlet and Jupiter Inlet that she and colleague Chris Johnson monitor each night for nesting sea turtles. It was the peak of nesting season for leatherbacks on that beach, and the researchers typically report three or four leatherbacks each night, though there were ten the night before I arrived. It was also early in the nesting season for loggerhead turtles, which are much more abundant on Juno Beach and peak in late June at 300-plus nests each night. After brief introductions, Stewart said she had already seen a loggerhead in the midst of nesting as she walked the beach to meet us, so we followed her several hundred yards along the high-tide line. With the darkness, the sound of the waves crashing, and concerns about an approaching storm, it would have been easy to miss the turtle just 20 yards up the steep beach. Stewart pointed out the inconspicuous track where the turtle had crawled ashore, which we followed to a dark lump lying immobile in a depression in the sand.

Using a red light so as not to disturb the animal, Stewart directed the beam toward the turtle's back end, and within moments we watched as her muscles tensed, her rear flippers curled slightly, and a ping-pong-ball-sized egg dropped into a hole the turtle had excavated only minutes before. The two-foot deep, flask-shaped hole lay at the rear of a triangular "body pit" in which the turtle remained for more than 30 minutes. Loggerheads typically nest from two to five times over several months between March and November, depositing 100 eggs in the sand each time. The night before, 140 loggerheads appeared on the beach to nest, though sometimes they are just "false crawls," when they return to the sea without nesting because of disturbances, poor nesting conditions, or other reasons. In a typical year, as many as 6,000 loggerhead nests are dug on the stretch of beach monitored by the researchers, out of a total of about 60,000 nests in all of Florida.

As we watched her, I noted that the turtle's shell was covered in algae, and small shells, barnacles, and other marine organisms appeared to be growing on it. Her head was massive compared to the size of her body, and when I carefully reached in to gently touch her rear flipper, it was much softer than I imagined, despite its rough reptilian skin. Just then, she finished laying her eggs and began to cover the nest. Using her supple rear flippers, she quickly pushed sand over the eggs. Then her front flippers took over, working in unison to push sand behind her and shifting her position after every few strokes until she was six or eight feet from the nest and kicking sand in all directions. By then, the actual nest location was uncertain to me and blended in somewhat with the surroundings. And then she slowly returned to the water, leaving a tractor-like trail in the sand behind her.

Renay and I continued to walk the beach for several more hours, noting three more completed loggerhead nests and several trails that led back to the water suggesting they were false crawls. Stewart returned to the Marine Life Center to join Johnson and await a report from their scouts driving the beach on all-terrain vehicles in search of leatherbacks. At 1:30 A.M., just as we were about to give up and head back to our hotel, Stewart called to report a leatherback 2 miles up the beach. When we got there, it was obvious even from a distance that it wasn't a loggerhead. She was huge! Her head was thick and mottled gray, with a pinkish mark on the top of her prehistoric looking face; her front flippers were longer than her body, with muscular shoulders; and her carapace was long and tall, not rounded or domed like most turtles, with a dry leathery feel to it.

The turtle was nearly finished covering her nest by the time we arrived, but she was clearly still working hard. She seemed to hold her breath while her flippers pushed sand around, then paused to exhale heavily, like the release of a high pressure steam valve. Her front flippers worked in unison, often tossing sand 10 feet behind her, while her back flippers alternated, making it look like she was swiveling her hips. Renay said the process looked like she was making snow angels, which everyone agreed was the perfect description. She continued working through a short downpour, and then began to turn back toward the water. Stewart called out "time to walk," but the turtle seemed to change her mind, tossed a few more piles of sand in the direction of her nest, then decided it was time to go.

The plodding walk to the water was the first time I saw all four of her flippers working in unison. Each stroke moved her forward about a foot—the length of her head—and after every eight or ten strokes she paused, then changed her angle slightly, creating a distinctive zigzag pattern in the sand six feet wide. After a few more strokes, she zigzagged again, eventually reaching the water, where tiny wavelets crashed froth over her head. One more pause and one more stroke and she was enveloped in the waves.

We learned later that this turtle had first been tagged at Sebastian Inlet by researchers at the University of Central Florida on May 2, 2004, and she was next seen at Indian River Shores on the Fourth of July of the same year, when she was observed laying eggs on the beach with fireworks illuminating the night sky over her head. The University of Central Florida researchers don't name the leatherbacks that they tag, but Stewart and Johnson do, and they decided to name this one Renay. My wife was thrilled, and even more so when I promised not to describe the 1,200-pound turtle as her twin.

Eventually, Renay (the turtle) may end up feeding on jellyfish in New England waters. While at first glance it looks like leatherbacks are only equipped to gum their food to death—which some might guess, incorrectly, would be adequate for a jellyfish eater—their scissor-like jaws have a sharp edge ideal for tearing apart soft-bodied invertebrates.

Jellyfish are abundant in New England waters, though at some times of the year and in many places they may be hard to find, primarily because most species are quite small. The term "jellyfish" is a generic label for any of a wide variety of gelatinous zooplankton that are jelly-like and transparent and that live most of their lives among the plankton in the ocean. The best known group of jellyfish in coastal New England is the medusa jellies, which include the very common moon jellies and lion's mane jellies upon which leatherbacks engorge themselves, while the lesser known and usually smaller ctenophores and salps are similarly gelatinous but are only distantly related.

The bodies of adult medusa jellies are often described as bell-shaped, although they look more like mushroom caps to me. While the bell encloses its internal organs, there aren't very many organs to enclose—they lack a brain, respiratory system, or circulatory system. Rather than a central nervous system, they have a nerve net distributed throughout their bodies that is sensitive to touch and that can perceive light and odor. Their digestive system is incomplete—their mouth and their anus are the same orifice, which is used to both feed and expel waste. Hanging from the bell are a number of tentacles containing nematocysts (stinging cells) and venom, which they use to immobilize their prey and for defense. They feed upon tiny crustaceans or the larvae and eggs of other organisms, including larval clams and fish. According to jellyfish expert Barbara Sullivan-Watts, a biology professor at Providence College, the muscles of medusa jellyfish "go in a circular band around the bell so they can scrunch up their bodies to shoot water like jet propulsion, which provides force for them to move forward," she explained. "Then, as they relax, they relax slowly so they don't propel themselves backward again. This ensures that they are not completely at the mercy of the currents; they can swim both vertically and horizontally, and they can take advantage of the currents to stay in a particular location if they choose."

What is perhaps most surprising about medusa jellies—of which there are about ten common species found in New England waters and many, many more around the world's oceans—is that they are closely related to corals. "Corals have little tentacles and stinging cells just like medusas do," said Sullivan-Watts, "and medusa-type jellyfish have a life stage that is very much like a coral. They start out as a little polyp attached to a substrate, just like corals, and then at a certain signal—water temperature or day length—it starts budding into tiny medusas that come off the top of the polyp and spring into the water column, where they live out the rest of their life."

Other than being gelatinous, ctenophores have little in common with medusa jellyfish. Also called comb jellies, ctenophores skip the polyp stage entirely and spend their entire life in the water column. Rather than having a muscular propulsion system like the medusas, they have a complex system of cilia—tiny tail-like projections—that beat in unison to propel themselves. Sullivan-Watts calls ctenophores stealth predators. "They move through the water in a slow, even pace without making a disturbance in the water in front of them, so the prey don't notice that they're there," she said. "Then other cilia draw the prey into their gut region to be digested." Salps, on the other hand, are small, barrel-shaped jellies with muscles aligned like rings around the barrel, which they squeeze together to create a pumping action for propulsion. Distinctive from all other jellyfish, salps are strictly herbivores, feeding entirely on phytoplankton.

Unlike those of jellyfish-eating leatherback turtles, the jaws of all other sea turtles are somewhat beak-like and are made for crunching down hard on crustaceans, mollusks, corals, and other hard-bodied marine animals. Of the six other species of sea turtles plying the world's oceans, three of them are found in varying numbers in New England waters each year. The most abundant of these is the loggerhead, which is probably the most commonly seen sea turtle in the region because it lingers in bays and lagoons where it feeds on crabs and other crustaceans. Named for its massive head and powerful jaws, it can weigh up to 250 pounds and its shell can grow to 3 feet in length. The very similar green turtle is the least common sea turtle in New England and is the only herbivorous sea turtle in the world. Weighing up to 350 pounds, green turtles were probably more abundant in the region 100 years ago when eelgrass was more plentiful in coastal waters.

The world's smallest sea turtle, Kemp's Ridley, may also be the most critically endangered. With a shell length of 2 feet and a maximum weight of about 120 pounds, it specializes in eating crabs and, as a result, is often found entangled in crab traps in the Chesapeake Bay. Adult Kemp's Ridley turtles remain in the Gulf of Mexico and the Caribbean Sea year-round, but juveniles often wander northward every year, and sometimes they can be found in large numbers in Cape Cod Bay. These inexperienced turtles often don't know when it's time to return south, and they become "cold stunned" during the first spell of cold weather in the fall. Malia Schwartz, who launched a turtle disentanglement program in Rhode Island in 2006, said "it's like a block of cold water hits them. Since they are unable to regulate their body temperature, the cold water keeps them from maintaining their metabolism high enough to stay active, so they end up popping up like little ice cubes and stranding on the beach. Sometimes they can be rescued, rehabilitated, and released, but often they have secondary problems like pneumonia and respiratory issues that complicate their recovery."

According to Sara McNulty, sea turtle stranding coordinator for the National Oceanic and Atmospheric Administration's Northeast region, most turtles reported stranded have washed ashore dead or barely alive or are found floating in similar conditions. While all species of sea turtles found in New England are occasionally found stranded, the majority are loggerheads and Kemp's Ridleys, while most of the turtles found entangled in commercial fishing gear are leatherbacks. Data collected by the Sea Turtle Stranding and Salvage Network indicate that 861 sea turtles of four species were confirmed stranded in New England from 1998 to 2004, the overwhelming majority from Massachusetts (799) and Rhode Island (49). Factoring in the 12 turtles stranded in Connecticut and 1 in Maine, the network data shows that 109 leatherbacks, 119 loggerheads, 21 greens, and, remarkably, 596 Kemp's Ridley turtles were stranded in coastal New England during those years. An additional 16 turtles were not identified to species.

In the fall of 2006, eleven sea turtles were rescued by Massachusetts Audubon and rehabilitated at the New England Aquarium and the National Marine Life Center. The following August, I joined a crowd of 1,000 people to watch as they were released at Dowses Beach in Osterville, Massachusetts.

It was an overcast, breezy day, and the water at the beach looked gray and unappealing, even for gulls and terns, which should have been abundant but were uncharacteristically absent. The town-owned beach located on the south shore of Cape Cod is divided by several low, rocky breakwaters. Visible in the haze to the southeast was Great Island, a peninsula extending from West Yarmouth, but straight south was open ocean, with only a bit of Nantucket visible on the horizon. The only boat I noticed amid all that water was the ferry departing from Hyannis to Nantucket. The turtle release was scheduled for four-thirty, but I arrived at three o'clock to a mostly abandoned beach where a handful of sanderlings flew back and forth in front of a lone willet standing knee deep in the water. A black-bellied plover flew by once, twice, and a third time before disappearing for good.

Despite there having been no public announcement about the release, crowds started arriving about an hour before release time, when a crew of college-age students began to set up a barrier of yellow caution tape around where the release was planned. Crowds of beachgoers and local families of all ages slowly arrived to watch, and by four o'clock the clouds parted and the sun came out like it was timed perfectly for the event. Newspaper and television reporters and photographers trickled in as well, and interns from the New England Aquarium passed out press releases for the well-organized photo op.

The scheduled time for the release came and went, as did the sun, while members of the huge crowd constantly repositioned themselves around the barrier tape in hopes of getting a clear view. At five o'clock, most of the small children were crying and throwing things, seemingly uninterested in what was to come. So I strolled toward the parking lot just in time to see an ambulance from the New England Aquarium Marine Animal Rescue Team back into a reserved parking place, just two spaces away from a station wagon that arrived carrying a large plastic tub in back.

And then things started happening rapidly. From the station wagon emerged four identically attired workers who quickly grabbed the tub and struggled to carry it across a sand dune toward the waiting crowd. In the tub was Cumin, the name given to the largest of the turtles being released that day, a loggerhead. It had been announced earlier that Cumin was the most anxious and unruly of the rescued turtles, so he was going to be released first and without much fanfare. Cumin, covered in wet towels and still in the tub, was rushed through the barrier and was quickly surrounded by onlookers, completely blocking my view. As the onlookers let out a gasp of excitement, I saw through a sliver of the crowd that Cumin was hoisted out of the tub and held aloft briefly with his flippers flapping anxiously. Two staffers then set him on the sand, and in less than a minute he made a mad dash into the water. Everyone cheered as he disappeared into the surf, but I missed most of it and worried that I was going to miss the release of the rest of them as well.

I needn't have worried. While the crowd was still savoring the release of Cumin, I strolled over to the ambulance with a small handful of other observers just in time to see a team of interns pull out ten small colorful plastic crates, nine of which held Kemp's Ridley turtles and the last containing a green turtle, all lying on colorful bath towels. Each turtle was about the size of a turkey platter, and they were mostly docile as the crates were carried to the nearest edge of the barrier and set on the sand where few people had congregated. With no one nearby, I got on my knees in front of two crates and had a spectacular close-up view. This was the beginning of what officials called the turtle parade, during which the crates would be set in front of every section of the crowd for lengthy views and commentary by local experts.

The interns responsible for each turtle wore rubber gloves to lift the animals out of the crates, then held them aloft for the crowd to see, much like kindergarten show-and-tell. In the crates, the turtles were quiet and hardly moved, but when they were picked up they all went into speed mode and continuously flapped their flippers in an effort to escape from the hordes of people. I was on my knees just inches from the first crate—no one had a better view than I did—and while the turtle was held aloft I even bent down further to get a view of its underside, though the turtle almost immediately pooped, barely missing my face and instead covering the intern's jacket and pants. It was a beautiful Kemp's Ridley turtle, colored mostly in a creamy ivory beneath and fading to an indescribable mocha above, both on its skin and shell, with scattered peach flecks. The one closest to me kept flailing its flippers, and it briefly opened its mouth to reveal a fat black tongue inside its parrot-like jaw. Its shell was ridged in the middle and pointed near the rear, and it appeared to have a single toenail emerging from the curve of its front flipper.

After getting more than my fair share of viewing, I moved out of the way so others could view the turtles, and then the animals were moved along the barrier for the next group to see. After about 20 minutes, everyone had seen the turtles well, so the interns carried them to the middle of the roped off area and set them down in a row about 30 yards from the water, like they were being lined up for a race. As soon as the turtles were released, the crowd began cheering loudly, as if they were encouraging their favorite racehorse, but the race took a long time. Some turtles barely moved at first, perhaps frightened by the crowd, while others made steady progress only to hesitate for long periods before aggressively moving forward again. As each arrived at the water, it waited until the next wave crashed in front of it and pulled it into the surf, at which time it made one last aggressive push with its flippers and it was gone, not to be seen again. From the moment they were engulfed by the waves, their heads or shells never broke the surface of the water, with the exception of one satellite-tagged Kemp's Ridley whose antenna was visible for perhaps 10 seconds after it first went under water, even as two waves crashed over it, and then even it disappeared for good.

It had been a spectacular show, which the audience celebrated with great enthusiasm, and then the crowd of onlookers quickly dispersed to their cars, only to get caught in traffic exiting the beach parking lot. Just a small number of observers lingered with me, staring out to sea in hopes of getting one last glimpse. And then even we headed home. Despite the delay and the impatient children, it was a most satisfying event. I've dreamed about sea turtles since I was eight years old, wanting to see one in the wild and swim with one. While I still haven't encountered one under water, the release at Dowses Beach was a tremendous first step.

Most of the turtles released that day had been rescued after having been distressed from natural environmental conditions. But the challenges that are faced by leatherback turtles are anything but natural. The prime cause of the historic decline in their population numbers has been poaching, both killing the animals outright and digging up their eggs on nesting beaches for food. These activities still take place in some poor countries, especially in West Africa, where people need the resources to survive and where there are no economic incentives to end the practice, but it is less of a problem in most of the Caribbean where ecotourism efforts have made the turtles more valuable alive than dead. Development along their nesting beaches around the world is also a major continuing factor in their decline, and unintentional capture of leatherbacks in fishing nets has historically caused high levels of mortality. The latter may be a leading cause of why the Pacific Ocean population is on the brink of extinction; however, Kara Dodge isn't prepared to point solely to commercial fisheries as the culprit.

"Leatherbacks face an interconnected web of threats," she said. "A lot of people want a smoking gun so they can solve the problem, and people often latch on to things that they can regulate. So fisheries jumps right out because you can do something about it. That's why a lot of the focus has been on fisheries. They are a problem—[turtles] are getting tangled up in long lines and gillnets and in our local waters we have them getting tangled up in vertical lines in the pot gear. Is that the primary threat they're facing? I don't think we can say that."

Nonetheless, it was a serious factor along the coast of the southern United States as recently as a decade ago, and the issue may resurface in the not too distant future. The fishery that was responsible for most of the sea turtle by-catch, including leatherbacks, was the shrimpers south of Cape Hatteras, North Carolina, and in the Gulf of Mexico. In the early 1980s, a trapdoor contraption called a turtle-excluder device was developed for use with shrimp trawlers that was successful at allowing 97 percent of turtles to escape from the nets while losing only a tiny percentage of shrimp. But the fishermen hated it and undertook a 20-year campaign to defeat regulations requiring its use, mostly because the fishermen were unfamiliar with the technology and they didn't think it would work. But it does. Fishing gear researcher David Beutel called the shrimpers' campaign "a large ignorant backlash."

Beutel, a former commercial fisherman himself who still works closely with the industry through the Rhode Island Sea Grant Program, showed me a 6-foot model of a drag net used by bottom trawlers to illustrate how the turtle excluder device works. To his office doorknob he tied the narrow closed end of the net—called the cod end by northern fishermen and the tail bag in the south—and he held open the wide mouth of the net to demonstrate how it moves through the water. Weights or chains are attached to the lower edges of the net to hold it on the seafloor. The whole net looked to me somewhat like a horizontal funnel. Beutel said that the solid plastic grid of the turtle excluder is installed near the narrowest point of the net, which allows the weak swimming shrimp to pass through the grid and into the net while deflecting turtles upward (or sometimes downward, depending on the design of the net) and out a trap door before the turtle becomes stuck. Early versions of the device were too small to allow the massive leatherbacks to escape, but that problem was eventually remedied in 2002. The gear modification has finally become accepted by shrimpers throughout the South.

According to Beutel, most of the sea turtles that escape from the nets due to the excluder device are mollusk-eating bottom feeders like loggerheads and greens. Since leatherbacks spend most of their life in the upper 100 feet of water feeding on floating jellyfish, the fishing net is usually far below them and of little concern. In New England waters, where there are few shrimpers and where fishermen trawling for bottom fish aren't required to use turtle excluder devices, the greater concern for leatherbacks is what Beutel calls the "up-and-down lines"—the rope that extends from a buoy at the surface to lobster pots, whelk traps, gillnets, or boat moorings anchored on the bottom. It's in these ropes, usually within 10 feet of the surface, that leatherbacks in New England most often become entangled. They may be attracted to the ropes because of seaweed or other organisms clinging to the lines, and as they investigate it the rope gets wrapped around their flippers. Then the turtle panics and begins to struggle, further entangling itself and sometimes making it impossible to reach the surface to breathe.

The established protocol for fishermen, recreational boaters, or anyone else who sees an entangled turtle is to immediately report it to the National Marine Fisheries Service, to a local turtle disentanglement hotline, or to a rescue team like those at Mystic Aquarium in Connecticut or the Center for Coastal Studies in Provincetown, Massachusetts. The boat is then supposed to stand by the turtle until a disentanglement team arrives. More often than not, however, the Coast Guard or a state environmental agency is called, or in the case of fishermen, they try to disentangle the animal themselves.

Beutel and Sea Grant colleague Malia Schwartz are the first responders to entangled turtles in Rhode Island waters, and they bring with them a kit containing all the tools they will need. "When a turtle is entangled in an up-and-down line, it's like they're on a leash," explained Beutel. "The key is to take the tension off the turtle from the weight of the gear below. We use a device like a grappling hook to grab the rope beneath the turtle, tie on a new buoy to that rope, and then cut the line connected to the turtle. That separates the turtle from the gear and keeps the gear afloat. Then it's simply a matter of untangling the remaining ropes wrapped around the turtle, which is generally not difficult." One important key to the process is to complete the job without getting in the water. "These are big animals, and they're not happy, so you've got to be careful," he added. "If you get in the water with it, you could get hurt from getting a flipper slashed across you. You also might get entangled yourself."

The one bit of good news that comes from the entanglement of leatherbacks in New England waters is that it allows researchers access to the turtles to study them to learn more about their behavior, migratory patterns, physiology, and health. Kara Dodge's research is largely dependent on being on the scene when a leatherback is disentangled so she can attach a satellite tag to the turtle.

"My primary objective is to study the fine-scale behavior of leatherbacks up here in coastal waters in New England," she explained. "One of the things that intrigues me is that we seem to have so many leatherbacks that pass here within half mile of shore, which is pretty unusual . . . I'm interested in what they're doing here. Are they just passing through on their way to Canada, which is an established foraging ground for them, or are they spending the summer and fall here foraging in the shallow shelf waters? I want to also use as much other data that's being collected as possible to characterize their movements—remotely sensed data like sea surface temperature and chlorophyll A, and buoy data about wind speed and direction and fine-scale temperature information. I want to look at all of that information to characterize their preferences—what do they like in terms of habitat."

So she spends her summers hanging out on Cape Cod, making contact with fishermen and charter boat captains in every harbor, maintaining regular contact with regional disentanglement teams, and waiting for a phone call alerting her to an entangled leatherback. In 2006 it was a long wait. Just two turtles were reported all season long, both on the same day, which got her rethinking her entire project. But 2007 was a little busier, and 2008 was a banner year. Her aim was to deploy satellite tags containing global positioning system technology on as many turtles as possible.

"The GPS technology has never been used on leatherbacks before, because it has only been miniaturized enough for them in the last two years," Dodge said. "We're charting new territory. Even the tag companies are learning from us. The tags collect location data as well as depth, temperature, and dive duration. When the turtles surface to breathe, it transmits the data to a NOAA weather satellite that's orbiting and listening for our tag."

Part of the challenge is getting to the entangled turtle in time. Too often, by the time she drives to the nearest marina, hops in a boat, and arrives at the site, a boater has already disentangled and released the turtle or the turtle has swum out of sight. Her first successful tagging of a leatherback in 2007 occurred the day before the release of the rehabilitated turtles at Dowses Beach. Working as a team with her husband Mike, Scott Landry of the Provincetown Center for Coastal Studies, Connie Merigo of New England Aquarium, and Mark and Sean Leach of the *F/V Sea Holly*, they struggled to place a fabric harness around its front flippers to control the turtle, extended a homemade ramp out the stern of the boat, and hauled the leatherback up the ramp. When the turtle was on deck, Landry removed the ropes and Merigo, who is doing the first baseline health study of non-nesting leatherbacks, began collecting blood samples and nasal and cloacal swab cultures. While that was going on, Dodge was entirely focused on tagging.

"We do a surgical prep because we're actually drilling into the shell to do a direct attachment of the tag," she explained. "Their shell is really good at keeping things off of it, which is why most leatherbacks you see have a very clean shell—no barnacles growing on them. They have a natural sloughing agent in their oil, a natural antibiotic, so epoxying a tag to their shell is out of the question. It just sloughs right off. Most researchers in the past have used a backpack system. We're trying to get away from that because we think that design is rather cumbersome—it's really big and bulky, the two shoulder straps cut across the animal's flippers, and we've got so much pot gear in the water, we feel that putting a harness system on them would just provide additional points of entanglement all over it. So we're trying to get something really compact and directly attach it to the animal. We attach the tags by creating two small horizontal holes through the central ridge of the turtle's shell. We then thread tethers, cushioned by surgical tubing, through the holes to attach the tag to a silicone putty base on top of the ridge. We're nowhere near any vital organ, it's a really simple procedure, and it's in keeping with our goal of reduced hydrodynamic impact to the turtle."

When the tag is attached and the turtle is returned to the water, the data collected by the tag are transmitted via the Argos satellite system directly to Dodge's computer. One of the five entangled leatherbacks that she tagged in August and September 2007 was dubbed Scusset, named for the beach in Sandwich, Massachusetts, near where it was found entangled. Dodge and a turtle disentanglement team from the Provincetown Center for Coastal Studies and the New England Aquarium responded to a call about Scusset from fishermen on September 22. Once they arrived at the scene, the team found the turtle swimming freely but with a rope wrapped around its right front flipper and neck. So they grappled the line trailing behind the turtle, cut away the rope, and hauled it on board.

In an e-mail Dodge sent to me later, she wrote, "This turtle turned out to be a juvenile, with a shell length of 137.5 centimeters and an estimated weight of 200 kilograms. The turtle was bright, alert and responsive, rather feisty and deemed an excellent candidate for our satellite tagging study. We attached a GPS-linked satellite transmitter directly to the shell and collected data for complementary health, genetics and stable isotope studies. The turtle was then promptly released with much fanfare from all involved, especially the environmental policemen who had never seen a leatherback turtle before that day!"

During the ensuing 184 days, Dodge tracked the precise movements of the turtle as it traveled 7,612 kilometers from Cape Cod Bay to the Caribbean. It remained in the bay for a month after being tagged, then rounded Long Point at the tip of Cape Cod on October 19 and headed for the open ocean, where it swam along the edge of the continental shelf for several weeks, looping back occasionally, and then headed south into the warm and rapidly moving waters of the Gulf Stream. Swimming up to 60 kilometers per day, Scusset passed just east of Bermuda in late January and appeared to be heading directly for leatherback breeding and nesting grounds in the Caribbean, but veered west in late February to a point 430 kilometers north of Puerto Rico. The turtle then moved slowly west-northwest toward Florida, and on March 24, 2008, the last day of satellite transmissions before the tag's battery died, Scusset was 250 kilometers east of the continental shelf.

For Dodge, it was satisfying to know that this turtle had made it back to the region where it had probably been born and had a good chance of reproducing as it matured. Every time she tags a leatherback like Scusset, she recalls a family legend that was partly responsible for her career path.

"My dad actually entangled a leatherback in his lobster pots in the 1960s, so I grew up with the legend of the giant turtle," said Dodge, whose childhood in Scituate, Massachusetts, spawned her love for the ocean. "No one had seen these animals around here before, so he thought it was a tropical stray that was going to die if it didn't get out to the Gulf Stream. He disentangled it and brought it in and put it in the lobster pound for a week, and people came from all over the state to see it. Eventually, with help from a local Scituate family, this turtle was brought all the way out to the Gulf Stream and released. It grew into this huge family legend—the turtle got bigger every time the story got told. That always intrigued me. That was the first time I had heard about sea turtles in these waters. That's what was intriguing to me—we do have sea turtles up here during certain times of the year, but people just don't see them or don't know anything about them."

After earning a degree in biological anthropology from Harvard and spending a semester studying marine ecology in the Caribbean, Dodge went to Barbados to work on a hawksbill turtle project, then to St. Lucia to track reef fish, and then on to a job with the National Marine Fisheries Service studying herring acoustics, during which she went to sea for prolonged periods of time over the course of 2 years. She then got wooed into coordinating the sea turtle stranding and disentanglement network for 5 years before shifting gears and returning to graduate school. Hopefully, a Ph.D. lies at the end of her leatherback study. But she still has a long way to go.

So do the leatherbacks nesting on Juno Beach, Florida. Renay and I started our second night of walking the beach at 9:30, and just 5 minutes later, with a smidgen of light still evident in the sky, we watched as a loggerhead emerged from the water 40 yards ahead of us and slowly crawled up the very steep beach. The turtle chose a location in front of six towering condominiums where the grassy dunes were just a few steps from the high tide line. At 9:55, she began digging her nest. Shifting her body back and forth and kicking with her rear flippers, she enlarged the body pit and then dug a hole in which to deposit her eggs. Egg laying commenced at 10:10 and continued for 20 minutes, her front flippers dug firmly into the sand as if she were holding on to the rail of a hospital bed. As she was nearly finished, Renay and I glanced behind us to see another loggerhead briefly emerge from the surf and then quickly return to the water. The nest was well covered by 10:46, but the turtle used her front flippers for another 6 minutes to shift sand around in a seemingly haphazard fashion to camouflage the nest site. She then headed downhill quickly toward the water, but she stopped and turned around to face us—or her nest—pausing for a brief moment as if to say goodbye, then completed her full pirouette and was carried away by a big wave. The entire process took just 78 minutes.

We walked back toward the Marine Life Center, spotting three more loggerhead tracks along the way—two completed nests and one false crawl—and one loggerhead still in the process of laying her eggs. When we arrived, Stewart was preparing to send dozens of leatherback turtle skin samples to a lab while Johnson reported the totals for the night before: three leatherback nests, fifty-eight loggerhead nests, and thirty-three loggerhead false crawls.

The leatherback research project led by Stewart and Johnson is designed to answer questions about population dynamics—including total population numbers, survival and reproductive rates, and shifts in nesting locations—to update the federal recovery plan for the species. They began the project in 2001 and now record between 50 and 100 leatherbacks nesting each season. When they find a turtle, they wait until she has completed laying her eggs; then they measure the carapace, collect a skin sample for genetic analysis, check for injuries from boat strikes or fishing hooks, then attach a simple metal tag to the inside of the right flipper. Some turtles they see just once, while others are seen as many as nine times in a season. Between March 27 and my visit on May 25, the researchers tagged twenty-three new leatherbacks and noted fifty-two others that had been tagged in previous years.

Leatherbacks mate at sea—the males never return to land after hatching—and females lay 60 to 100 eggs in each of three to six nests per year. Eggs hatch about 55 days later, and the hatchlings emerge from the sand and make their way to the water. The primary threat to the turtles on their nesting beaches in Florida is increasing development and lighting that disorients the hatchlings.

"The area is definitely getting more urbanized," said Johnson. "It's incredible the number of people we see on the beach in the morning. They've built 30,000 new homes nearby, all within a short distance of the beach. And it's getting brighter on the beach compared to when we started, and that means that the hatchlings might go the wrong way after hatching. The longer they remain on the beach—even if they're just paralleling the shore and not going up into the dunes—the greater the chance that ghost crabs or fire ants will get them.

"The good news is that the people of Juno Beach feel a sense of ownership of their turtles. It's a protective culture here, as you can see by the turtles on signs all over the place. They've tried to take measures to reduce light on the beach to protect the turtles, though some people don't always respond appropriately."

At 1:05 A.M., a call came in reporting a leatherback just north of the one we'd seen the previous night. We arrived not knowing exactly where the turtle was located, and Johnson first led us to what he thought was a turtle but turned out to be a pile of seaweed. When we finally found and approached the turtle, it was immediately clear that this one was even larger than the first one. She was already covering her nest, and her massive front flippers were throwing sand in every direction, carving out large pits in the beach. I asked Stewart about what looked like large slimy tears dripping from her eyes, which I mistakenly guessed were to clear the sand from her eyes. "Turtles are always crying big gobs of salty goo," she replied, explaining that their large tear ducts rid their system of salt.

A quick look at her tag confirmed that this turtle was Julianne, who was tagged on Jupiter Beach on May 12, 2005, nested four times in 2006, and was just then completing her third nest of 2008. Measurements confirmed that she was still the same size as when she was first tagged—her carapace was 156 centimeters long and 106 centimeters wide—which made her about an average sized leatherback.

As we watched Julianne continue to cover her nest, I silently reached to touch her rear flipper, which was surprisingly soft and supple, feeling sort of like the fat on an undercooked steak. I also touched the turtle's head; it was hard and smooth, like touching an exposed skull. But just behind her head on the upper part of her neck, her flesh was as soft as her flipper. It was quite an unexpected contrast.

Just then, a group of twenty college students from Alabama arrived. They were taking a sea turtle course and spending a week in Florida on a field trip. Renay and I had seen them crowded around a nesting loggerhead earlier in the evening, and they had just returned to their hotel rooms when they received word about the leatherback. Every one of them was awestruck at their first glimpse of Julianne, with each exclaiming some variation on "Wow" and "Oh my God!" I was pleased with their obvious appreciation for the incredible animal, and we stepped aside to let them get a better view and enjoy the experience.

With a single-mindedness of purpose that allowed her to ignore our presence, Julianne continued to cover her nest for the next 40 minutes, but she kept shifting northward and eventually she had displaced sand in an area 12 feet wide and 30 feet long. The deep pits she had created with her front flippers earlier in the process had been filled in, so that when she was finished, the sand hardly looked disturbed at all. It was amazing that she worked so hard over such a large area simply to cover a nest the size of a 5-gallon bucket.

Like the night before, Stewart noticed a change in Julianne's demeanor, quietly called out "It's time to walk," and the turtle began to walk. With powerful thrusts of her flippers in unison, she moved toward the water, zigzagging less than Renay (the turtle) had the night before, then straightened out her path until the waves crashed over her and she disappeared for good. I stared out to sea as the students returned to their vehicles, wondering where Julianne was headed, when she would be back (9 days later, it turned out), and how many of her eggs would survive to hatch and return to nest on that beach. And I wondered how many years it would be before these nesting beaches are inhospitable to nesting sea turtles. But more than anything, I was pleased that these remarkable prehistoric creatures have been able to withstand the pressures of a growing human population, and, at least in the Atlantic, find a way to thrive.

8

Bay Scallop

The laboratory looked like it came right out of the pages of a comic book, or perhaps from a bad science fiction movie about human cloning. On shelf after shelf stood dozens of flasks of many sizes, each containing a beautiful but unnatural-colored liquid—fluorescent green, bright yellow, tangerine orange, and numerous variations in between. A glance inside a modern refrigerator in the corner turned up more flasks, these much smaller, filled with similarly colored fluids. In a greenhouse adjacent to the lab were twenty even larger glass containers, each about the size of an old-fashioned household hot water tank and bubbling loudly from hoses connected to nearby compressed air jets. Seated in the middle of it all were college students wearing traditional white lab coats, staring dutifully into high-tech microscopes, and occasionally taking notes about what they were seeing.

If it weren't for the unusual-colored liquids, the room might pass for a biotechnology research facility, though without the sterile environment required in the biotech industry. Most visitors would be hard pressed to guess that this was an aquaculture lab for raising bay scallops, because not a scallop was anywhere within sight. Instead, all of the activity was centered on growing algae to feed to the 200 scallops being raised to spawn in a nearby section of the lab.

The food budget for one scallop is 1 million cells of algae per day, according to Karin Tammi, the shellfish hatchery manager at Roger Williams University, so a majority of the activity in her aquaculture lab is culturing algae to feed the scallops. The students at the microscopes were counting how many cells of algae are in a small quantity of water so they know how much liquid to feed a given number of scallops. It looked like incredibly tedious work, but the students were happily going about the task, chatting and tapping their feet to the rhythm of the air pumps in the adjacent fish tanks, which held seahorses, clownfish, and other ornamental fish being raised for another research project.

It wasn't until I went around the corner to a section of the lab that looked like the industrial laundry I once worked in at Yellowstone National Park that I finally saw my first live bay scallops. They sat on the bottom of a cage placed in a large stainless-steel sink, in which water pumped from Narragansett Bay was continuously circulating. The scallops were surprisingly beautiful, colored in a stunning variety of patterned earth tones, from coffee and chocolate browns to the rainbow of pale orange variations found in the rocks of the Grand Canyon. Most held their shells slightly open, and small reddish-orange tentacles were visible around the entire rim of the upper and lower halves as they filtered the water of microscopic particles of food. Occasionally, a scallop quickly closed its shell tightly, which forced water from the shell and resulted in the scallop repositioning itself in the cage. I couldn't tell if it was an intentional effort by the scallop to relocate or simply the result of an unconscious movement, like when a dog's leg twitches during a dream.

My answer came when I reached into the tank to pick one up and several scallops repeatedly clapped their shells together, lifting themselves off the bottom of the cage and retreating to the opposite corner. Startled, I pulled back, but eventually I got my hands on a 2½-inch diameter adult scallop and lifted it out of the water. By then, its shell was clasped tightly closed, but placed gently on my open palm, it soon opened slightly. Again, I was somewhat startled, because peering out from between the open shell were dozens of tiny blue laser beams, like the piercing eyes of the Jawas from the first *Star Wars* movie, whose faces were concealed by their brown cowls but whose yellow eyes emitted a sickly glow. The blue dots were indeed eyes, of which each scallop can have a remarkable total of 42!

The scallop hatchery at Roger Williams University got its start in 2002 and has become a key research and production center for the small bay scallop industry in the region. It gathered its initial brood stock in Nantucket and Martha's Vineyard and has been culturing scallops ever since. The circulating water from Narragansett Bay in which the scallops sat was slowly being warmed up, by 1 degree per day, from the typically cold late winter temperatures when I visited to between 68 and 75 degrees. During this 6-week process, the scallops are fed a diet of three or four microalga or phytoplankton each day. When the water reaches the proper temperature, the scallops are ready to spawn, as is evidenced by a change in the color of their gonads, from a pale cream to soft peach to bright orange. Tammi has even developed a color chart to know when the scallops are ready to spawn. When a scallop that is on the verge of spawning is opened, it looks somewhat like a fried egg, with the orange gonad surrounded by pale tissue. As hermaphrodites, bay scallops produce both sperm and eggs, and when they are ready, they eject the sperm first, followed soon after by the eggs.

"It's broadcast spawning, so they sort of spit out a little bit at a time," Tammi said. "They'll do a little spit or puff, almost like someone smoking a cigarette. The eggs will be shot up into the water, and they'll sort of mix around in the water column with the sperm. Mother Nature mixes and mingles it with the tides."

In the hatchery, Tammi's staff collects the sperm and eggs in separate containers so they can control the fertilization process. "A five-gallon bucket of scallop eggs in water needs only an eyedropper of sperm," she noted. "Over-fertilization can result in deformities, so controlling the egg-to-sperm ratio is the most critical stage in the hatchery."

The newly fertilized eggs are then transferred to one of nine 1,000-liter tanks where the larval scallops spend their first 7 to 14 days. By then, still microscopic in size, they're ready to attach themselves to the side of the tank. If allowed to do so, Tammi said, they appear as "tiny specks like freckles on the tank." That's when they are gently collected from the tank and placed in a mesh downweller, which uses circulating water to encourage the young scallops to attach to a screen. "We can also use the Asian method, which instead of using the downweller system uses mesh placed in the tank, and the scallops will attach throughout this mesh three-dimensionally into the tiny openings," Tammi said. "Either way, when the scallops are big enough, they are then placed in a spat bag, which is no bigger than half a pillow case, and we tie it up and hang it off the dock. If the timing works out and all this happens around the end of March or the beginning of April, we can then have Mother Nature feed the scallops. Eventually we change spat bag sizes or give them more structure by placing them into a lantern net, which is part of the Asian farming technique." That's where they stay, hanging off the boat dock at the Roger Williams University campus in Bristol, Rhode Island, through July, when they are transferred to a spawning sanctuary in a local salt pond or estuary, where managed populations of scallops are concentrated to increase the likelihood that they will successfully spawn naturally the following year.

Bay scallops (*Aequipecten irradians*) are the rarest shellfish in coastal New England. Originally found in shallow waters from Massachusetts to Virginia, wild bay scallops are very difficult to find anywhere today. Their preferred habitat is sheltered bays and harbors with sandy or muddy bottoms where eelgrass grows in abundance, but a dramatic decline in eelgrass beds has threatened their survival. Easily recognizable by their fan-shaped shell consisting of up to twenty ribs radiating from a hinged base, bay scallops are one of the most rapidly growing shellfish on Earth. Their short life cycle and rapid growth allow them to become sexually mature in just 1 year, but they also have a very short life span, seldom living more than 3 years, unlike many clams and oysters that can live as long as 20 years if left alone.

The upper and lower shell of a bay scallop are identical, though the lower shell is usually paler in color, and they are held together by a single adductor muscle, the only part of a scallop that is edible. Unlike most shellfish, which have either a foot that they use to dig into the sediment or a mechanism that permanently attaches them to a rock or other structure, adult scallops simply sit on the bottom to feed. That's not to say that they are unable to attach themselves to something if they so choose. Most wild larval scallops initially settle out of the water column and land on the upper reaches of eelgrass blades, where they attach themselves using a sticky, hair-like byssal thread to keep them away from bottom-living predators like crabs or snails. As adults they sometimes use that same byssal thread to attach to a rock or other solid structure, especially in rocky habitat or turbulent conditions, but this attachment is always temporary and much weaker than those used by mussels. Scallops can also break the attachment instantly if they need to move quickly.

As the young grow, they drop off the eelgrass and settle on the bottom to feed. "They orient themselves in the water with their shell slightly open and their tentacles out so the current will pass the water through the mantle cavity," explained Tammi. "Once the water passes through the mantle, it will hit a series of feather-like gills, somewhat like the gills on a fish, but more intricate and delicate. The gills capture microscopic particles, which will move along the edge of the gill and into a groove like an assembly line and then flow into the mouth of the animal. The gills act as a way to trap the food and move it along to the mouth. The tentacles help with that as well by grabbing food particles and moving them into the gills.

"Their mouth is pretty small, though, smaller than 60 or 80 microns for an adult, and it will trap anything that's in the water. So they select particles, and anything they don't prefer they will just spit out. I call it flocculent vomit. When you start to see that they don't like the food source, you can actually see this flocculent pseudo-feces. So they clearly have the ability to sort particles."

Even as adults, bay scallops are vulnerable to predation by crabs and sea stars, many of which can easily break open their shells. Seals have also been known to eat bay scallops, as do gulls, diving ducks like scoters and eiders, and even tautog and other fish. Winter storms are also a threat as they may cast an entire scallop bed up onto the sand. These dangers are why scallops have learned to swim by clapping their shells together and relocating themselves via jet propulsion. It's also why they have evolved so many eyes. While their eyes cannot see images, they are sensitive to light and can help detect approaching predators.

As the water cools in the fall and temperatures sink below 50 degrees, bay scallops enter a state of hibernation when they continue filter feeding but seldom move. Instead of growing during this period, their energy is used to thicken their shell, which leaves a raised ring that allows scallops to be aged—the number of growth rings indicates the number of winters through which it has lived. Following reproduction in the spring, they undertake a major growth spurt.

Because eelgrass is such an important part of the survival of bay scallops, I joined Sue Tuxbury, the eelgrass restoration coordinator for Save the Bay, an environmental group in Rhode Island, as she and a team of volunteers collected eelgrass from a healthy bed off Jamestown and prepared to transplant it elsewhere in Narragansett Bay. The project is a key component of a bay scallop restoration program the organization launched in 2007. In an open water test, Save the Bay placed adult scallops in cages in the lower bay and hung spat bags in the water column nearby so larvae from spawning adults would settle onto the bags. The method proved successful in protected salt ponds, so the next step was to test it in an unprotected location where the scallop larvae would move at the whim of wind and currents. Yet even if it is successful, scallop restoration in the bay will, in large part, be dependent upon the success of eelgrass restoration.

Eelgrass is a vascular plant, more closely related to terrestrial plants than to seaweeds, and because it needs considerable light to grow, it is only found in high-quality shallow waters where turbidity is low. Growing up to three feet tall, each stem can reproduce either by sending up lateral shoots from the side of the root or by flowering and dropping seeds that later germinate. Scientists at the University of Rhode Island have developed an eelgrass seeding machine to aid in the spreading of seed, but the germination rate of seeding is very low compared to transplanting individual shoots, primarily because crabs eat the tiny sprouts.

The habitat created by eelgrass beds not only supports bay scallops but also serves as a nursery area for many important marine species, especially winter flounder, tautog, and lobsters. It provides shelter for these animals while also attracting the invertebrates like snails, crabs and worms upon which they feed. A Save the Bay study of newly restored eelgrass beds found a significant increase in the abundance and diversity of invertebrates at transplant sites. According to Tuxbury, the plant also serves as a buffer protecting the shoreline from the effects of storms and reducing beach erosion.

While brant and Canada geese eat eelgrass, they weren't the cause of its decline. Instead, a natural fungus known as eelgrass blight killed most of the eelgrass beds on the East Coast in the 1930s. In southern New England, the hurricane of 1938 also caused considerable damage. Because of their dependence on eelgrass, bay scallops nearly went extinct as a result of the eradication of the eelgrass beds, and it wasn't until the eelgrass began to bounce back 30 years later that the scallops began to show signs of recovery. Soon after, however, the increase in coastal development throughout the region led to sewage discharges and runoff into coastal waters that increased nutrients in bays and harbors, which resulted in extensive algae blooms that cut off light to the plants, and oxygen depletion that hindered their growth. As coastal waters have become somewhat cleaner in recent decades, eelgrass is again showing signs of recovery.

But not without help. Save the Bay started a series of test plots at several locations in Narragansett Bay in 2001 in an effort to identify the most favorable sites for transplanting eelgrass. In 2002 the group selected three sites for large-scale transplantation—Fogland Point off Tiverton, the west side of Prudence Island, and Poplar Point off North Kingstown. "Year to year and site to site survival is very variable," said Duxbury. "In 2002 we had a really good year with lots of growth and high survival rates, but in 2003 we had lots of rain and runoff, so survival was low. Two thousand four was good, though Fogland was declining after doing really well the first two years, so we switched to Coggeshall Point off Portsmouth, where survival rates have been seventy to one hundred percent a year, which is really good."

Historically, eelgrass was found throughout Narragansett Bay, including all the way up to the Providence River, where it hasn't been seen in decades due to water quality issues. Maps from 1996 suggest that just 100 acres of eelgrass was left in the Bay, though a more thorough analysis in 2007 found that the total area was closer to 300 acres.

Today, it is found most prominently at the southern end of the east passage of the bay, where the water is deeper, it is less turbid, and the constant flushing of seawater from the open ocean results in fewer pollutants.

My visit to one of the last few healthy natural eelgrass beds in Narragansett Bay occurred on a hot day in late August at a cove next to a full RV park with the Jamestown bridge visible to the north, Dutch Island within swimming distance to the northwest, its lighthouse bell occasionally clanging, and the University of Rhode Island's Bay Campus due west, where its research ship *Endeavor* had recently docked. But there was little time to pay attention to the beautiful view. Two scuba divers were 75 yards offshore in 10 feet of water, their dive flags clearly visible, and a kayaker stood at the ready to transport eelgrass from the divers to a team of sorters on the beach. The divers used a garden trowel to dig up small clumps of eelgrass and place it in large mesh bags, which they handed to the kayaker, who in turn gave them an empty bag so they could continue their work. When the kayaker reached shore with bags of eelgrass, it was placed in a plastic laundry basket in ankle-deep water so the tiny waves would wash some of the mud away. Then the sorters—senior citizens, college kids, and a teenager doing a community service project for school—counted each stalk of eelgrass, straightening and aligning each shoot, and binding them in bundles of fifty. When they were transplanted to Coggeshall Point the next day, each bundle was placed in a one-quarter-meter quadrat, delineated by PVC piping. With every quadrat receiving fifty plants, it will be easy for the Save the Bay researchers to determine the success of the transplantation from year to year.

Maria Martinez, a blonde Save the Bay research assistant and one of the divers that day, said the bright sunshine made it a great day for the project, since the sunlight penetrated the water and made for excellent visibility. She was pleased to have seen an adult bay scallop—her first in the wild—and noted that starfish, green crabs, and rock crabs seemed to be everywhere. Her strategy under water was to search for a sandy spot amid the eelgrass where it was easiest to dig, and to carefully unearth each plant. "You can't stay in one place long because, even if you find a nice place to harvest, you stir up the bottom so much that you can't see much for long," she said. "And you also have to be careful because crabs tend to think the catch bag is a great place to explore, and they crawl right in."

Her enthusiasm encouraged me to take a look at the eelgrass myself, so I grabbed my mask and snorkel and walked into the cool water. I was just thigh deep when I reached the edge of the eelgrass bed, so I bent over and put my face in the water. Most of the plants were covered in a brownish mossy mess that looked like it could be accumulations of silt and sediment, but I learned later that they were epiphytes (algae) growing on the leaves. As I started swimming on the surface and reached deeper water, the epiphytes virtually disappeared and the plants were a lush green, making it seem like I was swimming over a beautiful garden. The bottom had a soft sandy or muddy feel to it, and starfish and broken shells were abundant. While there were occasional patches of open ground, most of the eelgrass appeared to be as thick and healthy as a cattail marsh.

Swimming above the slowly undulating eelgrass were several small schools of silversides, 2-inch-long minnows with a silver stripe down their side and a body that looked nearly transparent. Occasionally I saw a red bearded sponge that looked like a fat bloody finger sitting on the bottom or growing from an eelgrass blade. Where the leaves were greenest and shafts of sunlight turned the clear water a beautiful yellowish hue, I repeatedly noticed that many eelgrass leaves had a small red or gray or zebra-patterned patch on them, the early growth of sponges and other tunicates. While they apparently aren't harmful to the plant, I noted that few of those shoots of eelgrass were being collected for transplantation.

While wild bay scallops have been effectively extirpated from Rhode Island waters, there are several nearby locations where they can still be found, though in most of those places the scallops are managed intensively. Nantucket may be the last place where bay scallops grow naturally in the wild without human intervention. In fact, they are doing so well there that a commercial harvest of wild scallops is thriving.

"This year [2007] the scallopers are going nuts," said Bob Kennedy, director of natural sciences for the Maria Mitchell Association on

Nantucket. "There are a lot of scallops out there and the scallopers are getting their limit of five bushels a day in just a couple of hours."

The commercial scallop harvesting season on Nantucket runs from November 1 to the end of March, and the family scallop season—whereby one bushel of scallops per week can be harvested for personal consumption—begins a month earlier. Kennedy said that Nantucket has close to 150 licensed commercial scallopers who use a dredge dragged behind their boat that glides over the surface of the seabed to harvest the scallops. Most of the scallops are found in Nantucket Harbor, Madaket Harbor, and around Tuckernuck Island, just west of Nantucket.

Why are bay scallops doing so well in Nantucket? "The most obvious reason is that Nantucket is thirty miles out in the ocean, so our water source is excellent," explained Kennedy. "We have a large population on the island, but it's not like elsewhere where you're getting a lot of runoff from streets and roads contaminating the harbors. We do have a lot of boat traffic in the summer time, and that's the biggest worry, that they're putting things into the water like gasoline and detergents and human wastes."

After decades of healthy scallop populations around Nantucket, the harvest was way down in 2005 and 2006, causing some fishermen and biologists to worry that the scallops were on their way out. So for the first time in recent memory, the wild population was seeded with 1 million farm-raised scallops that were raised off-island but were from native Nantucket scallop stock.

"We don't know why we had those bad years," Kennedy noted. "It could be anything from pollution affecting the larvae to increased predators. The harbor hasn't frozen in the last two years, and we feel there might be some relationship between the scallop population and the harbors being frozen over and being protected. A lot of the predators like green crabs die back when the harbors freeze and the water temperature is too cold. But we don't know for sure." There is also speculation that the scallop population around Nantucket cannot support 100 commercial scallop boats and that overfishing may have had a role in the recent down years, though Kennedy doesn't think that's a concern. Nonetheless, he conducts regular research and monitoring of the population to learn more about them and to try and head off future problems.

One thing he has found is that Nantucket scallops don't spawn consistently even under normal circumstances. "In a classic sense, scallops spawn in water that's about sixty-eight degrees, which means June or early July here, but a couple of times we've had peaks of spawning in August and even into September. This year we put out our spat bags about the fifteenth of August and we had an average of 2,500 scallops in one spot in the harbor. That's a lot, especially when the average for the last few years has been fifty. And that's also very late, and we don't know why."

Despite these inconsistencies and uncertainties, Kennedy is "guardedly optimistic" about the future of wild bay scallops in Nantucket. "We certainly hope that we can hang on to this population because it's part of the Nantucket culture," he said. "We just implemented a new harbor management plan; there is a lot of interest in making sure the harbor is clean and eelgrass beds are protected; we've maxed out on the number of mooring sites in the harbor; and we're trying to address the street run-off and other sources of pollution into the harbors. So if we can manage these things and get it all under control, we will reduce human impact on the harbors and we'll have a scallop population for a long time."

Next to Nantucket, Martha's Vineyard may have the healthiest population of bay scallops in New England, primarily in Lagoon Pond on the north central part of the island, just south of Vineyard Haven harbor and the ferry terminal. It's there that U.S. Environmental Protection Agency biologist Marty Chintala has been monitoring the scallop population on a regular basis as part of a research program to assess habitat and link it to reproductive success. She isn't convinced that eelgrass is a necessary ingredient for a healthy scallop population, so she is starting from scratch to find out how variable the habitat can be and still harbor scallops.

"In Lagoon Pond they have a good population of scallops, but there's a lot of manipulation that goes on," she explained. "They do a lot of different techniques, one of which is a spawning sanctuary. They put about thirty big rafts in the water—a mesh cage with floats along the top—and put about two hundred scallops in each cage. The whole purpose is for the scallops to spawn and produce larvae. They also put a spat bag out in the pond to collect the juveniles and take them to places in the pond where they know they've done well in the past, and they dump them there. They're seeding scallops based on collections from the pond."

To determine how well the scallops are doing, Chintala and several colleagues don wetsuits every September and count the number of scallops they find along 25-meter transects in thirty-two randomly selected locations in the pond. They assess the composition of the habitat along the transect line, take sediment samples, count and measure all of the scallops they find, and count any scallop predators, including blue crabs, green crabs, sea stars, and a variety of inch-long snails called drills that use their teeth to drill through the shells of mollusks to feed upon their flesh.

"We just completed the third year of the survey, and we're finding that the scallops are never in the same place twice," Chintala said. "There are some historical places where we've found scallops every year, but for the most part we don't have similar numbers each time. We tried to predict where we would find them using our Habitat Suitability Index, and the predictability was better for finding adults than for juveniles, which might indicate that for juveniles, habitat isn't the predominant driving factor. For them, it might be something else, like water circulation patterns. Maybe where the scallops end up depends on where your spawning adults are and where the currents take the larvae. That might be why they move around so much."

Chintala noted that the weather might also play a significant role in determining scallop abundance and location. Lagoon Pond is lined with houses with septic tanks, many of which seep nitrogen and other nutrients into the pond during heavy rains. When that happens, algae blooms soon follow, which provides food for scallops. But the summer and fall of 2007 were very dry and few blooms appeared in the pond, so many of the scallops the biologists collected that September were emaciated and malnourished. They also found an unusually large number of ctenophores—small, transparent jellyfish that prey upon algae, zooplankton, and shellfish larvae. The unexpected abundance of ctenophores may have denied the scallops adequate food resources.

Despite a perfect week of weather during their scallop survey and feeling confident that they recorded nearly all of the scallops along each transect, the biologists found that the scallop population in Lagoon Pond was way down in 2007. The numbers of adults were particularly low, which may be a bad sign for future years. According to Chintala, the low food availability may make it difficult for adult scallops to have the energy necessary to reproduce. On the other hand, she also noted that there is tremendous variability from site to site and from year to year. At one site they found 4.2 scallops per square meter in 2005 and 80.3 scallops in 2006, falling to 6.9 in 2007. Another site went from 0.6 scallops in 2005 to 53.7 in 2006 and 25 in 2007. So perhaps the low numbers in 2007 can be attributed to natural variability in Lagoon Pond. Continued annual monitoring may provide answers.

Regardless of what they learn in the pond, however, Chintala and other scallop biologists will still be worried about the future of bay scallops, because they are faced with an increasing number of threats, both natural and human-induced, that raises serious questions about their long-term viability as a completely wild creature. For instance, while scallops have evolved to cohabitate with predators like blue crabs and eastern sea stars, the accidental introduction of new predators into the coastal marine environment, including the European green crab and the Chinese mitten crab, are placing increasing pressures on them. More intense rainstorms, due in part to the effects of global warming, have caused freshwater intrusion into bays and estuaries, reducing salinity levels below that which scallops can survive. Increasingly severe storms also cause wind-driven currents to transport larval scallops into deeper water and away from appropriate habitat. And repeated "brown tide" blooms in the waters of southern New England, New York, and New Jersey in recent decades have decimated remnant scallop populations by preventing them from feeding properly and killing eelgrass.

New and unexpected threats are also emerging. Perhaps the most surprising is the impact that the overfishing of sharks is having on bay scallop populations, particularly in the southern portion of its range. Research in 2007 by the late Ransom Myers of Dalhousie University in Nova Scotia and Charles Peterson of the University of North Carolina found that as large shark numbers have declined, populations of skates and rays—which feed on shellfish—have increased. They focused their research on great white sharks, which typically keep in check the numbers of cownose rays, but fewer sharks have meant more rays. The rays feed voraciously on shellfish, easily consuming bay scallops sitting on the seabed and digging into the sediments to harvest clams and other mollusks as well.

Another group of scientists has raised an even more dire concern for the future of scallops and other shellfish. The team of twenty-five researchers from around the world noted that the expected doubling of carbon dioxide emissions into the atmosphere by the end of this century—mostly from fossil fuel combustion and one-third of which is absorbed by the oceans—will alter ocean chemistry by lowering the pH level of the water to the point where shellfish will no longer be able build their shells. When excessive amounts of CO_2 dissolve in the ocean, it forms carbonic acid, which damages coral reefs, corrodes shellfish shells, disrupts the formation of corals and shells, and interferes with the ocean's supply of oxygen. Pre-industrial concentrations of atmospheric carbon dioxide were 280 parts per million, while today's concentration is about 380 parts per million. In the absence of major efforts to curtail emissions, concentrations are projected to reach 760 parts per million in 2100.

One additional major threat to bay scallops is harder to predict—oil spills. On January 19, 1996, the oil barge *North Cape* and the tugboat *Sandia* ran aground on Moonstone Beach in southern Rhode Island after the tug caught fire, spilling more than 800,000 gallons of heating oil. The oil spread throughout Rhode Island Sound and the coastal salt ponds, including the Trustom Pond National Wildlife Refuge, resulting in the closure of an area totaling 250 square miles to fishing. The spill killed 2,100 seabirds, 9 million lobsters, 800 pounds of shellfish, and 244 pounds of finfish, putting numerous fishermen out of work and requiring an expensive and time-consuming effort to rebuild stocks. Bay scallops had already disappeared from Rhode Island by then, but if they hadn't, the spill would likely have pushed them over the edge.

As a result of the spill, the barge and tuboat owners agreed in 2000 to pay more than $7.5 million to help restore what was lost, including $1.5 million for shellfish restoration, part of which was used to reintroduce bay scallops to the state's salt ponds. Karen Tammi, now the scallop hatchery manager at Roger Williams University, was hired to oversee the project. She grew up spending summers on Cape Cod exploring beaches and tide pools, certain that she was destined for a career in marine science. During her junior year at UMass–Dartmouth, she worked on a boat in Alaska "cutting open halibut, pollock, and cod and pickling whatever was in their stomachs," she recalled. Later she studied oyster diseases in New Jersey before earning a master's degree at the University of Rhode Island. That led her to an effort to restore bay scallops in Westport harbor in Massachusetts. Bay scallops had contributed $9 million to the local economy in Westport in 1985, when 66,000 bushels of scallops were harvested, but the population soon crashed and there was no commercial harvesting of scallops for nine consecutive years. "So we devised a restoration strategy in Westport around spawning sanctuaries and spat collection," explained Tammi, "and it worked. We placed over five thousand artificial spat bags in the estuary, and we even developed a nonprofit group that worked with the school system. It was designed to get people passionate about cleaning up the estuary."

But the 2 years Tammi spent trying to restore bay scallops to Rhode Island following the oil spill weren't nearly as successful. She contracted with one of the few bay scallop hatcheries on the East Coast to scatter 500,000 juvenile scallops in a salt pond adjacent to Rhode Island's recovering fishing port of Point Judith. "We tagged one percent of them with the hopes that the following year, when we did our dive surveys, we would see them and know they came from us . . . . [They] can take a hit from crab predation and burial in the sand in the winter, and if that happens, well, welcome to the ranks of scallop restoration. The number one way to bring scallops back here in Rhode Island has been to buy seed from somewhere else, toss it in the eelgrass beds, and say a few Hail Marys and hope something happens." But nothing did. Nor did it work well the next year when the same thing was tried in Green Hill, Ninigret, Quonochontaug, and Potter ponds further west along the Rhode Island coast.

"We've really altered our salt ponds here in Rhode Island with runoff and eutrophication [low oxygen]," Tammi said. "There's no vegetative buffer around the ponds that would take up any runoff. We're talking about a scallop that's like the salmon of our salt ponds. It prefers pristine, highly oxygenated water and a hard bottom to survive, and the offspring are even more temperamental. They need the eelgrass blades or other structure to settle on. So now we're forced to do some sort of enhancement. Maybe artificial spat collection in conjunction with seeding in conjunction with spawning sanctuaries is the way to go. In Westport it was. The first commercial harvest there came in 1996 after we started our restoration in 1993. We need more than one tool in our tool box to bring back the scallop."

EPA biologist Marty Chintala thinks that one of those additional tools needed for scallop restoration is more and better information, particularly about what happens to scallops when their habitat is altered. So I met her, colleague Eric Weissberger, and intern Adam Pimenta on a hot and hazy day in June 2007 to check up on the health of scallops they had placed in cages around Point Judith Pond a month earlier. "What we're trying to do is link habitat assessment to population dynamics," Chintala explained. "And if you have a habitat that might be altered, what does that mean to the population of scallops?" By placing the cages in a wide range of habitat types in the pond, the researchers hope to determine survivorship and productivity rates. "We're trying to calculate rates based on a number of habitat types, including eelgrass, algae, bare substrate," she said. "The common tenet is that scallops need eelgrass, but we're finding them in algae, cobble, shell, bare areas. If they have structure that suits the purpose of attachment for the settling larvae, they're probably going to use it, as long as there isn't something else going on that's detrimental to them."

We climbed aboard a small EPA boat at a state boatyard a stone's throw from Rhode Island's major fishing port and adjacent to Succotash Marsh in the tiny village of Jerusalem, Rhode Island, one of my favorite birding locations. The boatyard was protected by a pair of osprey that were feeding several nestlings as we prepared to launch. Great egrets, snowy egrets, green herons, and glossy ibises flew back and forth from the marsh to the pond as we slowly rode to the north end of the pond, which is surrounded by an odd mix of million-dollar homes and modest beach houses. Dozens of recreational boaters competed with wind surfers and divers snorkeling for clams on what turned out to be a perfect summer day.

Our first stop was in a quiet cove by a small orange buoy that marked cage number 14, which was in about 5 feet of water, 30 feet from shore. Wearing wetsuits, masks, and snorkels, Weissberger and Pimenta jumped into the water to check the cage, but they quickly returned for weight belts because the buoyancy of their wetsuits prohibited them from reaching the cage at the bottom. After about 3 minutes under water on their second attempt, they returned to the boat carrying a yellow mesh bag containing five scallops. "It's murky, murky, murky, with algae all over the place," said Weissberger, who noted that those conditions would be typical at most of the cages located in quiet coves where there is little movement of water. Back on board, he opened each scallop to assess whether it had spawned yet. He inserted the blade of a pocketknife between the shells to pry it open slightly, and then he carefully cut the scallop's adductor muscle and opened the shell completely. Scraping away a black mass revealed the scallop's gonads, the color of which indicates its reproductive status—bright orange means it's ready to spawn, and pale peach means it isn't or it already has. Of the five scallops he checked, one was dead—he called it a box—and the other four weren't yet "ripe" or ready. Ten minutes after arriving, we were ready to move on to the next site.

At site 12, also located in a quiet cove, Chintala, Weissberger and I jumped into the water and found the cage in just two feet of water. We scraped our bellies on the bottom as we approached, and despite the shallow water it was virtually impossible to see the cage until we bumped into it with our heads. The cages were custom made for the project, constructed of a wire mesh like a lobster trap, about 3 feet long, but bottomless so the scallops can maintain contact with the bottom of the pond. The edges of the cage are pushed down into the sediment to prevent predators like blue crabs and gulls from getting in and eating the scallops. Attached to the cage was a gauge that measured temperature and light intensity, and at each site we also collected a water sample to determine salinity. After opening the scallops we took from the cage, we saw that none of them had bright orange gonads, though Weissberger speculated that they had all already spawned. During the previous week's visit, they hadn't yet spawned, so the spawning must have occurred just a few days earlier.

We then headed to the next cove near a YMCA camp where twenty kids were practicing kayak skills while others learned to windsurf. From a great distance, cage 13 was clearly visible above the waterline, with a herring gull sitting on top of it. It was an easy cage to check, but the murky water meant we still had to find the scallops by feeling around with our hands blindly. Cage 10 was located next to a rocky spit where an active osprey nest was built on the ground, the first time any of us had seen such an unusual location for a nest. All the scallops in both cages had already spawned. But all the scallops in cages 9 and 11 were dead, perhaps because the pond bottom there was so soft that the scallops may have sunk into the sediment and couldn't breathe.

Eventually we got to three sites that Chintala called "classic scallop sites," where eelgrass grew from the sandy bottom and a wild scallop was found the previous week. At one shallow site, the eelgrass was short and scattered among piles of razor clam shells, while at another the water was deeper and the eelgrass grew 2 or 3 feet tall in a thick forest. It was about as pristine a site as one could find at Point Judith Pond, so I took my time snorkeling back to the boat after collecting our five scallops from the cage. Pimenta pointed out the blooms and seeds on some of the eelgrass blades, and Chintala handed me a tiny invasive green crab, which she warned are aggressive and pinch, though I didn't get the message until the crab crunched down hard on my finger tip.

By the end of the day, almost all of the sites with live scallops were recorded as "four pale, one medium," which meant that four scallops had already spawned so their gonads were pale peach, and one was medium in color, so it could have been getting ready to spawn or, more likely, had recently completed spawning and its color was fading. It would take a while before the data from the study would shed new light on scallop productivity and survivability in various habitats, but Chintala was certain they would learn more than they did the previous year at nearby Ninigret Pond, when freshwater intrusion into the pond from major rainstorms lowered salinity levels and killed most of the scallops.

·   ·   ·

While bay scallops are struggling to hang on in the wild, their larger relative, sea scallops, are driving the fishing economy in one of the country's largest fishing ports, New Bedford, Massachusetts. Sea scallops—which have 120 blue eyes, compared to the bay scallop's 42—are found at depths of up to 500 feet from Cape Hatteras, North Carolina, to the Grand Banks off Newfoundland, with one of the most intensively fished areas being at Georges Bank off Massachusetts. Approximately 300 commercial fishing vessels have permits to drag for sea scallops, making it the highest value fishery landed at U.S. ports. The New Bedford–based scallop fishery contributes $300 million per year to the regional economy.

Bay scallops will never bring in that kind of money, but aquaculture may provide opportunities for a sustainable harvest of the species. "When New England was first settled, scallops were fed to the pigs," said scallop hatchery manager Karen Tammi. "They were considered a trash shellfish. It wasn't until an influx of European settlers that it finally transcended to our palate. Now they're considered a delicacy." Yet the world's leading producer of New England's native scallop is China, which grew its industry from a small number of scallops sent from Nantucket. Techniques for scallop aquaculture have been developed in Asia and are finally making their way back to New England, but not very quickly. Rhode Island has about thirty aquaculturists who grow shellfish, and only three of them focus on scallops because the success rate is so low.

"Scallop culture throughout the world utilizes a spat bag. They use a farming technique out in the waterways with lots of structure, lots of suspended gear," explained Tammi. "If you can visualize raising some kind of a farm animal, at a certain stage you have them in a small pen, then you move them to a bigger pen, and maybe you then have to build an even bigger house for them. It's the same sort of philosophy for scallops."

But why hasn't large-scale aquaculture caught on here?

"It basically comes down to water usage in our estuaries," she said. "The culture techniques for scallops involve hanging things off piers or placing lots of buoys in the water with long lantern nets off them. Just imagine a Rhode Island recreational boater in Narragansett Bay trying to negotiate that on a hot summer day. It just wouldn't happen. The sailing vessels will win out over the aquaculturists for use of the water."

Tammi believes that small-scale scallop farming might work, though, particularly since she is convinced that fresh, native scallops are larger and sweeter tasting than those raised on large Chinese farms. She envisions creating a "Beaujolais scallop for white table-cloth restaurants" from bay scallops cultured in southern New England, and she is already working on a scallop cookbook. "But the days that the old timers remember, when you could walk across Point Judith Pond on scallops—those days are long gone."

9

Atlantic Wolffish

When a net is dragged behind a commercial fishing vessel to catch groundfish like cod, haddock, or flounder, the various species of fish behave somewhat differently in their efforts to escape the all-consuming net. Haddock, a high-value fish that experienced a strong population surge in the 2000s, typically swim upward when the net approaches, while cod, whose stocks are perilously low, and flounder swim downward. To exploit these different behaviors, a team of fishermen reconfigured a standard otter trawl net to allow the species that swim downward to escape while efficiently capturing the upward swimming haddock. The upper and rear portions of the net have the regulated 6-inch mesh to capture the haddock, while the lower portion of the net has an 8-foot mesh that easily allows the cod and flounder to escape capture.

In 2006 and 2007, Rhode Island Sea Grant fisheries researcher Dave Beutel was contracted to scientifically test the effectiveness of the new configuration. He conducted more than 100 side-by-side trials with the net on Georges Bank—one vessel equipped with the tra-

ditional otter trawl and another with the new net dubbed The Eliminator—and he was impressed with the results. "The new gear catches
just as much haddock as the existing gear, but without catching the
species of critical concern," he said. "And it virtually eliminated all of
the by-catch like flounders, cod, skates, lobsters, and dogfish."

The results were so good that the net won the grand prize in the
2007 International Smart Gear competition, which was established by
the World Wildlife Fund to find innovative solutions to reduce the
capture rate of vulnerable and other non-target species. Perhaps more
important to the fishing industry, the net also won the approval of the
New England Fishery Management Council in 2008 for use by fishermen on "B days" in areas it manages. Fishermen are allowed a certain
number of days at sea—called A days—when they could potentially
catch species of concern like cod and flounder. They are also allowed
additional days at sea—B days—as long as the gear used on those days
does not affect overfished species. Because the standard otter trawl net
captures all groundfish indiscriminately—cod, haddock and flounder,
among others—that gear can only be used on A days. But the new net
now allows fishermen to selectively fish for haddock on B days.

The capture of non-target species—called by-catch—is a monu-
mental problem. Worldwide, about one out of every four fish captured in fishing gear is unwanted or unintentional catch, according to
the United Nations Food and Agriculture Organization. That means
that every year millions of tons of fish are tossed back into the water,
either dead or dying, because they have no market value or are too
small to be legally caught or the fishermen don't have the proper permits to catch them or simply because they aren't what the fishermen
wanted to catch that day. And it's not just fish. Dolphins, sea turtles,
seals, whales, and seabirds are also accidentally caught and drown in
fishing gear. The shrimp fishery is perhaps the worst offender, as between 2 and 10 pounds of other species are caught and discarded for
every pound of shrimp captured. The issue even creates conflicts
among fishermen, as species caught and discarded by one fishery may
be important to another fishery. Not only is by-catch a major waste
of natural resources, but the discarded animals can no longer contribute to the health of their ecosystem. Young fish captured and
thrown back dead aren't able to grow up and breed to rebuild de-

pleted populations, and by killing these animals, food is being taken away from numerous species of mid- and top-level predators that only eat live prey.

The problem of indiscriminate fishing is one that the fishermen would like to solve as much as anyone. By-catch costs them time and space on their boats, and it is a significant contributor to the critical problem of overfishing, which is threatening their livelihoods and jeopardizing their future revenue. The issue is primarily driven by the lack of selectivity in the fishing gear. All of the traditional fishing methods—hook and line, traps, gillnets, and bottom trawling—are apt to catch whatever fish happen to be in the area. That's why the development of adaptations to fishing gear, like The Eliminator, is so important, especially for trawlers. Most of the by-catch from bottom trawling is unlikely to survive because it is brought up from deep water too quickly, it's crushed in the net, or it's thrown back too late.

When Beutel returned to sea on the last day of May 2008 to test The Eliminator on a smaller commercial fishing vessel, he invited me to join him. It was my first time on a trawler, and it was a great opportunity to see firsthand the problem of by-catch. Just like the earlier trials on Georges Bank, two trawlers participated in the side-by-side trials—Beutel in the *F/V Stormy Weather* equipped with The Eliminator, and me aboard the *F/V Lady Victoria* using the traditional net. We left the harbor in Seabrook, New Hampshire, at 4:30 A.M. under gray and threatening skies with the expectation of occasional thunderstorms and very breezy conditions. Captain Puggy Felch, a commercial fisherman for 43 years, was headed to Gloucester, Massachusetts, after the trials were completed that day for the midnight start of the groundfishing season. But he was pleased to have the opportunity to help test the new net, and he provided me with tremendous insight into the industry from a fisherman's perspective.

Built in Nova Scotia and named after his wife, Felch's 12-year-old boat was a 45-foot combination trawler and gillnetter that he used to catch cod, haddock, pollock, and other groundfish. Since his usual fishing grounds are closed in April and May, he and his crew—son Puggy Jr. and deckhand Rian Fogg—had spent the last few weeks doing maintenance, including painting the boat's entire interior and installing new rugs. The vessel has four narrow bunks below deck plus one more in the wheelhouse, and the fishing deck was filled with stacks of black, green, and white plastic totes and a multicolored trawl net wrapped around an overhead net reel, with several fish still entangled in it from the previous day's tow.

Felch didn't have much positive to say about the current state of fishing regulations, which he called draconian. He prefers individual fishing quotas rather than the complex "days-at-sea" formula. Depending on the equipment he uses (trawl or gillnet), each actual day spent at sea counts as 1½ or 2 days toward the total allotment he has from his four fishing permits. He believes the regulations are part of the reason for the decline in the number of commercial fishing boats based in Seabrook from fifteen in the 1990s to just two in 2008. "The regulations are totally crazy," he said. "We could sit here and talk about it all day long and not understand it. The people who manage the industry don't know how to do it. It's mismanagement at the highest levels."

After traveling 6 or 7 miles south-southeast from Seabrook, the deckhands prepared to deploy the net for the first time at 5:30 A.M. at an area Felch referred to as the winter shrimp ground, a sandy-bottomed spot in 39 fathoms of water off the far northern shore of Massachusetts. Wearing their bright orange oilskins, Puggy Jr. and Fogg guided the net as it was unraveled into the water, dropping remnants of the previous day's catch to an aggressive flock of herring and great black-backed gulls. Near the end of the process, they pointed out to me the circular, cookie-like "rockhoppers" that line the mouth of the net and bounce along the seafloor to keep the mesh net from snagging on anything on the bottom. Then they unhooked two 5-foot, heavy metal doors from the outside edges of the boat and dropped them into the water to help herd the fish into the net and hold the net open. It took 10 minutes to set the net, and then the deckhands removed their rubber boots and oilskins and took a nap until it was time to haul it back in.

From a distance of 50 yards, it was impossible to tell that the net that Beutel had deployed from the *Stormy Weather* was any different from the one that dragged behind the *Lady Victoria*. The two vessels then traveled just out of shouting distance of each other at 2.8 knots for exactly an hour, a speed that Felch said was typical for catching cod, adding that he usually goes 2.4 knots if he's targeting flounder. It felt like we were barely moving forward, but the captain said that traveling any faster than 3 knots causes the mouth of the net to collapse and close.

At 6:40, the net was slowly hauled back in. It seemed to take a long time, but it may have just been that my anticipation of seeing the results was so high. Once the bulging net was on board and hanging from the reel overhead, Puggy Jr. gave a hard tug on a rope on its underside to release its contents. I felt like we were opening a big Christmas present or like we had just given a piñata a good, solid hit as its contents spilled out everywhere. The variety of fish that poured onto the deck was impressive. The most obvious were the cod—gray-green or golden backs, heavy white bellies, and three dorsal fins—which were caught in a wide variety of sizes. There were also lots of small flounder of four or five different species, from tan and brown ones to bluish-black specimens, all with bright white undersides. Haddock, our target species, was also caught in abundance, though since they are smaller than the cod they seemed to be hidden among the rest of the catch. And then there were the unexpected oddities: a dozen sculpin colored in gorgeous earth tones with bloated bellies and large spiny fins; an 8-pound female lobster with hundreds of eggs and no claws; several ugly gray wolffish with nasty-looking teeth; one very large monkfish, a basketball-sized creature with a huge mouth and comparatively tiny tail; at least two species of skates, square flatfish with long tails that are closely related to rays and sharks; and a few other things I couldn't identify.

The deckhands immediately began sorting the fish by species into different totes, and after getting most of the big ones out of the way, they set the net again. To compare the different catch rates between The Eliminator and the standard trawl net, everything brought up in the net had to be weighed, a process that took about 30 minutes and was conducted by Alex Brickett, a recent graduate of the University of New Hampshire who came along specifically to collect data on the catch. The final tally included 585 pounds of cod (including 55 pounds of small fish that were below the legal size limit); 341 pounds of haddock, with just 8 pounds below the limit; 218 pounds of flounder, though one quarter of it was too small to keep; and five wolffish totaling 97 pounds.

The total quantity of by-catch was smaller than I expected. Just the undersized cod, haddock, and flounder, as well as the skates, sculpin, and a few others (all of which were dead), were tossed overboard. Everything else was kept because there is a market for it, even the monkfish—though only its tail is eaten, and very few people will eat that, not even the vessel's captain. However, considering that our target fish was haddock, it could be said that everything except that species, nearly three-quarters of our catch and a total of more than 1,000 pounds of fish, was by-catch. Cod, which may be the most overfished and imperiled species in the region, represented more than half of the total weight of the tow.

As gulls feasted on their entrails, the fish were put on ice and stored below deck. That's when I walked over to the tote holding the wolffish, the species that I had come to see that day. Sitting there dead in a green plastic box and weighing between 10 and 25 pounds each, they were pretty frightening. I can only imagine what it would be like to see one coming at me in the water. They looked somewhat eel-like, with one long dorsal fin along the entire length of their bodies and a faint tiger striping on their blue-gray sides, which are absent of pelvic fins. But it was their mouths that made them look especially fearsome—large tusk-like teeth projecting forward from both jaws, and behind them a series of smaller teeth. On the roof of the mouth behind the canine-like tusks was a series of molars for crushing the shells of their mollusk prey. By the looks of them alone, it's a creature that most people would be happy to avoid. Unfortunately, it's also a species that has declined considerably in New England waters.

Atlantic wolffish (*Anarhichas lupus*) are among the most formidable creatures in the region, known to fishermen for their tremendous biting ability and ferocious temperament. They are reputed to be able to bite through broomsticks, break steel knives, and crush steel fish baskets, and legends claim they have gnawed scars onto anchor chains. Found throughout the Gulf of Maine in waters between 100 and 700 feet deep (but most often from 150 to 250 feet), they have been reported from as far north as Greenland, Iceland and Norway. A high concentration of antifreeze-like proteins in their system lowers the freezing point of their blood, enabling them to tolerate waters as low as 30 degrees Fahrenheit, though their abundance is highest where temperatures are in the 40s. Solitary except during the mating season, they live in protected nooks among large piles of rocks and stones on the seafloor.

"Their mating and denning system is relatively unique, especially for Gulf of Maine fishes," said Peter Auster, science director of the National Undersea Research Center at the University of Connecticut, who has observed them on Jeffrey's Ledge and Stellwagen Bank in the waters between Provincetown and Cape Ann, Massachusetts. "The gulf has a series of reefs, especially in the near shore to 80 meter range, that are remnant glacier eskers—long trains of linear boulder reefs—and wolffish occur in these kinds of places." Auster said that wolffish excavate dens beneath the rocks at the margins of these boulder reefs, where they typically are at the top of the food chain. "Wolffish probably don't have any competitors there. Other resident fishes in boulder reefs, like cunner and Acadian redfish, crabs, and lobster, are more likely to be their prey," he noted.

The wolffish diet consists mostly of mollusks, crustaceans, and echinoderms, the group of marine invertebrates that includes the starfish, sea urchins and sea cucumbers. Wolffish may even be a key factor in controlling the density and distribution of this group of animals. Because their teeth quickly become worn from crushing these spiny and hard-shelled species, their teeth are replaced annually after the spawning season. Sometimes growing to 5 feet long and 40 pounds, Atlantic wolffish don't spawn until about age 6. Females produce between 5,000 and 12,000 eggs, which are laid in clusters and aggressively guarded by the male, who fasts during this 200-day brooding period while he waits for his teeth to grow back.

According to Auster, the population of Atlantic wolffish in the Gulf of Maine has declined precipitously since the mid-1990s, and their average size declined by 50 percent from 1980 to 1999. The annual spring trawl survey conducted by the Northeast Fisheries Science Center caught an average of 1 to 2 kilograms of wolffish per tow between 1968 and 1988, but since then the trend has steadily declined, leading the National Marine Fisheries Service to list it as a species of concern in 2004. The biggest factor in their decline has been their capture as by-catch by commercial fishing trawlers.

"There is no targeted fishery for them," Auster said, "but there is a market for them. You can sometimes see them on menus as ocean catfish. Back in the seventies they were a poor man's fish, but now that so many other species have been fished out, all these obscure and bizarre species became gourmet items."

For species like wolffish, however, it is difficult to develop an accurate assessment of their populations because their preferred rocky habitat is difficult to survey.

It is obvious to Auster, based on the trawl surveys, that the catch is declining. But he said that the survey mostly catches fish that stray away from the boulder reefs, which is what makes them available to the trawl gear. "As populations decline, wolffish retreat to their preferred habitats, and ultimately the catch index gets very low, but we still don't know how many are left in the boulder reefs because the trawl surveys don't go there. Which means that we don't really know how rare the species is. It's still clear to me, though, that their overall population has declined severely."

While the greatest issue facing Atlantic wolffish is clearly commercial fishing by-catch—and to a lesser extent, recreational fishing in protected areas that are otherwise closed to fishing—another troubling effect of commercial fishing that may threaten wolffish is habitat degradation. That's a major reason why the Canadian government listed it as a species at risk. Trawling damages benthic habitat, stirs up bottom sediments that can release settled toxins, smothers spawning areas, and can harm their gills.

"Small boulder piles where wolffish live can also be rolled over by trawl nets, and that might have an effect on the fish and the habitat, too," Auster said. "I've got no data to back that up, but until there's another glaciation, these kinds of habitats are not recoverable."

A 2005 report by the Deep Sea Conservation Coalition, an alliance of more than 40 international organizations, says that bottom trawling is the world's most destructive type of fishing. Focusing mostly on large offshore trawlers but also including near shore vessels, the report summarizes dozens of scientific studies analyzed by the U.S. National

Academy of Sciences. The report described some of the ways that trawlers impact habitat: "Weighted with massive bobbins, rollers or rockhoppers, the trawl nets stretch up to 40 meters in width and are held open by pairs of seven-ton steel trawl doors. Trawler footropes can roll 18-ton seafloor rocks. Both rolled-boulders and trawl doors can plow deep gouges in soft sediments. A trawler towing at three to four knots for a period of four hours directly impacts an area of 2.5 kilometers . . . Trawlers sweep a vast area of seafloor, crushing corals, sponges and most of the other living things that they hit. The estimated total area swept annually by trawl nets (the same area is often trawled many times a year) is equivalent to about 50 percent of the world's continental shelf area, or approximately 150 times the area of forest that is clearcut worldwide."

In New England, a report by the Massachusetts Institute of Technology Sea Grant Program the same year raised similar concerns about coastal fisheries. It cited research that found that fishing gear disturbs physical features on the seafloor that are attractive to juvenile fish, leading to increased predation. One study predicted that disturbance of just 1 percent of the estuarine habitat of juvenile menhaden could lead to a 58 percent decline in the menhaden population over 10 years. Under a worst-case scenario, another study suggested that fishing gear could alter the integrity of entire marine ecosystems. Given how tied wolffish are to their boulder habitat, they are unlikely to come away unscathed.

Nathalie LeFrancois is less concerned about by-catch and the effect of fishing gear on wolffish habitat than she is about how changes in the marine environment are going to affect the species. The research professor at the University of Quebec at Rimouski was the first person in North America to raise wild Atlantic wolffish in captivity and get them to reproduce. She said that the most interesting thing about wolffish is "their sex life, that they actually have one, and that they keep their mate for as long as they do."

Because the fish are so sedentary, because they occupy the same burrow for years at a time, because their pre-spawning and spawning periods are so long, and because the males can spend more than half a year guarding their eggs without feeding, they are very susceptible to environmental changes. "The main issue to me is climactic," said Le-

Francois. "They are one of the most sensitive fish out there because of their life cycle. Fish that can move away and reproduce anywhere won't be the first to show signs of problems. It will be the one who will be less mobile, like wolffish, that will rapidly suffer. Fluctuations in the environment—temperature, oxygen levels, salinity—can be worse for them than living in poor but stable conditions."

LeFrancois studies the physiology of wolffish in captivity to try to understand how to improve survival rates. She said that there is a great deal that is unknown about the species—like their nutritional needs and the effect of stress—but her main focus is on what she calls "egg quality." What does the egg need to survive long enough to hatch? Fifty percent of Atlantic wolffish eggs survive to hatching, which is an excellent rate compared to most other fish, but they lay far fewer eggs than most species—cod, for example, may spawn millions of eggs—which she believes may be one clue as to why the population is in decline. Once a wolffish egg hatches, however, its survival rate is excellent.

While wolffish are known for their aggressiveness, in captivity that behavior trait mostly disappears. "I call them by their names, and they almost come to me," LeFrancois said with a laugh, only partly joking. That's why she thinks it is an excellent species for commercial aquaculture. She said that they get along surprisingly well together, even in high densities, which is unusual for wolffish, though the wild brood stock must be kept in lower numbers. "They take well to feed, they are very simple to rear, you only need a low volume of water, and once you get the egg to hatching, you have it for life," she said. Out of a concern for the environmental effects of aquaculture facilities in the open water, she recommends that wolffish aquaculture be developed as a land-based system. "It's not a fish that swims much, it's a fish that stands on its pectoral fins, so it doesn't need a lot of space and it doesn't use up much energy."

But is there a demand for farm-raised wolffish in the marketplace, I asked her. She assured me there is. "It is looked upon very well by the fish connoisseur. It has big white fillets, a mild taste, and no bones. It is building markets, especially at high-end restaurants, and in Europe it's popular as Loup de Mer. Marketing it as wolffish is perfectly feasible, too. It already won first prize at the Boston Seafood Show as the best new product."

. . .

In the wild, however, the Atlantic wolffish is still in trouble. In 2000 it became the first marine fish to be protected under Canada's Species at Risk Act, and a management plan was issued for it in 2008 that focuses on research, public education, habitat protection, and monitoring and mitigation of human activities. In the United States, almost all of the fish listed as endangered or threatened by the Endangered Species Act are types of salmon found in the Pacific. Among species found in New England, just the Atlantic salmon and shortnose sturgeon—both of which spawn in a few rivers in the region and spend only part of their lives in salt water—are listed. But Atlantic wolffish might be next.

The Conservation Law Foundation, University of Hawaii marine biologist Les Watling, and Boston-based veterinarian-turned-lawyer Erica Fuller filed a petition with the government in September 2008 asserting that wolffish are imperiled enough to be listed as endangered, too.

"I heard tales about wolffish growing up," Fuller wrote me in an e-mail, "but they didn't have much relevance to my life until I heard two of my law school professors talking about needing a student to do some research on imperiled fish species . . . The hope was to find a species which would meet the listing criteria of the Endangered Species Act and might ultimately have critical habitat designated. The Endangered Species Act is always somewhat controversial, but this looked like a situation that required it—the wolffish are going to become extinct in the very near future without our help and the species is in enough trouble that it should meet most of the listing criteria in the ESA."

Fuller became so obsessed with preparing the endangered species petition—it took her 3 years—that her children started calling her Erin Brockofish, a reference to the single mother who fought to expose the contamination of drinking water by Pacific Gas & Electric that caused widespread illness in Hinkley, California, in the 1980s.

"I scoured the earth to find anyone who would talk to me or map the data for me so that I could write this thing," she said. "I wrote the largest chunk of it while sailing with my brother and two others from Seattle to Hawaii two summers ago. It is truly a collaborative effort at this point though, and I hope that it will be successful at least in bringing some more attention to imperiled species in the ocean."

But Atlantic wolffish isn't the only fish species living among the boulder reefs in the Gulf of Maine that is apparently in trouble. Cusk is, too. In fact, if Fuller hadn't written an endangered species petition for Atlantic wolffish, she would have written one for cusk. Closely related to Atlantic cod but the only member of its genus, cusk (*Brosme brosme*) are shaped somewhat like wolffish, with a long eel-like body and a single dorsal fin extending all the way to their tail. Solitary, sedentary, slow-moving, and slow to mature—all features they share with the wolffish—they like deep water between Newfoundland and Cape Cod, though the bulk of the population seems to be off southwest Nova Scotia and throughout the Gulf of Maine. Cusk grow up to 3 feet in length and 20 pounds, feeding on crustaceans, small fish, and starfish.

Like wolffish, there is no targeted fishery for cusk, but there is a market for those captured, especially in Canada where fishermen earn more per pound of cusk than for cod, haddock, or pollock. With no regulations governing their capture in either U.S. or Canadian waters, concern has been growing over a severe decline in population indices since the late 1960s. Not only is the total number of fish caught at record lows, but the average length and weight of those fish has dropped dramatically, and they are being found in a smaller and smaller area each year. In 2008 the status of cusk was being reviewed in both countries, which may lead to commercial fishing restrictions, a step that Canadian fishermen worry will have a significant effect on their livelihoods.

By-catch is the biggest cause of mortality for cusk, but trawlers seem to be less of a concern for them. Instead they are more often caught in gillnets, longlines, and lobster traps. The Atlantic halibut survey I joined in the spring of 2007 in Downeast Maine was redefined as a halibut and cusk survey in 2008 to take advantage of the fact that cusk were being caught in significant numbers and so little was known about the species.

"We established randomly selected stations across the state in federal waters—more than three miles offshore—and set three hundred hooks baited with frozen herring or frozen mackerel at each station," explained Trisha Cheney DeGraaf, a marine biologist with the Maine Department of Marine Resources. "We then let the hooks soak for five to twenty-four hours and then hauled them back in. During a typical set, we'd catch two cusk. Last year [2007] we had fourteen stations and caught a total of thirty-nine cusk all year. This year we decreased our stations and we still caught thirty-six cusk. They're out there, and they're widely distributed."

One particularly unexpected result was the capture of four cusk on four consecutive hooks on one longline. "That's something new," she said with excitement. "They're supposed to be solitary, so to have four come up in sequential order is pretty amazing. It might be that we were right on top of their preferred habitat, or it might have been a spawning aggregation—if they have them. That hasn't been documented before."

DeGraaf said that the plan had been to run the survey throughout the month of May, but by late May when dogfish moved into the area, almost every hook had a dogfish on it after just 5 hours in the water, ending the project. The aim of the research was to document the incidence of cusk in the region and collect biological information about them. Unfortunately, unlike the halibut that were also targeted in the study, few of the cusk captured survived the experience.

"Since they're slow-moving animals that don't move across the pressure gradient very often, they can't adjust the pressure in their air bladder as quickly as cod can," DeGraaf said. "So when they're brought to the surface, their eyes are bulging out and their air bladder pushes their stomach out of their mouth. From those fish, we collect biological information—maturity information, genetic samples, weight and measurements, and otoliths [an ear bone] for aging."

DeGraaf hopes that this study will help to shed some light on cusk life history and learn whether the areas protected from fishing are benefiting the species. And she hopes to follow up the project with a study in 2009 of discard mortality—how many cusk survive being caught and returned to the sea. One concern she has is that it is a very tasty fish. "It's not normally seen in the fish section of most local grocery stores, but a lot of maritimers have historically had a lot of cusk available to them. It's fairly soft and takes the flavoring of anything you cook it with."

By the time the deckhands on board the *Lady Victoria* had cleaned and stored the fish and hosed down the deck from the first tow, it was time to haul the second tow. This time, when the piñata dropped its contents on the boat, it had similar varieties of fish but far fewer cod and more haddock. And no wolffish. It did, however, have one big striped bass and a few spiny dogfish—the smallest and most abundant shark in New England waters. By-catch was way down, but so was the total catch, so the sorting, weighing, and cleaning took far less time. That meant the deckhands had time to go back for another nap before deploying the net once again.

The boats continued on their course to the south-southeast for a few miles before the call went out to set the net. The weather had been getting unexpectedly clearer, but the wind picked up and made the water conditions more difficult, which is apparently typical off Cape Ann. Coupled with the smell of fish guts and diesel, it made me a little queasy. The third tow ended up in 44 fathoms of water just a couple miles off Rockport, Massachusetts. A steady stream of gulls remained alongside us, along with an occasional immature gannet, when three sooty shearwaters darted in and zipped back and forth between the two fishing vessels for the last 20 minutes of the haul. Unfortunately, the net brought up mostly cod—we were already past our quota for the day—and very few of our target haddock. Dogfish numbers were up, but the rest of the by-catch was way down.

As I watched the sorting and weighing of the catch, I couldn't help but be impressed with the speed at which the deckhands were tossing fish from the deck to the proper totes for each species, and how they could determine with hardly a glance whether a fish was of legal size or not. Some they had to measure against a ruler that they always had handy, but they even did that with speed and agility that were surprisingly impressive.

As we turned around to steam north again, the water conditions grew calm but the skies darkened again. A steady rain forced most of us into the protection of the wheelhouse, and intermittent lightning worried me just enough to forget about my queasy stomach. At 11:00 we began the final tow of the day, with the gulls, gannets, and shearwaters still by our side hoping for a handout. The result was similar to the first tow, which was expected since we had retraced our path and were back to the winter shrimp grounds where we started: about 50 percent cod, including some big ones over 40 pounds, 25 percent haddock, three large lobsters, one scallop, and four wolffish. With too much cod on board and little on the *Stormy Weather* due to the success of The Eliminator, we slid up beside her and tossed some of our cod to our partner vessel. And then the day was done.

I caught up with Dave Beutel a few weeks later to learn how well The Eliminator net worked that day. When he showed me the data sheet listing all of the fish caught in each tow, I was stunned that it was all on one page while the results from the Lady Victoria took up four pages. That's because all of the species that sit on the seafloor—lobsters, flounders, skates, and more—were completely absent. Using The Eliminator, the *Stormy Weather* caught cod and haddock and almost nothing else other than a couple of wolffish and a couple of dogfish. Clearly, the net was a success. Or so I thought.

"The New Hampshire fishermen were ecstatic with the net when we tested it," Beutel said. "They thought it worked great. But it caught a few more codfish than I anticipated, though that was partly because there were a lot more codfish in the area than I anticipated. It reduced the cod catch by 50 to 70 percent, but I was hoping for an 80 percent reduction. It clearly minimized the by-catch, but it also didn't catch as much haddock either, so that worries me a little. But remember, this is a smaller sized net compared to the others we tested. We're trying to make this tool available to all sizes of boats. For some reason, the cod reduction was bigger on the bigger net on the bigger boat."

Nonetheless, given that it was approved for use on B days by the New England Fisheries Management Council, The Eliminator is clearly a step in the right direction. And given that by-catch is such a serious threat to wolffish and cusk and to dozens of other species of fish and other organisms, the new net is an important step toward protecting the health of the marine environment.

As for the future of Atlantic wolffish and cusk in New England waters, UConn's Peter Auster is concerned. "The only way to improve the outlook is to reduce fishing mortality, both recreational and commercial, because it's hard to see any signal from pollution or other threats. In the nineteen sixties and seventies there were very many more of these fish. It doesn't portend well for how well we've managed these populations. I think it's something to worry about, and there's an obligation under several federal laws to do something about it."

10

Harlequin Duck

Deer Isle, Maine, located halfway up the coast on the eastern edge of Penobscot Bay, is connected to the mainland by a narrow bridge that some claim has been under construction 24 hours a day for years. I reached the bridge in total darkness, waited interminably for my turn to cross, and finally arrived 30 minutes later in the small fishing village of Stonington at the southern terminus of the island. It was well after the staff had gone off duty at my motel, but I found an envelope with my name on it, checked myself in, and climbed the unlit outside staircase to my room.

At dawn I got my first view of the gorgeous landscape—rocky shoreline, spruce covered islets, quaint harbor, and a pink sky hinting at rain. It was early November 2007, and while I was prepared for whatever the weather had in store, I was slightly embarrassed by my obnoxiously bright orange parka, though later I would also be pleased I brought it. I met Glen Mittelhauser in the harbor parking lot preparing to board the mail boat to Isle au Haut, when a crew member on the boat brought Mittelhauser the talon of a large raptor that had been found on a nearby beach. It was too large to have been from an osprey. Mittelhauser tentatively identified the talon as that of a bald eagle, but he stuffed it in a baggie in his backpack and assured the crewman he would confirm it back in his lab later.

Mittelhauser seemed to be known for his ornithological prowess by everyone coming to and from Isle au Haut that day, and he was genuinely pleased to share his latest projects with whoever asked. We climbed aboard the mail boat with Megan Smith, a graduate student at Antioch College who grew up in Bar Harbor and had volunteered to join us for the day. She was finishing up her master's thesis on the birds living in aspen groves in Grand Teton National Park in Wyoming and was happy for a day of fieldwork away from her computer.

The boat left Stonington at seven o'clock on quiet water and with the view of a beautiful sunrise reflecting on the windows of the houses in town. It was a 40-minute trip past scattered uninhabited islands, and I spent most of the time scanning the water for birds. Several common loons gave us a cursory glance, one long-tailed duck darted across the bow, and six black guillemots swam quickly out of our wake before taking flight. As we approached the harbor at Isle au Haut by first scooting along the eastern edge of Kimball Island, duck numbers skyrocketed. Dozens of common eiders floated casually in a multitude of plumages—warm chocolate females, handsome black and white males with a hint of mint green on the back of their gently sloping heads, and numerous mottled first- and second-year birds somewhere in between. The only flock of bufflehead we were to see that day disappeared quickly under the water's surface as we approached, unlike the flock of seven long-tailed ducks that gladly modeled their finest outerwear for us. Formerly called oldsquaw, long-tailed ducks are difficult to find at my usual winter birding haunts in Rhode Island, so every time I see them I marvel at their unique look—bold black and white plumage that somewhat reverses itself from winter to summer, and two daring and conspicuous long black tail feathers that make it one of the longest ducks from beak to tail of any in North America. It's my second favorite duck, next to the one Mittelhauser and I had come to see.

Lying seven miles off the Maine coast, Isle au Haut (High Island) can hardly be called a tourist destination. Save for a gift shop and a bed-and-breakfast, there is little for typical tourists to visit—no quaint stores to wander in, no fancy lodging and no restaurants. But the scenery is spectacular. Like most of the islands in the Gulf of Maine, it was formed by debris left behind by the receding glaciers. Isle au Haut was probably inhabited by Native Americans a thousand years ago, most likely those from the Penobscot tribe of the Abenakis, a branch of the Algonquin Nation, though the island's first residents are today often referred to as the Oyster Shell People for the mounds of shells they left behind from their great feasts. The island was named in 1604 by the French explorer Samuel de Champlain, for whom the island's highest peak is named. The first European settlers—mostly English and Scottish—came to the island in the late 1790s, and the population peaked at about 275 in the late 1800s, thanks to the establishment of a lobster cannery on the main thoroughfare at the north end of the 12-square mile island. The population has slowly declined ever since, with just 79 year-round residents recorded in the 2000 census and even fewer today, though the number nearly doubles in the summer.

The main attraction to visitors is the 60 percent of the island included in Acadia National Park, the first national park east of the Mississippi River, which maintains miles of trails and several campsites. When the mail boat arrived at the town dock, Mittelhauser and I were met by the park ranger, who graciously loaned us his truck for the day, and we headed off on a slow drive on narrow rutted roads through a red spruce forest to the south end of the island. A short hike along Goat Trail wound through ankle-deep bogs where thick mats of mosses covered the trail and the smell of spruce boughs brought to mind Christmas wreaths and holiday decorating. The trail led us to Merchant Cove, a cobblestone beach with beautiful views of granite boulders and rocky cliffs topped by spruce and firs. It was there that we began our search for harlequin ducks (*Histrionicus histrionicus*), a somewhat common duck in the West but one whose Eastern population is frightfully small.

Upon scanning the cove with my binoculars, I saw numerous birds in the distance—loons, eiders, a large flock of herring gulls, a couple red-necked grebes, and far to the east a distant flock of harlequin ducks. Mittelhauser was somewhat surprised they were there, since the ducks are seldom found in that cove except during bad weather when the surf is too rough in their preferred locations, so he speculated that they had probably just arrived from the north and hadn't yet joined the larger flocks nearby. After months apart, the birds we were watching were probably reestablishing their pair bonds with a series of chases, flutters, and what looked like intimate dances that included a cute little tail wiggle. We walked in their direction to get a better view, but as we approached they were well hidden in a tiny, rocky inlet. Eventually they came out but soon disappeared around another rocky outcropping and continued further away from where we intended to go, so we turned around and headed in the opposite direction. After returning to Merchant's Cove, we circled the shoreline and walked slowly out to Merchant's Point, a narrow spit of land that extends about 300 yards into the bay. When we arrived at the point, dozens of harlequin ducks were already there, many perched on a series of rocks just off shore and others feeding, swimming, and bonding.

Harlequin ducks are among the most striking ducks in North America, with males attired in a distinctive slate blue with several bold streaks of white bordered in black on their face, neck, and sides, and soft cinnamon patches on their flanks. Mittelhauser said they are "so different looking, you really can't confuse them with anything else. The males are a wash of color, with a blue that's hard to describe and that takes on different colors depending on the light conditions." Females are a warm chestnut brown with several white facial patches. Besides their unmistakable look, harlequins often hold their tail up at an angle that, when seen in silhouette, Mittelhauser said can sometimes appear like a spinnaker.

Biologists have identified four distinct populations of harlequin ducks—an abundant western population that winters along the Pacific shoreline from Alaska to northern California; an Iceland group of about 12,000 to 16,000 birds; a Greenland population that is unstudied but may number roughly 10,000 individuals; and the eastern North America population that winters in New England. This latter group consists of about 3,600 birds, up from fewer than 2,000 a decade ago when hunting pressures limited an already depressed population.

Perhaps the rarest duck in eastern North America, harlequins occupy a unique habitat niche that they share with no other waterfowl—

a preference for breeding adjacent to clear, fast-moving rivers and streams, with those in the eastern population breeding exclusively in the forests of Quebec and Labrador. Harlequin ducks are uniquely able to move with agility in turbulent waters to feed on the aquatic insects that inhabit river bottoms. While not known to breed in New England, nearly the entire Eastern population winters here along the rocky coastlines, preferring to dance within the crashing surf of the shallow intertidal zone where they feed on amphipods, snails, mollusks, and a wide variety of small marine invertebrates.

While the bulk of the population winters around ocean-facing points and small islands in Maine—the largest numbers being at Isle au Haut—smaller groupings are found as far north as southern Newfoundland. "The ice limits the northern end of their winter range," explained Mittelhauser, "and the northern coast of Newfoundland tends to get encased in ice, so you wouldn't see them there. But Cape St. Mary's is a good place for them, and good numbers winter along the Nova Scotia coast." South of Maine, he said, harlequin numbers dwindle considerably, with small numbers returning each year to Cape Ann and Martha's Vineyard in Massachusetts and to the southern points of Aquidneck and Conanicut Islands in Narragansett Bay in Rhode Island. Beyond that, only Barnegat Bay, New Jersey, is a consistent wintering location, and there only a handful of birds are found each year.

What the birds are attracted to in each of these locations are rocky, wave-exposed shorelines. I've been watching harlequin ducks in Rhode Island for 25 years, and I'm always amazed that they seem to prefer coastal locations where the water is rough and where rocks lie dangerously close to the surface. Like all the surfers I know, who look forward to gales building ever taller waves from the south, harlequin ducks appear to enjoy diving beneath crashing waves and riding out the turbulence. But it's not the "fun" factor that they base their habitat preferences on. Instead it's the availability of food. "It's not just a flat rock that the water in these locations is boiling over," Mittelhauser said. "It's a mangled rock with all these little crevices and things, and I bet you'd find clouds of amphipods in these little protected crevices on the rocks. My hunch is that there are a lot of amphipods that cling to the seaweed attached to those rocks. So the harlequins are keying in on those sites where they can get access to those clouds of amphipods."

What is particularly noteworthy about their choice of wintering habitat is how committed they are to returning year after year to the same tiny patch of shoreline. One of Mittelhauser's first harlequin duck research projects attempted to assess their movement on their wintering grounds by banding ducks from one location and observing their movement and rate of return in subsequent years. "It was really a site fidelity study, and we've really teased out some interesting bits of data," he said. "It's clear that they are highly site specific. The harlequins we banded on this one section of shoreline on the east of Isle au Haut hang out here on this ledge and maybe move another ledge or two over, and that's it. That's their entire winter range: less than a mile. And they come back here year after year. There's another group that hangs out on the other side of Isle au Haut [a mile away], and they stay over there. You can speculate that they're getting to know a site really well so they know all the microsites where they can find amphipods in the dead of winter."

But that's not the only reason they are so closely tied to a small wintering area. It also helps them find their mates. On their breeding grounds, harlequin ducks split up soon after their eggs are laid. The female sticks around to raise the young while the male flies to the coast to molt. Since they mate for life, they need to find each other again before the next breeding season, which they do by returning to the same narrow wintering ground. "They need to both go back to the same winter site, they pair up again, and year after year it's the same pair that meets up again here in winter," Mittelhuaser said. "It's the monogamous part of the breeding cycle in this duck that helps to tie them to really specific areas in this fine detail."

Mittelhauser grew up in coastal Connecticut, where he took to the water early and did a great deal of sailing without paying much attention to the birds. He went to Maine to study whales at the College of the Atlantic, but got sidetracked by his ornithology and botany classes. He began studying harlequin ducks after volunteering to conduct fieldwork at Acadia National Park, and he later worked there part-time cataloging plants, animals, and birds at park-owned islands. Eventually he started a nonprofit agency, the Maine Natural History

Observatory, which is dedicated to inventorying and monitoring species and habitats along the Maine coast. He spends his winters studying birds and his summers studying plants, with his in-between time
spent producing island-specific field guides. And he can't imagine
wanting to do anything else.

My visit to Isle au Haut was an extension of Mittelhauser's site
fidelity study. Since 1996 he has banded about 400 harlequin ducks in
the waters off Isle au Haut, and many of those bands have letter and
number combinations that are large and distinctive so they can be read
from a distance without having to recapture the birds. Our plan for
the day was to watch the ducks coming and going and hope that they
climbed on some of the exposed rocks and turned their bodies just
right so we could read their bands from a telescope 75 yards away.

As we reached the observation point, Mittelhauser mentioned that
the birds are often alarmed by bright colors, so he advised me to remove my orange parka and drop my red backpack before I emerged
from the forest. Thankfully, the temperature had increased slightly
and the short hike had warmed me up a bit, but I knew that eventually I would need the coat again. As we settled in for several hours of
observation, I leaned against a tree to take in the scene. The rocks
upon which Mittelhauser said the birds would occasionally perch rose
about 15 feet out of the water on the western end and slope downward to the east where tiny ripples of surf occasionally rolled over
them. A great black-backed gull stood at the highest point of the rock,
but all of the other birds around were harlequins. Most were in the
water, diving for food or swimming in tight groups, but others were
perched on the rocks a foot or two above the water line. Perhaps
three-quarters of the ducks were males, and there were generally 40
to 50 harlequins in sight at any one time, though they were constantly
flying in and out of our viewing area so we probably saw 100 or more
different individuals during our 3-hour stay.

Mittelhauser quickly announced that he saw five harlequin ducks
on the rocks with white "field-readable" bands, but reading them at
such a distance was a challenge. Since the bands may be a decade or
more old, some have cracked or the printing has faded, and more
often than not the bands were twisted on the bird's leg in such a way
as to make it impossible to read from our vantage point. So we stared

through our binoculars and telescopes and hoped that the birds would switch position just enough so we could pick up on their distinct letter and number combinations. Before I could even find a banded bird in my binoculars, Mittelhauser and Smith found one bird that both agreed had a band imprinted with the letters EP, though upon further study they changed their minds and decided it was FP. That was a male harlequin that had been banded before its first birthday at the next cove to the west on April 16, 1999. It had been observed twenty-nine times since then, always within a mile of the Merchant Point Ledge where we were standing. When I finally figured out which bird they were watching, I could see the band but could not make out any lettering whatsoever, even through the telescope, so I assumed my nearsightedness was probably going to make the job of band-reading impossible for me. But I kept trying.

Shortly, a lobsterman motored in to the opposite side of the rocks and began to haul several traps. I was sure his arrival was going to frighten the birds away, but most ignored him, and those that took note just swam slowly away. That boldness is a helpful characteristic when approaching a group of ducks, according to Mittelhauser. "When you come up to the shore, there's often a bunch of eiders with the harlequins and sometimes other ducks, too, but the other ducks, especially the eiders, skitter away and just the harlequins are left. If you're looking for harlequins, you don't have to pay any attention to whatever is skittering away; you just watch what's left. The harlequins will flush eventually, but they tend to group up and take some time to decide what to do, so you've got some time to get a scope on them."

Another behavior that is seemingly unique to harlequin ducks is their propensity to swim in extremely tight groupings. Mittelhauser said that few other sea ducks move in such close arrangements, and those that do "tend to be feeding and aren't interacting with each other, except to give one an occasional poke when it's too close. When harlequins are in a tight group, there are lots of interactions going on— they're chasing each other, especially in the larger groups, there's a fair amount of squeaking going on, and they're much more active socially."

As we continued to watch the ducks, hoping to find one with a band that my poor eyes could read, I noted a tight group swimming with their faces in the water, peering in search of a meal. Then, almost in unison, they seemed to gently jump upward before jack-knifing beneath the surface in a feeding dive. Another group—seven males and one female—hopped out of the water onto the rock like penguins, so I grabbed the scope to get a better look. With the sun directly on them, they looked like models posed for the perfect cover photo. Their gorgeous plumage suggested eighteenth-century royal outfits, though they still seemed to act more like adolescents, constantly shuffling places, then jumping back into the water when another group flew in and landed nearby.

Mittelhauser pointed out another bird with a readable band—readable to him anyway. He debated with himself whether it was N9 or NP, eventually settling on N9 after staring at it for another 10 minutes. That bird had been banded nearby on April 20, 1999, but had only been seen once before in 2002, though its appearance again that day meant that it had likely been around every year since then. As Mittelhauser and Smith debated the letter combination on another band—"does that say JY?"—I simply enjoyed the antics of the ducks. They regularly flapped their wings vigorously, as if flying in place, perhaps just to stretch their flight muscles, but in doing so they often splashed water a great distance in the air, so maybe it was intended as a bath. Their frequent chases took on the appearance of either faster-than-normal swimming after one individual—usually several males swimming toward a lone female—or a short run or brief flight across the water's surface that generally split the group up momentarily before they all regrouped once again. The comings and goings of the harlequin ducks were certainly entertaining to me, but I was somewhat embarrassed that I was contributing little to the band-reading effort.

Eventually the sun moved directly in line with the rocks, making it very difficult to see the birds clearly and virtually impossible to read the bands, so we grabbed our lunches and relaxed for a bit. As we did, three herring gulls joined the lone great black-backed gull that was still perched atop the rock, and later a double-crested cormorant arrived and stood with its wings outstretched in the sun to dry. A flock of about thirty purple sandpipers eventually joined the other birds as well, though they were mostly out of view on the other side of the rock. The shorebird with the northernmost wintering range on the

East Coast, purple sandpipers are commonly found on the same rocks as wintering harlequins, but they wander around much more than do the ducks. Mittelhauser said that purple sandpiper resting locations are a good indicator of where harlequins may turn up next. He recently completed a 5-year census of purple sandpipers in Maine, which found about 12,000 of the hardy little birds wintering in the state, about half of which were on the mid-coast where most of the harlequins are found.

While we continued to eat lunch, two harlequins separated from the rest of the birds and slowly swam in our direction. As they approached, I noticed for the first time how small they were—closer in size to the smallest of the freshwater ducks, the green-winged teal, than to the rest of the sea ducks with which they are usually found. The birds didn't notice us until they were just 20 feet away, at which point I was hoping they were going to climb out of the water where I could finally get a chance to read their bands, but then they noticed our movement and cautiously circled back. They stopped, however, by the edge of a low rock protected from the surf. The female then seemed to flatten herself out and lower herself in the water, where-upon the male mounted her and they mated. It happened quickly, and yet I felt honored and somewhat embarrassed to have observed this intimate act so closely. But the act also appeared somewhat casual and they quickly returned to the rest of the flock. Mittelhauser interpreted their behavior as that of a long-term pair that had just found each other again after separating on the breeding grounds, and their mating was likely used to reestablish their pair bond.

With the sun in our eyes and the tide going out and exposing more rocks, behind which many of the ducks perched, we relocated about 200 yards away to get a different angle on the birds. As soon as we resettled, I located a group of six ducks through the telescope and was stunned—again—by their spectacular plumage. With the sun reflecting off the white markings on their faces, they reminded me of a mime in full makeup. But their face markings weren't the only white that appeared particularly bright. One duck's band was positioned just perfectly, and a brief glance was all it took for me to read it—9O. Mittelhauser reported that this bird had been banded in that exact spot on April 17, 2000, and observed 30 times since then, almost always there at Merchant Point Ledge, though a few times it was seen a half mile away at Squeaker Cove. When I pulled my eye away from the scope, I saw a small group of harlequins take off from the rocks and fly straight at us, veering off just before it appeared we could reach out and grab them, causing the three of us to call out in awe. That was the sign that told us to call it a day. In all, we had read the bands of eight harlequin ducks, all of which were captured and banded between 1998 and 2001 within a half mile of where we saw them that day.

As we left, Mittelhauser mentioned that eight of the 400 harlequin ducks he has banded in Maine were also fitted with satellite transmitters in 2000 to learn more about the long distance movement of the birds. About the size of a matchbook, the transmitters were surgically implanted in each bird's abdominal cavity by veterinarians with the Canadian Wildlife Service, and each had an antenna extending out from an incision in its back. "The biggest thing we learned from the satellite tags was that some of our males go to Greenland to molt, and that was totally unexpected," Mittelhauser said. "They winter in Maine, they breed in Labrador or Quebec, but some go to Greenland to molt. It seems bizarre, but not out of the ordinary for sea ducks. It's called the molt migration—migrating to a new site to molt that's safe from predators and has a good food supply, then migrating back here to Maine to winter." The females don't undertake this molt migration, because they remain on the breeding grounds to raise their young. Whether the females take an unexpected detour of their own somewhere remains a mystery for now, as they are too small to be fitted with satellite transmitters.

No one has been able to explain why the West Coast population of harlequin ducks is close to 100 times larger than the Eastern population, but speculation is that the Eastern group has always been small, perhaps never having been more than 10,000 individuals. Hints from the historical evidence suggest that the population had declined to just a few thousand by 1940 and to a low of 1,000 in the 1980s, primarily due to hunters interested in a trophy of the brightly colored males. Hunting of harlequin ducks was banned in the Canadian Maritimes in 1986 and in the rest of the Atlantic flyway by 1990 when they were designated as endangered by the Committee on the Status of Endangered Wildlife in Canada. They were listed as a threatened species in Maine, but as hunting pressures eased and the population began to recover, the U.S. Fish and Wildlife Service rejected a proposal to list them on the federal endangered species list in 1998. As their recovery continued, they were down-listed to "threatened" in Canada and to a "species of special concern" in Maine in 2001.

But that doesn't mean they are out of the woods just yet. With a population estimate of just 3,600 individuals wintering on the East Coast, harlequin duck numbers are half that of one of the rarest breeding birds in New England, the roseate tern, which is endangered in the United States and trending downward. Harlequins face a wide range of predators on their breeding grounds, especially hawks, eagles, mink, and marten, and flooding of breeding habitat by an increasing number of dams for hydropower in Quebec is a considerable concern. On their wintering grounds, Mittelhauser said there are no smoking guns. Harlequins are unusually skittish and flee from gray seals, but there is no evidence that seals kill harlequins. Oil spills on critical wintering territory could wreak havoc with the ecosystem, but there appears to be plenty of additional available habitat the birds could move into, at least along the Maine coast. Fishing and fishing nets don't seem to be a problem at this time, nor does increased aquaculture along coastal waters. "I'm encouraged that the population is coming up," Mittelhauser said, "but if that trend levels off and they quit increasing, then something else we don't know about is going on. Sitting on this coast, I don't see a whole lot of threat . . . My biggest concern would be if the state put them back on the hunting list. There's talk that if we get enough harlequins on this coast that [the hunters and state regulators are] going to want to put them back on the hunted list. If they did that, then I would be concerned that the take would be too high. A long-lived species with slow reproduction rates like harlequins can't take the same harvest levels as the freshwater ducks. I'd be very concerned if that happened."

While a return to hunting harlequins may have serious repercussions for the future of the ducks in eastern North America, another less obvious threat may already be taking its toll—mercury. The Biodiversity Research Institute—the same group noted previously for

studying contaminants in Leach's storm petrels—is a nonprofit research group focused on examining mercury contamination in a wide
variety of wildlife across the country, from loons and eagles to cray-
fish, otters, and salamanders. No one had evaluated mercury levels in
sea ducks before, so the group began the process by capturing 125 harlequins from Maine, Massachusetts, and Rhode Island in 2008 and
collecting blood and feather samples for laboratory analysis.

"Mercury contamination is a pretty wide-scale problem," explained
Lucas Savoy, the research biologist at the institute who is coordinating the harlequin study. "North America is getting quite a bit better,
and the Environmental Protection Agency has implemented some
strict regulations, but it is still a serious issue. A lot of the mercury
comes from local sources like hospital or hazardous waste incinerators
and construction waste like light switches and thermometers, as well
as from coal-burning plants in the Midwest. In Maine, about fifty percent of mercury pollution comes from outside the area—air deposi-
tion from the Midwest coming our way—and fifty percent is from
local incinerators."

Mercury that finds its way onto the land and water is converted by
bacteria into its most toxic form, methylmercury. From there it slowly
works its way up the food chain, from bacteria to phytoplankton to
insects and ultimately to birds and fish, accumulating in greater and
greater quantities the higher it goes. Savoy calls estuaries and salt
marshes a "breeding ground for mercury" because mercury from local
sources finds its way into the substrate exposed at low tides and accu-
mulates in mollusks and other aquatic invertebrates that filter out the
contaminants. It can be particularly problematic for those species, like
harlequins, that return regularly to the same breeding or wintering
site. If that site is near a local source of mercury, the contaminants ac-
cumulate year after year.

"Birds can't shed the mercury from their body," Savoy said. "They
can dump their body burdens of mercury into their feathers, but once
they fill their feathers, then it starts building up in their body tissues
again. So long-lived species like loons, eagles, and ducks are accumulating loads of mercury. It's a neurotoxin that affects their brains. It
can alter their behavior, like laying fewer eggs and not attending their
nests as long."

Before he started this study, the only clue Savoy had to the potential for mercury contamination in sea ducks came from a few samples collected from harlequin ducks from Kodiak Island and Unalaska Island in southwestern Alaska. Those samples varied tremendously, perhaps due to varying levels of local industrial effluent, with males and older birds containing slightly higher levels of mercury than females and juveniles. With nothing to compare it to, Savoy is uncertain whether the levels recorded were considered high or not and whether the mercury was having any noticeable impact on the health of the birds.

U.S. Environmental Protection Agency biologist Rick McKinney said there may be one more threat to harlequin duck wintering populations. He's worried about human disturbance of wildlife that use coastal habitats, particularly since development along the coastlines has never been greater. "Harlequins always intrigued me because they always seemed to be different from other wintering waterfowl in the area," McKinney said from his office at the EPA's Atlantic Ecology Division in Narragansett, Rhode Island. "In southern New England, there are these established wintering locations from the coast of New Hampshire to Rhode Island, and I was intrigued by the fact that they were using such discrete habitats. So my question is, why are they using such discrete habitats, and are humans having an impact on them because the birds have less flexibility in where they go?"

To answer those questions, McKinney examined the landscape around 12 harlequin duck wintering locations in Massachusetts and Rhode Island, calculating the extent of urbanization and other characteristics of human impact and comparing them to nearby sites where harlequin ducks were not found. As he wrote in *Northeast Naturalist* in 2007, harlequins "may be particularly vulnerable while concentrated on their wintering grounds, where even small, localized disturbances can affect substantial portions of the population . . . We found that the presence of harlequin ducks at a given site was negatively influenced by the extent of developed land within a 100 meter radius of the site. Thus, harlequin ducks that winter in southern New England are exposed and apparently respond to impacts from human disturbance." He noted, however, that the wintering sites he studied also had more food available to the ducks, so it is possible that the birds "are enduring the costs (e.g., increased migration, higher disturbance) of wintering at more southerly sites in order to take advantage of more abundant and accessible prey."

My wife Renay and I decided to visit several of the sites that McKinney studied in a whirlwind tour of Rhode Island to get a snapshot of the harlequin duck population in the state. Rhode Island is the southern anchor of the harlequin wintering population, with more ducks found in the smallest state than in all of Massachusetts, yet the dynamics of exactly where they are found has been shifting in recent years. According to a population analysis conducted by University of Rhode Island graduate student Christine Caron in 2006, about 150 harlequins winter in Rhode Island, almost entirely at three locations—Sachuest Point National Wildlife Refuge at the southeastern tip of Aquidneck Island, Beavertail State Park at the southern end of Conanicut Island, and Sakonnet Point in the town of Little Compton. Most of the birds have historically been found at Sachuest, but they have spread out a bit in recent years.

"The population at Beavertail is much more recent," Caron said. "There were very few individuals at Beavertail in the nineteen eighties and nineties, but since 2001 there have consistently been twenty or more birds there every winter." She believes that the reason for the population gains at Beavertail is that the increasing numbers of birds at Sachuest through the 1990s forced some harlequin ducks to look nearby for appropriate habitat.

Maine biologist Glen Mittelhauser noted that the Rhode Island population of harlequin ducks had slowly increased while the coastal Maine and Canada numbers were dropping due to hunting pressure. That may have been because hunting has long been prohibited at the Rhode Island sites. But Rhode Island numbers are leveling off now while Maine numbers are showing modest growth.

It was just 16 degrees at 7 A.M. on the Saturday after Thanksgiving in 2007 when Renay and I went in search of Rhode Island's harlequin duck population. Arriving at our first stop, Beavertail, after passing multi-million-dollar homes well hidden behind gates and naturally landscaped yards on the road leading to the park, we scanned the west side of the point and saw little but a small flock of common eider, mostly females and juveniles. A double-crested cormorant flew by as we glanced around, and a common loon sat low in the water way off in the distance, but otherwise it was very quiet, save for the park's foghorn. When we reached the southern point, where the foghorn was located, the pulsing electronic sound was intense and almost painful. Not a cloud was in the sky, let alone fog, so there appeared to be no reason to sound the horn, but it blasted away every 15 seconds anyway. So we avoided the point—thankfully there wasn't much in the way of ducks to see there anyway—and headed around to the east side of the park and slowly worked our way northward.

Barely past the park's historic lighthouse we saw our first pair of harlequins, quite close to shore. They were mostly preening, riding the lightly rolling waves in and out, and occasionally diving for food. The glare of the sun made it difficult to get good looks at them, so we kept walking and scanning the nearby water. Fifty yards further north, three eiders were floating alongside a group of nine harlequins—six adult males, two females and one juvenile male—all actively diving and feeding. A flock of seven more harlequins flew by in a tight formation, then circled back and landed next to the first group. The new flock swam in such close quarters that it was difficult to even count them, but eventually they loosened up and mixed with the others. As we turned to walk away, we heard the sound of their nasally whistle call, which made Renay laugh, remembering the story I had written earlier that year about my confusion one morning between the sound of a distant wood thrush and the sound of her nose whistling. Just then, all of the harlequins flew off together, quickly separating into what I suspected was their original flocks, with the group of seven returning to the north while the others circled way out over the bay, turned south, and disappeared into the glare.

Continuing along a ridge overlooking the rocky shoreline, we aimed toward what appeared to be the northernmost point on the eastern side of the park, where we could see a flock of more than thirty eiders loafing and preening. As we approached, we passed a flock of ten harlequins well camouflaged on a low rock covered in green and brown algae. At the end of the path, we climbed out on the rocks to complete our survey and noted one last flock of nine harlequin males swimming tightly amid growing waves while chasing a lone female. It looked like the males were jockeying for position at the start of an automobile race, with the female serving as the pace car just a few lengths ahead. When they disappeared around the point, we turned to retrace our steps, noting for the first time the tiny frozen tide pools and numerous vein-like intrusions of quartz in the rocks we had walked upon.

According to geologists, 550 million years ago the rocks at Beavertail were part of an island off the coast of Africa that eventually moved across what became the Atlantic Ocean. The rocks were fractured and folded when the continents of North America and Africa collided about 250 million years ago, which transformed them from sedimentary rock to metamorphic phyllite, somewhat like slate. Evidence of the African origin of the rocks at Beavertail is found in the fossilized trilobites found there, which are the same species as those found in Africa and Europe.

Twenty-five minutes later, Renay and I arrived at Sachuest Point National Wildlife Refuge, a military post during World War II used by the Army as a fire control point and by the Navy as a small arms firing range and communications station. We walked the perimeter path, starting on the west side overlooking the deserted Sachuest Beach, which is mobbed with bathers in the summer. The water is always quiet on the beach side of the point, so harlequins are seldom found there. Instead, a large flock of buffleheads mixed with three red-necked grebes, one horned grebe, and a flock of female goldeneyes glided through the still water. At the point, where one can usually find large numbers of eiders along with black, surf, and white-winged scoters—all commonly seen wintering sea ducks—just one common loon was in view. Around the corner, however, was our first flock of eiders, perhaps a dozen of them, and then a group of eight male harlequins chasing two females. Then another group of five male harlequins and one female appeared, eventually mixing with the larger group. But just like at Beavertail, the glare of the sun made it difficult to watch them for very long.

The east side of the refuge is usually where most of the sea ducks are found, but it was unusually quiet, perhaps because the water was too still for their liking. As we walked, I raised my binoculars several

times to look at several black lobster buoys that I thought were scoters. Six fishermen, each with multiple rods, stood on the rocks waiting for the fish to bite, and their activity may also have explained the
absence of birds, though four brants—seagoing geese that feed on eelgrass—stood on a rock near the fishermen, oblivious to or uninterested in the human disturbance.

At Island Rocks, where the harlequins, scoters, and eiders are usually abundant, the very low tide exposed seldom-seen rocks, the water
lapped at the shore, and a loud family enjoying the holiday weekend
walked the beach. Few of the usual birds were visible. We briefly saw
two flocks of harlequins, totaling about twenty-two birds, mostly
males, but they swam to the back side of the furthest rocks and disappeared from sight. Several more flew in to the same spot, while others
flew back out, making it hard to know exactly how many birds were
in the area. On a very distant small rock emerging from the surf to the
north of Island Rocks sat three harlequins, while four more caroused
in the water. As we squinted through our binoculars to watch them,
a flock of about 100 purple sandpipers flew off en masse, circled over
the open water, and disappeared behind the largest of the Island
Rocks, then returned to their starting point only to fly off once more.
Five kayakers boisterously paddled through, so we moved on. Across
the water, we glanced at Sakonnet Point, our final stop of the day.

When we arrived there an hour later, workers were removing the
floating docks from the tiny Sakonnet marina beside a boarded-up
restaurant that was probably quite magnificent in its day. It had been
15 years since I had last been to the point, so I wasn't entirely sure
where to expect the ducks, and a quick glance around didn't provide
any clues about where to start. So we walked to the end of a seawall
protecting the harbor to get a view of a section of rocky coastline that
looked auspicious. The water was clean and clear with a good view of
the sandy bottom and gently swaying seaweed 6 or 8 feet below, but the
only birds we spotted were herring and great black-backed gulls. We
walked a short distance in the opposite direction, but while we saw
no other birds we did spy some promising coastline in the distance.

So we drove around the corner and down a dead-end street, parked
illegally, and walked along a cobble beach posted with signs indicating that it was only for town residents and their guests. Despite their

massive size, most of the homes appeared unoccupied and locked up tightly for the winter, so we proceeded through the gate anyway. We quickly noted a handful of ducks leaping off a rock 50 yards from the shoreline. As we approached to get a better view, two harlequins took flight, but five more—four males and a female—remained along with three eiders and two buffleheads. Soon they, too, disappeared into the rapidly retreating sun, leaving us to study an unexpectedly large variety of seaweed exposed by the tides. My seaweed identification skills were still in their infancy, but I tried to give each a name anyway. One that looked like bright green grass, probably gut weed or stone hair, covered the tops of most of the rocks, while a red parsley-like variety was almost certainly the wonderfully named Turkish washcloth. The flat, greenish-brown fronds of Irish moss were interspersed with several varieties of rockweed, including one with air sacs that looked like chicken's feet. We also noted an olive-green species with a disk-shaped air sac from the genus *Ascophyllum*, as well as another with the disturbing yet descriptive name of dead man's fingers. All are quite common along the New England shoreline, but I still was pleased to have been able to give a name to most of them.

I was less pleased with all the private roads in the area that stymied our further attempts to find another access point to view what appeared to be more good harlequin duck habitat nearby. Yet in the end, I was content that we had found about half of the total number of harlequins that winter in Rhode Island. And with their New England wintering population steadily on the rise after a worrisome decline, it is satisfying to note that the clown of the waterfowl world seems somewhat secure for now.

11

Basking Shark

"If it's a big fish, then I'm infatuated with it."

It sounded funny when he first said it, but after talking with Greg Skomal for a while, it's easy to see how passionate he is about big fish. While he collaborates on research about giant bluefin tuna, and he did a little work with marlins in the 1990s, the big fish he's usually talking about are sharks. If you want to know something about sharks in New England waters, Skomal is one of the most knowledgeable people to talk to. That was the case when the producers of my favorite television show, *Dirty Jobs*, were looking for a shark expert to follow, and that's often the case when documentary filmmakers are looking for footage of sharks in the region. And it hardly matters what species of shark they're interested in.

"If there's a shark that occurs in New England waters, I'm doing something with it," he said. "I've got a big project going on with porbeagle sharks; I'm dealing with blues, makos, and threshers, which are the most common sharks here; my holy grail is the white shark, which I dabble with and continue to find; and then I do a lot of work with coastal species that rely on estuarine habitat—sandbar sharks, duskies, sand tigers, smooth dogfish, and spiny dogfish. And I collaborate with people studying sharks in other parts of the world, too—bull sharks in Louisiana, black tips and lemons in the Caribbean, gray reef sharks in the central Pacific, and Greenland sharks around the Arctic Circle."

A relaxed and friendly guy with windblown hair and an easy laugh, Skomal looks like he has spent his whole life on the water. And while that's not entirely true, he certainly knew from a very young age that he wanted to pursue a career in the marine sciences. He grew up in southern Connecticut, and his family had a home in the Caribbean that they visited regularly. It was there that he fell in love with the ocean and became obsessed with fish. But at the time he was sure that his future was going to revolve around studying coral reefs, which he found a way to study in high school and continued while earning two degrees at the University of Rhode Island.

"The big crossroads of my life, when sharks entered the picture and coral reefs spun out, was when I was a senior in college and I volunteered for the Cooperative Shark Tagging Program with the National Marine Fisheries Service," he recalled. "I was supposed to be spending my final semester in the Caribbean, but I was offered an opportunity to study shark biology. And that was it."

That experience lasted through graduate school and led to his current position as a shark biologist with the Massachusetts Division of Marine Fisheries, based on Martha's Vineyard. I tracked him down in the summer of 2007 because of his reputation as New England's leading expert on basking sharks (*Cetorhinus maximus*), the second largest fish in the sea and the largest by far in New England waters. As their name suggests, basking sharks are often found basking at the surface of the water in the summer and early fall in the Gulf of Maine, Cape Cod Bay, and other adjacent waters. But very little is known about them, which is surprising given their massive size—up to 35 feet long and weighing as much as 5 tons. In an effort to learn more about their life history and discover where they go when they leave New England, Skomal tags basking sharks to learn their secrets, and he invited me to join him.

"The basking shark is kind of like a whale trapped in the body of a shark," he said. "Their most outstanding attribute is their large size, but as far as sharks are concerned, they're atypical because they're planktivores—they feed entirely on plankton. But for being such a conspicuous animal, it's remarkable that we don't know much about how it lives, how long it lives, how it spends its time, even its general distribution is still a bit of a mystery."

I met Skomal at a marina in Scituate, Massachusetts, early one September morning on board the *Wake Up Call*, a luxurious 61-foot Viking sportfishing yacht owned by a local hotel executive and registered in the Marshall Islands with a full-time crew of two. It wasn't the typical vessel from which Skomal conducts his research, but a documentary film crew had chartered the boat for 2 weeks to shoot footage of basking sharks, and Skomal was their guide. Despite our early arrival, we didn't depart the harbor until 8:50, long after Skomal had hoped, as the film crew took their time getting ready and insisted on a full leisurely breakfast, even though Skomal assured them that it was better to start early to beat the approaching weather conditions. As we finally left the dock and rounded the breakwater, Skomal clapped his hands together with excitement and shouted "Here we go!" in anticipation of a successful day of basking shark tagging.

I had never been on such a fancy boat before, and since we had a 30-minute ride ahead of us before arriving at our destination, I decided to explore the accommodations. The interior of the main level had a leather upholstered U-shaped couch that seats eight, a fully stocked kitchen with stove, three bedrooms—two with queen-sized beds and multiple dressers and closets—and a large bathroom with shower and mirrored ceiling. After climbing up one level using an outside ladder, I found Captain Bob at the controls, which looked by its abundance of electronics like the NASA control room and had additional seating for ten. There were two more levels above that were primarily used as observation decks, the uppermost of which has additional controls for operating the boat but can barely squeeze three standing bodies.

We were headed for a point on the southwest edge of Stellwagen Bank, just north of the line between Boston and Provincetown, where the water was 200 feet deep and about 62 degrees. On our way out, very little wildlife was about—just a few gulls, a handful of common and Forster's terns, and one greater shearwater gliding across the water's surface. When the boat stopped, two shark spotters climbed to the top of the tower where they stayed for the remainder of the day. The rest of us scanned the water while waiting for the arrival of a small plane hired to search the region for congregations of basking sharks. A smaller boat pulled up alongside us as we waited, and Skomal and most of the film crew jumped aboard so they could get closer to any basking sharks we might find. Two humpback whales spouted off in the distance, and then Captain Bob pointed out some thrashing in the water nearby that might have been feeding tuna.

Finally the plane flew over and checked in on the radio, then departed in search of sharks. Twenty minutes later, when the pilot still hadn't reported any shark sightings, Skomal and the film crew started to worry. Just as they began discussing alternative plans, the pilot reported a single basking shark four miles north, and after a short discussion to decide whether it was worthwhile to chase a single shark—they were primarily looking for large groupings to film—we raced off to find it.

The plane circled overhead as we arrived at the site, and the pilot began giving detailed instructions of where the shark was in relation to the boat. "It's eight or nine boat lengths away, off at twelve o'clock. Now he's ten lengths at two o'clock coming right at you. No, now he's turning, now four boat lengths off the stern." No one in either boat had yet seen the shark, but the view from the plane directly above was apparently quite clear. For nearly an hour, the pilot tried to guide the small boat close to the shark, but the fish repeatedly changed course or casually glided too deep for us to see it. As we continually maneuvered the boats following the directions from above, a fin whale coasted by us and for a moment everyone aboard wondered aloud if the plane's pilot had mistaken the whale for a basking shark.

But he hadn't. The pilot announced that the basking shark had a large white patch behind its dorsal fin, which the spotters in the tower claimed to see momentarily, yet despite their efforts to point it out to me, I never could find it. It was a frustrating time for the entire crew because the animal was uncharacteristically moving around a great deal, making it impossible to approach. With a big grin and a hint of sarcasm, Pete Rudd, the first mate on the *Wake Up Call*, called out sarcastically to everyone within earshot that "this basking shark is basking at eighteen knots!"

Discouraged with the time lost unsuccessfully chasing that one shark, Skomal told the pilot to go off in search of a larger grouping of sharks, and that was when the single shark decided to make an appearance close to the boat. It quietly glided beneath the bow to much excitement, yet all I could make out was a blurry whitish patch in the water. And then it disappeared again, this time for good.

Basking sharks (*Cetorhinus maximus*) range throughout much of the Atlantic and Pacific oceans, as well as in the Mediterranean Sea, the Sea of Japan, and in the waters to the south of Australia. They appear a mottled grayish-brown in color and, due to their large size and conical snout, they are often mistaken for great white sharks. They have as many as 100 rows of tiny teeth, which surprisingly serve very little purpose. Instead, they have long gill slits that extend almost entirely around their bodies and bristle-like gill rakers that enable them to filter huge quantities of plankton from the water simply by swimming around slowly with their enormous mouths wide open.

"Their feeding ecology is very similar to that of the right whale," noted Skomal. "They expand their buccal cavity—their mouth—as wide as they can, taking in massive quantities of water. Then the water passes over the gills like over the baleen of a whale. They capture their food in mucus on the gill rakers and it is funneled down their throat. They eat mostly copepods, and they seem to require high concentrations of these creatures in order for them to feed. It takes a lot of energy to open up their umbrella—their mouth—and push it through the water, so it's got to be worthwhile for them, which means there has got to be high concentrations of copepods. It's generally considered that basking sharks are fond of productive areas off the New England coast that are loaded with these copepods, so we find large congregations of basking sharks forming in our waters."

The copepod preferred most by basking sharks is *Calanus finmarchicus*, a small crustacean somewhat like a shrimp about the size of a grain of rice. Despite their small size, they are tremendously rich and nutritious—sort of like eating butter, according to one expert.

The congregations of basking sharks feeding on *Calanus* provide great insight into the sharks' behaviors, though they also raise as many questions as they answer. Spotter pilots flying over Cape Cod Bay and the Gulf of Maine in search of tuna or right whales have reported several hundred basking sharks feeding together in dense patches. Some biologists speculate that it may be courtship or mating behavior, while others believe the sharks have simply found a dense aggregation of copepods in a preferred water temperature.

When they get together in these groupings, it's not uncommon to find them doing what Skomal calls cartwheeling, which is "when you get a few to a couple dozen animals swimming nose to tail in a circular pattern. In the three dimensions of the water column down several meters, you get these animals stacked on top of each other in a circular pattern. Perhaps it's courtship behavior or a precursor to mating behavior. 'We're all together feeding anyway, guys, so why don't we screw?' But that's entirely anecdotal. No one has ever seen the mating behavior. But from diving in these groups, I don't think that's the case. We've not seen a single male in those groups—it's all females. It points to sexual segregation that's occurring here. If it's not for mating or courtship, then why are they following each other nose to tail? It could be a means to orient to a patch of food and orient to each other in a productive feeding area. If you find a patch and you keep turning, you stay in the patch."

Another basking shark behavior that Skomal says is particularly noteworthy is breaching—jumping out of the water and landing with a big splash. It's a basking shark behavior that is seldom observed anywhere but in New England waters and occasionally off the coast of Great Britain. "We don't even know why whales breach, so we're certainly light years away from understanding why basking sharks breach," he said. "Typically, when a fish breaches, it's trying to remove some sort of parasite, which is a possibility with basking sharks, too. Many have large parasitic lampreys on them, which can do some destruction to their tissues. Maybe it's some sort of social or communication mechanism, though I have no reason to believe that's the case. Maybe it's some other physiological mechanism, or maybe it's to clean their gill rakers. We just don't know."

There is plenty more that isn't known about basking sharks. For instance, their reproductive biology, growth rate, age at maturity, life span, and population are all big question marks to the scientific community. It is believed that their eggs hatch in utero and they give birth to live pups after a gestation period of perhaps 1 or 2 or 3 years. No one knows how large they are at birth—the smallest basking shark ever recorded was about 5½ feet long—or how many young are in a typical litter. And because they are seldom seen in the winter when they are likely giving birth, many of these questions will be difficult to answer.

Lisa Natanson, a fisheries biologist with the National Marine Fisheries Service's Apex Predators Investigation, working in collaboration with Sabine Witna from South Africa, has tried to learn how to determine the age of a basking shark, but the usual methods don't seem to work.

"For standard age and growth studies of fish, you need their backbones," she said. "Basking sharks sometimes wash up on shore off Cape Cod, so over the years I had collected seven backbones to analyze. Sabine had collected additional samples from all over the world, including some pretty old ones, but many of them didn't have much information about where they came from or when they were collected. Normally when you do age and growth studies, you can count pairs of bands in the vertebrae, like tree rings, and there is one band pair per year, but that doesn't seem to be the case with basking sharks."

If each band pair represents one year in its life, as has been proven with most fish, every vertebra from the animal's head to its tail should have the same number of band pairs. But what Natanson found was that the number of band pairs changed dramatically along the vertebral column of each individual shark. There were often many fewer band pairs in a vertebra analyzed from near the neck or tail than from one in the middle of its column.

"The bottom line is that we don't think the bands are annual," Natanson said, "so if you just count the bands you would not get an accurate age. Instead, we think that band pairs are related to growth rather than time. So they grow a certain amount and put on a band, grow a little more and put on another band. And the bands are calcified, which means they are probably more structural than anything else."

Much of the basic anatomy of basking sharks was learned in the middle of the 1900s when a harpoon fishery for them developed in the waters of New England, the Canadian Maritimes, and Great Britain to harvest their livers for oil. Basking sharks have a massive liver that accounts for approximately 25 percent of their entire body weight and that makes them nearly neutrally buoyant. While the fishery helped to develop a basic understanding of these magnificent creatures, it also led to a dramatic decline in their population. And it also created a great deal of confusion.

"The scientists in the eastern Atlantic that were cutting them up in the fisheries in the nineteen fifties found evidence that basking sharks lose their gill rakers in the winter," said Skomal. "So based on this, they surmised that basking sharks must shed their gill rakers in the winter and go into deep water, stop feeding, and hibernate. This hypothesis lasted for decades. We had anecdotal reports of basking sharks in the Gulf of Mexico and off the coast of Florida every now and then, but given the large numbers that occurred in the summer and fall off New England and Great Britain, there was still the feeling that maybe they just disappear in the winter. But there's no evidence that any species of shark hibernates."

The mystery started to unravel when new fish tagging technologies were developed in the 1990s.

Skomal's objective on the day of my visit was to use a long pole to attach a satellite tag to several basking sharks without having to get in the water with the animals. He had tried tagging sharks while under water with them, but it was very difficult to get enough leverage to sink it beneath the shark's tough skin while swimming alongside them. He knew that if he could get the boat close enough to the animal, he could poke the tag right behind the dorsal fin without even getting wet.

But back on board the *Wake Up Call*, we hadn't heard from the pilot for more than an hour. Everyone speculated he was having lunch in Provincetown while we waited expectantly for the crackle of his call on the radio, when finally he reported in at 12:45 that a group of five basking sharks was 8 miles away. So we dashed off to find them, passing a group of four humpback whales and a flock of thirty rednecked phalaropes along the way. By the time we arrived, the sharks had dispersed and gone deep, but then the pilot announced that a group of three of them had resurfaced a quarter mile ahead.

When we got there, I was the first to spot a dorsal fin at the surface—not sharp or scythe-like as in most sharks and whales, but more like a fat triangle with slightly rounded sides—and the small boat with Skomal and the film crew moved in to get a closer look. It was disappointing to me that the vessel that I was on had to stay a hundred yards away while the other boat approached the basking shark, but as it did so, the animal disappeared. As we lingered in the distance, the first mate started taking pictures of the spotters in the tower and me one level below. While we stared toward the camera, a basking shark appeared in the water right behind the photographer, swimming about five feet beneath the surface and less than 10 feet from the side of the boat, parallel to us on the starboard side. Standing on the third level, 20 feet above the water, I stared straight down at it, my first clear look at a basking shark. It was about 25 feet long—nearly half the length of the boat—and it appeared to be an odd pale blue-green color, clearly the shape of a shark and not a whale, with its tail undulating from side to side like a fish and not up and down like a whale. I didn't notice any mottling in its coloration, but in my excitement it was difficult to take in all the details. It disappeared quickly, but it didn't give me any time to celebrate the sighting. Moments later it circled back and swam directly beneath the boat, but it was deeper, perhaps 10 or 15 feet below the surface, so all I saw was a blur. By the time Skomal arrived on the scene, it was gone again.

And then I spotted another fin, about halfway between the boats. This one seemed to take its name seriously, basking at the surface, even as the boat slowly approached. I watched through my binoculars as both the shark's fin and the boat came into one field of view, and then Skomal lifted his long harpoon-like pole with the tag on it, looking like I imagined Queequeg did in *Moby-Dick*. My anxiety rose as the boat appeared well within range of the shark to tag it, and yet Skomal still didn't move. Then, with the boat almost on top of the basking shark, Skomal raised his body on his toes and thrust the pole downward with all his might, landing the tag perfectly just at the base of the shark's dorsal fin. The biologist then shoved down hard on the pole once more to ensure the tag had released from the harpoon, then yanked back on the pole, leaving behind the tag embedded in the shark. The animal responded to the irritation with a small splash at the surface, then dove deep.

As the whole team savored the success of a well-inserted tag, the spotters in the tower called out that another basking shark was 50 yards in front of us. Through my binoculars, I had a perfect view of the large shark at the surface, pointed away from us, basking content-edly. It looked muddier in color than the one I had seen well beside the boat earlier, and it had a bright red tag behind its dorsal fin. It was the same animal we had just tagged, back at the surface and seemingly unconcerned that we were still there.

The film crew diver had been in and out of the water with his bulky camera several times during the day, every time we were somewhat close to a basking shark, but he had never yet seen any sharks under water. The murky, plankton-filled waters made visibility beneath the surface less than five feet, and he was clearly frustrated with his in-ability to get any usable footage. But the cooperative, tagged basking shark was his best opportunity, so he slid into the water and resurfaced 5 minutes later with what he said were superb close-up shots.

The pilot went out again in search of additional basking sharks, and I took some notes while listening to the chatter on the radio of a dis-cussion between Skomal and Captain Bob about where to go and what to do next. I was surprised to realize that there had been no gulls or terns or other birds around for nearly 2 hours on a day when they should have been everywhere. The only bird present was a weary blackpoll warbler, a tiny songbird that nests in the boreal forests of Canada and migrates south almost entirely over water, taking off from New England and landing again in South America. The one that landed on the boat was exhausted or disoriented and seemed to need to catch its breath. I reached out toward it, and it allowed me to touch its feet before flitting to the upper level and eventually continuing on its way.

After an hour of chasing single basking sharks without any success, the pilot spotted a group of seven circling at the surface. Even with-out my binoculars I could clearly see three fins and one tail—the tail is much sharper and narrower than the dorsal fin, and the huge dis-tance between the fin and the tail suggested that this animal was a massive creature. While the diver slipped into the water and filmed spectacular images from the middle of the circle of sharks, those of us in the *Wake Up Call* noticed a big splash about 200 yards away and then saw masses of bait fish—what Captain Bob called half-beaks—escaping from a school of feeding tuna. Two of the tuna followed the half-beaks into the air, leaping from the water like dolphins, and when they re-entered the water with another big splash, even more half-beaks leapt from the water in a rush to escape, skimming the surface for 30 yards or more like they were running on the water.

When the diver was back in the boat, two more basking sharks sat quietly side by side at the surface beyond where the tuna had been. The small boat approached, going too fast by my judgment, yet one shark remained at the surface, and in one smooth motion, Skomal jammed a tag behind its dorsal fin. My line of sight was briefly blocked, but confirmation of the success of the tagging operation came when I heard Skomal exclaim loudly "Yeah," which he followed by pumping his fist in the air and then sprinting in place. It was quite a celebration.

We never saw that shark resurface, and we never heard from the plane again, so we turned the boats around and returned to port.

The tag that Skomal was using is called a real-time satellite tag. Every time the shark was near the water's surface basking and the tag's antenna poked into the air, it transmitted data about its location via satellite directly to Skomal's computer. The tag also collects information about water temperature, depth, salinity, and light levels, which helps to pinpoint its preferred habitat type. Skomal placed his first tag on a basking shark in 2001, but since 2004 he has been aggressively tagging as many animals as he can to try to answer some of the lingering questions about the life history of basking sharks, especially where reproduction occurs and where their nursery areas are located.

"We can't tell if there are any anthropogenic impacts on their young until we know where their nursery areas are," he said. "The fact that we haven't found it yet suggests that it's far away from us, and probably far from fishing areas. So we still have these questions about the movement patterns of these animals when they leave New England, and how do those movements fit into their life history."

What Skomal quickly learned from his first satellite-tagged bask-ing sharks is that they don't bask at the surface when they leave New England. That means that the tag's antenna never breaks the surface, never communicates with the satellite, and never downloads data about the shark's whereabouts after leaving the area.

"Satellite tags work great on animals that come to the surface to breathe, like marine mammals and sea turtles, but they don't work well on animals that don't," he said.

So he instead began using a pop-up archival tag, which is similar to the tags used on bluefin tuna and other species. When attached to an animal, it collects and archives data on the water temperature, depth, and light levels, and at a designated time typically 6 to 8 months—a release mechanism detaches the tag from the animal and the device floats to the surface, whereupon it transmits the data via satellite. Based on what is known about the temperature and depth of the world's oceans and the amount of daylight in a given day every-where around the world, those data can be used to recreate the three-dimensional movements of the shark. According to Skomal, this type of analysis doesn't provide the fine-scale movements that a satellite tag would, but it's relatively easy to piece together the movement patterns of animals that travel great distances.

And that is exactly what basking sharks do.

"What we learned about their distribution indicates that we had no clue of the extent of their movement patterns," Skomal said. "Bask-ing sharks are typically thought of as temperate species, but they're not. They move as far south as the equator and off South America, but also spend a lot of time in the Caribbean, the Bahamas, in the Sargasso Sea, where we never thought this animal even occurred. It has broad movement patterns of thousands of miles and great changes of depth. When they get to tropical waters, they prefer to stay at great depth in excess of 300 to 600 meters and as deep as 1,000 meters. That was re-ally eye-opening for us. It's pretty clear that the basking shark is mis-named. We found that sharks that leave New England move rapidly to depth and traverse these tropical areas where people never knew they existed. They seem to have a temperature range that is fairly re-stricted. They are ectothermic, which means that their body temper-ature is within a degree or two of the water temperature. If it's making broad movements to tropical waters where the surface temperature is warm, it goes down to depth to stay at its preferred temperature range. There's got to be some reason that makes it profitable to move from productive shelf waters to subtropical waters."

This discovery, while exciting, also points to more and more questions. Why are they traveling so far? Why not just go to the deep waters off Florida or Georgia rather than continuing all the way to South America? Skomal speculates that it may be that wherever they go after leaving New England is a stable environment with few predators where there is probably excellent foraging habitat for their young.

Unfortunately, the two tags Skomal placed on the sharks during my visit provided little additional insight. The tag on one basking shark apparently malfunctioned, as it never transmitted any data whatsoever, while the other shark remained in Cape Cod Bay through most of November and then disappeared for the winter, presumably to the deep sea somewhere. But that shark resurfaced the following year off the coast of New Jersey as it moved from its deeper winter habitat back onto the continental shelf for the spring and summer.

While previous tags on basking sharks have helped to learn a great deal about their movements, tagging has also contributed to what is known about the many other shark species that are found in New England waters. Lisa Natanson and her colleague in the NMFS Apex Predators Investigation, Nancy Kohler, showed me a map indicating where blue sharks tagged in the Northeast have traveled, and I was amazed to see that they've been recaptured almost everywhere in the North Atlantic, as well as in the Mediterranean Sea and the South Atlantic. "Sharks are highly mobile and pelagic species," Kohler said, "so it's not unusual to see them go this far. Few sharks are found in our waters year round."

Blue sharks are the species that recreational shark fishermen in New England are most likely to catch. The biologists said that the blue sharks in northern waters tend to be smaller than those in the south, while those in the Mediterranean are the smallest of them all, and it's the biggest individuals that tend to migrate the farthest.

There are 453 species of sharks worldwide, according to a 2005 taxonomical listing, and 39 species are managed along the East Coast and Gulf of Mexico, 19 of which are illegal to possess. While 15 shark species in total are likely to occur within 50 miles of coastal New England in a typical year, fishermen should expect to encounter only half that many in the region—blue, mako, thresher, porbeagle, tiger, dusky, sandbar, and white—not counting the spiny dogfish, the smallest shark in New England and one that is managed more like a groundfish than a shark.

One way that Natanson and Kohler study sharks is by monitoring shark fishing tournaments in New England to gather tissue samples. The fishermen generally take the meat from their catch but allow scientists to examine the body before they do so, which makes for an easy and inexpensive way for the biologists to collect information for their studies of shark aging, sexual maturity, growth, food, and habitat. They also collect weight and measurement data on all of the animals brought to the dock at these tournaments.

Shark fishing in New England started in the 1960s and 1970s as a way for sport fishermen to capture big fish early in the season before tuna arrived in the area later in the summer, but it has become an industry unto itself and now shark fishing tournaments are held from June through September. Kohler said that these tournaments are managed well and have stringent rules, so they are not a threat to the population of any shark species.

"New England has no specific threats to sharks that we can pinpoint," she said. "But the general threats to sharks worldwide affect sharks here because our sharks are highly migratory."

The biggest threat to sharks worldwide is finning, the practice of cutting off the fins of sharks and throwing the still-living fish back into the ocean to die. Dried shark fins can be sold for up to $400 per pound for use in shark-fin soup, a delicacy in Asia, or for traditional medicines. As many as 73 million sharks per year are killed worldwide for their fins, mostly in the waters of Europe, Asia, South America, and the Persian Gulf, to supply the growing Asian market.

The practice has contributed to what some scientists are calling a global collapse of large shark populations. While finning is illegal in U.S. waters, that doesn't mean that it hasn't impacted the sharks that spend part of the year here. According to Julia Baum at Dalhousie

University in Nova Scotia, some of the shark species that once had been dominant along the East Coast, including tiger, dusky and scalloped hammerhead sharks, she now considers "functionally extinct." And the loss of the top predator in the food chain may be having far-reaching effects.

It is unknown how many basking shark fins are turning up in the Asian fin market, but Skomal believes that any that do are probably not being captured by American fishermen in New England waters. However, a paper published in 2007 in *Animal Conservation* by Jennifer Magnussen of the Guy Harvey Research Institute at Nova Southeastern University suggests that basking sharks are "exceptionally sensitive to overexploitation." And with the increasing demand for shark fins, she reported that one large basking shark fin was sold for $57,000.

Basking sharks are one of just three shark species in the world officially protected from overexploitation by the Convention on International Trade in Endangered Species. It is also fully protected from commercial harvest in the territorial waters of the United States and Great Britain, and partially protected in New Zealand. It is listed by the World Conservation Union as vulnerable throughout its range and endangered in the North Pacific and Northeast Atlantic regions, and in 2005 it was added to the Convention on Migratory Species that aims to strengthen international conservation efforts. But it is still facing hard times.

In her paper, Magnussen noted that it is difficult to assess the full extent of the basking shark harvest and trade because most nations don't collect information about their shark fisheries by individual species, and, more importantly, identifying shark products by species is extremely difficult, especially for non-experts like customs inspectors or fisheries enforcement personnel. Using genetic markers, Magnussen developed a way of identifying basking shark meat and fins, and she tested nineteen samples from fish markets in Japan and Hong Kong. She determined that sixteen of them came from basking sharks. She also used the test on shark fins confiscated in a law enforcement investigation by the National Oceanic and Atmospheric Administration in the U.S. and found two basking shark fins.

"Our unambiguous identification of several basking shark fins in a fin market survey, and documentation of contemporary illegal trade

in this species in a country with among the most regulated and en-
forced shark fisheries in the world, is consistent with the notion that
the high market value of basking shark fins will continue to drive ex-
ploitation and trade surreptitiously and otherwise," Magnussen wrote.

The fin trade isn't the only threat that basking sharks face, however.
Like the large whales that spend time at the surface of New England
waters, basking sharks often are found with scarring indicative of having been struck by ships or entangled in fishing gear, though seldom
are they actually observed entangled. While there is no evidence that
predators have killed adult basking sharks, Skomal thinks that "an am-
bitious killer whale might give it a go, and maybe even a white shark
or a big mako." There is also no evidence that pollution from anthropogenic sources is a problem for them, though he also notes that "any
species that lives in productive coastal habitat like we have will have
to deal with pollution."

But global warming is a different story. Warming temperatures and
melting ice caps are almost certain to have a significant impact on the
dynamics of the *Calanus* copepods that basking sharks primarily feed
upon, which means that the sharks themselves will be seriously affected as well. Andy Pershing, a professor at the University of Maine
and a research scientist at the Gulf of Maine Research Institute, has
been evaluating records of plankton abundance in the Gulf of Maine
from the 1960s to the present to try and match the changes in plankton populations to changes in the physical characteristics of the gulf.
What he has found is that two physical processes appear to strongly
affect *Calanus* abundance.

"Water masses at the bottom of the gulf—that is, layers of water
with a particular temperature and salinity that you can track—go back
and forth between a water mass that's warmer and saltier from a Gulf
Stream influence, versus water coming from the Labrador Sea that's
fresher and colder," he explained. "That shift in water masses seems
to affect *Calanus*. When it's warmer and saltier, *Calanus* seems to be
more abundant."

Pershing also noticed that in the 1990s, a large pulse of fresh water
moved into the surface of the Gulf of Maine, probably from the Arctic, which he said "turned the ecosystem a little on its head. We saw
Calanus numbers go down and a lot of smaller copepods increasing in

abundance at that time. We're not sure whether *Calanus* was responding to the physical changes, or whether it had to do with an increase
in herring, which feed on *Calanus*, too."

Now he is trying to predict what physical changes in the Gulf of
Maine will result from global warming and how that will affect copepod populations. His early guesses are somewhat surprising. While
the atmospheric temperatures over the gulf will certainly increase,
that doesn't mean the water temperature will, too. Some scientists
even think the gulf will get colder because most of the water that en-
ters the gulf comes from the north. Pershing thinks that the warmer,
saltier water from the south and the colder, fresher water from the
north will stratify the Gulf of Maine, creating layers of water that
have a significant contrast between the top and bottom.

"If you stratify the gulf, you're probably going to see a decline in
Calanus populations," he said, while admitting that he was just spec-
ulating about the possibilities. "In the 1990s, when the gulf was more
stratified, *Calanus* numbers went down. It's more of an open ocean
plankton species, and when the water gets more stratified it's usually
the coastal species that do well, which doesn't bode well for *Calanus*."

It also doesn't bode well for basking sharks. If Pershing is right and
the gulf gets colder and *Calanus* populations decline, then basking
sharks are going to struggle to bulk up during the crucial summer
feeding season. That means they may not have the necessary energy
stored up to fuel their long migration southward and the females may
be unable to provide for the needs of developing embryos. And if Pershing is wrong and the gulf gets warmer, *Calanus* populations may increase, but they will also probably move northward and no longer be
available for basking sharks in New England waters to feed upon.
Calanus in the gulf are already at the southern limit of their range—
the center of their distribution is in the Labrador Sea, the Greenland
Sea, and the Norwegian Sea—so if the water warms up by even a
little, they may retreat northward and disappear from the Gulf of
Maine for good.

To learn more about local efforts to study basking sharks, I joined marine biologist Krill Carson in July 2007 aboard the *Captain John II*, a

whale-watching boat leaving from Plymouth Harbor. Carson was the naturalist onboard and spent most of the trip talking on an intercom to a noisy group of tourists about the natural history of the many whales found in New England waters in the summer. But she has a personal interest in basking sharks as well, and in 2005 she started the New England Basking Shark Project to encourage recreational boaters, fishermen, and others plying the region's waters to report the sighting of any basking sharks they might come across. She hopes that these sighting reports will help to fill in the knowledge gaps about the distribution and seasonal movements of basking sharks in local waters. Carson passed out brochures about the organization to every passenger on the trip, along with sighting forms, business cards, and information about how to distinguish basking shark fins from those of other fish and marine mammals.

"When people on our trips see basking sharks, they get so excited because it's something they don't expect and it's a magnificent animal that we know so little about," Carson said. "This year we've only seen two so far from our boats, and we've had about ten other sightings reported by others, mostly from the Provincetown ferry. But in a typical year we have thirty or forty sightings."

Carson shares whatever basking shark data she collects with Bridgewater State College biology professor John Jahoda, who provides his undergraduate students with opportunities to serve as official observers aboard the *Captain John II*. Whatever they learn about the sharks is then shared with Skomal and other shark biologists around the region.

Just 20 minutes after leaving Plymouth on our way out to Stellwagen Bank to search for whales, the captain unexpectedly stopped the boat, which gave the passengers quite a jolt. He thought he saw a basking shark fin, and I jumped to the railing to get a look. Instead, it turned out to be an ocean sunfish, which, oddly enough, is often confused with a basking shark. Ocean sunfish are bizarre-looking creatures up to 10 feet long that lie on their sides at the surface of the water with their paddle-like dorsal fin visible above the water's surface like that of a basking shark. Their large fins and absence of a tail make them look somewhat circular, as if they are all head and no body. Weighing an average of 2,200 pounds, they are the heaviest bony fish—as opposed to sharks, which are mostly cartilage—in the world, and females produce more eggs than any other known vertebrate.

Despite having spectacular close-up views of humpback whales during the rest of the trip, which Carson described as "the most amazing of my thirty years on whale-watching boats," in the remainder of the day aboard the *Captain John II* we saw not a hint of a basking shark.

Thanks to the help of a spotter pilot scanning the waters from above, seldom does Greg Skomal miss out on seeing basking sharks when he is conducting his research. And whenever he can, he puts on his wetsuit, straps on an oxygen tank, and joins the massive creatures in their domain. He uses the opportunity to determine the gender of the sharks—males have modified pelvic fins called claspers that they use in reproduction—estimate their size, and get a closer look at specific behaviors.

"I've been in the water with a lot of species of sharks, and I find diving with basking sharks to be spooky yet peaceful," he said with a sense of wonder in his voice. "You're hit with a clash of emotions when you're under water with them, and it's largely dictated by the fact that you've got a multi-ton beast that's swimming silently in pea soup where visibility is less than ten feet and typically less than five feet, and you're having trouble finding what's up and down. Then out of the gloom come these large animals—half a dozen or a dozen—and you're within feet of them and you feel their mass as they go by you. The momentum of their swimming seems effortless, and the swish of their tail spins you out in a vortex. It's particularly unnerving when one breaches when you're in the water. When a shark breaches, you don't see it breach, you just see whitewater and the remnants of a splash, and when you surface the people in the boat ask if you're OK, and you don't know why they're asking. What would it be like for one of these animals to land on you or to hit you on the way up? I don't know which would be worse, and I'm glad it hasn't happened. But the bottom line is that when you come out of the water after swimming with basking sharks, it's a pretty powerful experience."

Acknowledgments

Given the vagaries of weather and marine conditions and the usually tight capacity on research vessels and fishing boats, it was more of a challenge to arrange to spend time in the field with biologists studying life in the marine environment than in my previous efforts to study land-based wildlife. And yet somehow the researchers made it happen for me. While there were plenty of last-minute changes in plans due to high surf, strong winds, and the availability of boats, the researchers and fishermen featured in this book were immensely accommodating to my requests to join them in the field, and for that I am sincerely grateful. Thanks are also due to the dozens of other experts I called upon to provide insight into the lives of the species featured and the intricacies of marine geology, physical and chemical oceanography, and other factors influencing the lives of New England's marine life.

Deciding which species to include in *Basking with Humpbacks* was a far greater challenge than I anticipated. Dave Beutel and Bob Kenney were especially helpful in that regard, as well as with identifying appropriate researchers studying their suggested species, as were Malia Schwartz, Molly Lutcavage, Peg Van Patten, and Trisha DeGraaf.

Thanks also to Charlotte Raymond and to Phyllis Deutsch and the staff of University Press of New England, including Sarah Welsch, Sherri Strickland, and Barbara Briggs, who helped make my experience promoting my first book, *Golden Wings & Hairy Toes*, such a delight.

Most of all, I am especially appreciative of my wife Renay, who stayed behind while I went on numerous adventures at sea and who spent far too many weekends entertaining herself while I was locked away writing. There's no way that this book would ever have been completed without your love and support. Thank you.

Bibliography

The primary sources for *Basking with Humpbacks* were the numerous biologists with whom I spent time in the field and the many others that I interviewed in person or over the telephone. Their encyclopedic knowledge of marine ecosystems and the species discussed in this book was most helpful. I also relied heavily on fact sheets, newsletters, and other material about rare and threatened species provided by the National Marine Fisheries Service Office of Protected Resources and the Atlantic States Marine Fisheries Council. These documents were extremely useful in understanding the life histories of the species, the threats that they face, and the steps being undertaken to protect them.

In addition, several chapters benefited greatly from the information I gleaned from one or two other primary sources. For instance, *Voyage of the Turtle* by Carl Safina provided tremendous insights about leatherback turtles; *The American Horseshoe Crab*, edited by Carl Shuster, Jane Brockmann, and Robert Barlow, is the definitive resource on that species; and *Bigelow and Schroeder's Fishes of the Gulf of Maine*, edited by Bruce Collette and Grace Klein-MacPhee, is the standard reference work for all the fish in the region. I also referred often to field guides to birds, marine mammals, fish, the Atlantic seashore, and seaweeds, especially to those guides in the Peterson and National Audubon Society series.

Beyond these general reference materials, I found myself turning again and again to scientific papers in *Northeast Naturalist*, news reports in the *Boston Globe*, *Los Angeles Times*, and *New York Times*, the newsletter of the Stellwagen Bank National Marine Sanctuary, and popular articles in the member magazines of the Ocean Conservancy, the National Audubon Society, and the Wildlife Conservation Society.